MW00781333

Believe Nothing Until It Is Officially Denied

Believe Nothing Until It Is Officially Denied

Claud Cockburn and the Rise of Guerrilla Journalism

Patrick Cockburn

VERSO

London • New York

First published by Verso 2024
© Patrick Cockburn 2024

All rights reserved
The moral rights of the author have been asserted

1 3 5 7 9 10 8 6 4 2

Verso
UK: 6 Meard Street, London W1F 0EG
US: 388 Atlantic Avenue, Brooklyn, NY 11217
versobooks.com

Verso is the imprint of New Left Books

ISBN-13: 978-1-80429-074-3
ISBN-13: 978-1-80429-076-7 (US EBK)
ISBN-13: 978-1-80429-075-0 (UK EBK)

British Library Cataloguing in Publication Data
A catalogue record for this book is available from the British Library

Library of Congress Cataloging-in-Publication Data

Names: Cockburn, Patrick, 1950- author.
Title: Believe nothing until it is officially denied : Claud Cockburn and
    the invention of guerrilla journalism / Patrick Cockburn.
Description: London ; New York : Verso, 2024. | Includes bibliographical
    references and index.
Identifiers: LCCN 2024016851 (print) | LCCN 2024016852 (ebook) | ISBN
    9781804290743 (hardback) | ISBN 9781804290767 (ebook)
Subjects: LCSH: Cockburn, Claud, 1904-1981. | Journalists--Great
    Britain--Biography.
Classification: LCC PN5123.C45 C63 2024 (print) | LCC PN5123.C45 (ebook)
    | DDC 070.92 [B]--dc23/eng/20240521
LC record available at https://lccn.loc.gov/2024016851
LC ebook record available at https://lccn.loc.gov/2024016852

Typeset in Sabon by Biblichor Ltd, Scotland
Printed and bound by CPI Group (UK) Ltd, Croydon CR0 4YY

To Jan, Henry and Alex and in memory of Kitty Lee

Contents

Preface:
'A Maquis of His
Own Devising'

Two months after Claud Cockburn, my father, fled Berlin hours before Hitler became German chancellor on 30 January 1933, he founded and largely wrote an anti-Nazi and anti-establishment newsletter, *The Week*, which had an influence in Britain and abroad in the 1930s out of all proportion to its size and circulation. 'Blum read it and Goebbels read it and a mysterious warlord in China read it. Senator Borah quoted it repeatedly in the American Senate and Herr von Ribbentrop, Hitler's ambassador in London, on two separate occasions demanded its suppression on the ground that it was the source of all anti-Nazi evil.'[1] *The Week* was one of the carefully chosen weapons in Claud's ceaseless campaign against the powerful on behalf of the powerless. He conducted his journalistic guerrilla warfare, as relevant today as in his era, with courage, originality and intelligence, demonstrating how those in authority can be challenged and harassed by a determined and skilful journalist, even one almost entirely without resources.

Claud's charm, likeability and talkativeness were such that they masked his achievements and his radicalism, neither of which I fully understood when I was growing up in Ireland in the 1950s, though I got on with him extremely well. Warm and engaging to children and adults alike, he was interested in everything I did, whether building a rickety dam out of mud and pebbles in the streams that ran near our house or, when I was a little older, what comic I was reading, or the latest gossip about our neighbours. We talked about whatever was in the news-papers, copies of which were often strewn across the drawing room floor, much to the irritation of my mother, Patricia. He treated me and my elder brothers, Alexander and Andrew, as if we were adults, fully capable of taking part in an intelligent conversation about current politics and past history. He had an air of gaiety and a sense of mischief combined with vast experi-ence of conflict and war. I might have been intimidated and put off by this as a small boy, but his conversation sparkled with self-mocking stories. For example, one such tale played down the misery of being penniless and hungry in Berlin in 1927 by giving a detailed and funny description of how he had persuaded a friendly butcher to provide a large Christmas dinner of nauseating-looking offal for a dog Claud was looking after. On taking the meal home, he carefully divided it into two equal portions, keeping half of it for himself and giving the rest to the dog, much to the animal's astonishment and distress. Episodes of high personal drama and danger were diluted with moments of farce. Telling how he had taken part as a volunteer soldier in a doomed attack of heroic but untrained Republican militiamen during the Spanish Civil War, a charge which was cut to pieces by machine-gun fire, he recalled how the belt of his ill-fitting military uniform had broken at a critical moment during the retreat. His trousers had fallen down, tripping him up and knocking him out. I was none too sure of the location of Berlin or Spain, but his adventures sounded agreeably exciting, though the circumstances in which they had taken place were as strange to me as those of the Wars of the Roses.

Claud's likeability meant that people usually did not think much about what 'made him tick'. A reason for this charm, felt by friends but equally by those violently hostile to his politics, was that he was an excellent listener. People become wary of relentless charmers, but not of those who show genuine engage-ment with their lives and opinions. By his own account, he never found anybody truly boring, and this was not an affectation.

Hope Hale, his first wife, said that she and her friends searched out notoriously tedious people to talk to Claud, knowing that he had a Proustian fascination with the details of the lives of others, prompting those written off as dull into telling interesting and amusing stories about themselves.

When it came to food, drink and general comfort, we lived well in Ireland, though our day-to-day way of life was closer to the first half of the nineteenth century than the second half of the twentieth. Claud and Patricia had moved into our beautiful but dilapidated Georgian country house, called Brook Lodge, when they arrived from England in 1947. One corner of the main building was tacked onto an older farmhouse with massive stone walls and stables for the horses, on whom we relied for transport to the ancient town of Youghal, a mile away on the estuary of the Blackwater River on the coast of East Cork. We had electricity but no car, so I would go to the Loreto Convent in Youghal in a horse-drawn gig or trap, while Claud bicycled into town to post articles to newspapers and magazines and drink in one of the many dark little pubs. We once had a telephone, but this was blown away in one of the periodic financial gales which struck our family finances, and it was not replaced. Bailiffs serving writs for the non-payment of bills appeared with some regularity on the drive outside the big French windows on the ground floor of the house that flooded its cavernous rooms with light. Patricia said that our house 'had writ-servers like other houses have mice'. Claud and Patricia joked ruefully about the plague of duns, though they were expert in negotiating their way out of trouble with local creditors. Living with this semi-permanent financial crisis must have been a fearful strain on them, but I did not really understand this at the time. I felt that it was sad and unfortunate, but not entirely out of the ordinary when some familiar piece of furniture, inherited by Patricia or bought cheap by her in London during the war, had suddenly disappeared from the house, sold off to meet some unusually pressing debt.

Claud earned just enough money to prevent us from capsizing totally, close run though it often was. Getting up at five or six in the morning – he was an early riser throughout his life – he wrote on an old Imperial typewriter a stream of articles for newspapers and magazines, as well as a three-volume autobiography and several novels and histories. One novel, *Beat the Devil*, made into a film by John Huston and Humphrey Bogart, which later achieved cult status, was shown in the cinema in Youghal to loud applause and, no doubt, much to the satisfaction of our local creditors. The relief from our money troubles was temporary, and I found agitated-looking jottings on the flyleaf of whatever book Claud was reading, showing a worrying imbalance between hoped-for income – freelance journalists are seldom paid much or on time – and long-overdue bills.

I did not fully understand until I was older that Claud's ability to earn money from journalism and books was hindered, rather than aided, by his political notoriety. His politics, while radical and revolutionary, were sophisticated and nuanced in a way that people found perplexing in the midst of the Cold War. At one moment, he was being attacked by Senator Joe McCarthy in the US as one of the most dangerous Reds in the world, while at the same time he was denounced by an old Communist friend, Otto Katz, shortly before he was executed in Prague after a show trial, in which he 'confessed' that he had been suborned by an agent of British intelligence, Claud Cockburn.

I think, looking back, that I was mistaken about Claud's character, as were nearly all of his friends. His likeability and warmth were certainly not a pose, but he was a far more determined, practical and even ruthless man than he appeared. Early in life, he had come to value George Bernard Shaw's advice 'to get what you like or you'll grow to like what you get'. He applied this to his politics, which wholly absorbed him, and also to his personal life. He would endure hardships and risk dangers, such as being mistaken for an enemy agent and almost shot in Spain or arrested by the Gestapo in Germany (to which he briefly returned on a badly forged passport). Many approved of him as an amusing gadfly, always ready to tweak the nose of authority, but he was a much more serous person than that. His friend Malcolm Muggeridge, one-time editor of *Punch*, saw a little deeper, saying of Claud that 'like all imaginative and sensitive people, Cockburn tends to lurk in a maquis of his own devising'.[2] As I researched Claud's life in the years before I knew him, I came to realise that he was a far tougher person than I had supposed. He never looked backwards at past mistakes or defeats, because he felt there was nothing to be done about them. He seldom quarrelled personally with people, be they wives, friends, political collaborators or even political enemies, but he did sometimes move on from them, letting them fade into the past. Above all, he was a serious revolutionary who wanted to improve the world.

Until the summer of 1932, Claud was a rising star at the *Times* as a correspondent in New York, having previously worked for the paper in Germany. He already knew Central Europe well, having been partly brought up in Budapest where his father Henry, a British diplomat, had taken a job. After leaving Oxford, Claud lived in the Weimar Republic in its heyday before going to the United States in 1929, having persuaded the *Times* to send him there as a staff correspondent. He did not tell the paper of another motive, which was that, having been influenced by revolutionary anti-capitalist ideas in Berlin and Vienna, he wanted to see for himself whether modern American capitalism had discovered the recipe for ever-greater economic prosperity – which made demands for radical political and social change obsolete. He arrived in America three months before the Great Crash, giving him an immediate answer to his question, though he stayed on in the US for three years, during which the Great Depression grew ever more cataclysmic. He remained in close touch with Germany, where the Weimar Republic was in its last days as economic catastrophe and political division propelled Hitler and the Nazis closer to taking power. Resigning from the *Times*, much to their outspoken regret, he returned swiftly to Berlin, where he found the situation to be even more disastrous than he had expected, forcing him to flee to Vienna twenty-four hours before Hitler became German chancellor on 30 January 1933.

Out of a job and almost penniless, Claud pondered how he might best oppose the Nazis and decided to return to London, a city he had scarcely visited for six years. He had no money, but a great deal of determination and a carefully worked-out plan to start a newsletter he would call *The Week*, to be written entirely by himself, which would expose the Nazis and those who were aiding or failing to resist them, by reporting news that the rest of the media was ignoring. Six weeks later, with forty pounds borrowed from a friend, he launched his newsletter, and by the summer of 1933 it was giving horrific accounts of the Nazi savagery, most especially about the persecution of the Jews, while explaining that Hitler's and Mussolini's expansionism made another war inevitable, unless the rest of Europe (including the Soviet Union) united against them. As Claud had hoped, his scoops and insider information, written up in an aggressive but authoritative style, soon began to impact the news agenda by influencing the opinion makers – the journalists, diplomats, politicians and intellectuals whom Claud calculated were dissatisfied with the established press. What Claud called his 'pirate craft' was soon waging a journalistic guerrilla war of surprise attacks against fascism and authoritarianism, two trends which Claud saw as closely intertwined. Just how *The Week* was established and why it was successful is explained in detail in the opening chapter of this book.

Claud believed in resistance to arbitrary government and fascism at all times and on every front. Counterattacks against the powerful might take the form of journalistic revelations about wrongdoing or street protests against repressive laws in Britain or military action in favour of the democratically elected government in Spain. He became a founder member of the National Council for Civil Liberties in 1934 and took part in hunger marches in Scotland and the North of England. He briefly worked part time for a Labour-supporting newspaper, but he felt that Labour was where he had been ten years earlier in Central Europe, when he viewed Germany sympathetically as the victim of an unjust Treaty of Versailles. He started writing for the *Daily Worker*, his first eyewitness piece of reporting being on the Gresford Colliery mine disaster in which 266 miners had died in an explosion and fire. He joined the Communist Party as the most committed, best-organised movement opposed to fascist dictators and capitalism. During the Spanish Civil War, he thought that the Communists alone had the fanaticism and discipline to give the Republic a fighting chance against General

Francisco Franco's professional army, backed by Germany and Italy. He helped organise 'Popular Fronts', the aim being to unite everybody, from deep-dyed Conservatives, through the political middle ground of liberals and social democrats, to radical revolutionaries like himself, against fascism. He later moved quietly away from the Communists before coming to Ireland, feeling that they had become ineffective as a force for radical change, yet he was determined not to denounce them or say anything that would bring joy to the heart of Senator McCarthy or look like an endorsement of the status quo.

Left-wing friends often wondered why he got on so well with High Tories and others on the establishment right who were hostile to his overall political viewpoint. He explained that he had a simple measurement by which he judged whether or not somebody stood fundamentally on the same side of the fence as himself: he would ask himself what stance the person in question would have taken in France during the 'Dreyfus affair', that huge scandal which had convulsed and divided France at the end of the nineteenth and the beginning of the twentieth century. A Jewish army officer, Alfred Dreyfus, had been wrongfully convicted of being a German spy on forged evidence and given a long prison term. Even when his innocence was proven, reactionary anti-Semites, monarchists and Catholics sought to keep him incarcerated. Claud asked himself: if, hypothetically, a person had been in France during the affair, would they have protested in person and in print in favour of Dreyfus and against his persecutors? In other words, was their opposition to injustice an overriding feature of their character which took precedence over their other political sympathies? If so, Claud labelled them as 'Dreyfusard', with whom he was happy to cooperate; if not, as 'anti-Dreyfusard', whom he viewed with suspicion. This curious political health check mystified those accustomed to more conventional labelling. People may applaud independent mindedness in theory, but they are disconcerted and alarmed by those who reject conventional political categories and allegiances.

When I was at school in Scotland, and later as a student at Oxford, I felt that Claud's derisive but unwavering suspicion of governments and the mainline media, always expecting the

worst from both, was the correct posture for a polemical journalist. This was the era of the Vietnam War, but also of giant
demonstrations against it; of the presidency of Richard Nixon,
but also of the Watergate scandal and his fall. I could see as a
young man that old-fashioned cultural rule-makers were still in
business, but the rule-takers were gamely fighting back and winning at least some of the battles. I was in favour of protests for
civil rights in the US and Northern Ireland, and against racism
and arbitrary government in any country. But, at the same time,
I did not feel that those in charge were inherently evil or motivated solely by the pursuit of profit and power. I had not seen
much of the world, but my first job was working for Paul Foot,
the great investigative reporter at *Private Eye*, so I had early
experience of scandal and corruption.

It was only after I went to the Institute of Irish Studies at
Queen's University Belfast in 1972 to write my PhD thesis that
I began to feel that Claud's profoundly negative view of government as essentially a force for evil, unless permanently battered
by opposition, had more going for it than I had previously
imagined. This was one of the worst periods of the Troubles in
Northern Ireland, where the British government's violent and
counterproductive support for one religiously defined commu-
nity against another had helped turn a confrontation over civil
and economic rights into a vicious low-level war that lasted
thirty years. It was my first real experience of seeing a government make a bad situation worse, but there were to be many
others. I can see how Claud's political attitudes would have been
similarly impacted, as a teenager and young student, by seeing
governments fostering persecution and pogroms in Hungary
and the rest of Central Europe.

I shifted from academia to journalism, travelling first to Leb-
anon at the start of the civil war in 1975, then going on to cover
crises and wars in Iraq, Israel, Chechnya, Afghanistan, Libya
and Syria. At other times, I was based as a foreign correspondent in Moscow and Washington, working for the *Financial
Times*, *Independent*, *London Review of Books* and the *i* newspaper. Over the years, Claud's reputed cynicism appeared to me
more and more like Realpolitik – simply an unsentimental

understanding of how the world really worked. I did not become disillusioned with the news business, any more than Claud had done half a century earlier, and was rather encouraged, as he had been, by the size of the vacuum of knowledge to be filled.

Claud believed that serious political conflicts were always information wars in which news outlets were partisan weapons. I found this was invariably true in places like Afghanistan, Iraq, Libya, Syria and Gaza. Claud thought this lack of objectivity was inevitable, but it mattered much less if the public was aware that they were getting only half the picture. Regrettably, this bias in news reporting has been the norm since the time when the Pharaohs were inscribing accounts of imaginary victories on their monuments. But in my professional lifetime, particularly since the start of the post-9/11 wars, official mendacity has become grosser and media credulity and lack of pushback more pronounced. In Afghanistan in 2001, I felt that the volume of official lies and self-deception had reached new heights, promulgated by sophisticated government PR machines which claimed that the US and its allies had eliminated the Taliban – something that I could see for myself was entirely untrue. In Iraq, the US and Britain first said Saddam Hussein had weapons of mass destruction, which he did not, and then that the war was over when I could see that it was only just beginning. In Libya in 2011, the NATO-backed rebels who overthrew the country's leader, Muammar Gaddafi, were presented by the West as liberals and democrats, rather than the criminalised warlords who have since ravaged the country. Complex conflicts in Syria, Ukraine and Gaza are presented as struggles between good and evil in which compromise is prohibited, while the terrible destruction inflicted by ceaseless warfare is understated.

After 9/11, historic progress appears to have gone into reverse gear, moving speedily backwards, especially since the populist nationalist triumphs of 2016 when Britain voted for Brexit, opening the door for Boris Johnson to become prime minister three years later, and Donald Trump was elected US president. Cold wars have turned into hot wars between Russia and Ukraine, Armenia and Azerbaijan, Israel and the Palestinians; as in the 1930s, permanent crisis has once again become the norm. Claud, who died in 1981, would have found much familiar in the political landscape today, with far-right nationalists in power and a war in Europe. But he would also believe that governments and media, which have together fostered or failed to prevent these serial crises, can be successfully resisted.

He thought – and to a large degree proved through his own actions – that a journalist without wealth or resources could fight and win in opposition to those who had great quantities of both. He was convinced that people commonly underestimate their own ability to oppose governments and powerful organisations of all kinds. The poor and the weak are encouraged to feel, so he would argue, that resistance is useless because the powers that be are so overwhelmingly strong that resistance is futile and should be abandoned. He would contradict the proverb, sometimes attributed to Napoleon, that battles are won by the big battalions, arguing that this was propaganda put out by big-battalion commanders to demoralise their small-battalion opponents. He said that rule-makers, who might be cabinet ministers, senior bureaucrats, army generals, big businessmen, newspaper proprietors or editors, were far more vulnerable to critical assault than they pretended. Ostensibly, their raw power might appear impressive and unassailable, but this was mostly for show, and they could be harassed, damaged and ultimately defeated by well-planned journalistic guerrilla warfare targeting known vulnerabilities. He did not think that those in possession of great power would be a pushover or delude himself that a journalistic David would necessarily overcome a big-media Goliath, but he did think that the odds could be evened if David took care to select the right sling-stone and the means to deliver it.

'Believe nothing until it is officially denied,' a saying attributed to Claud in dictionaries of quotations, accurately sums up his defiant disbelief in officially derived information.[3] He said that these warning words – apparently formulated by himself, though he suggests they are an old Fleet Street adage – came into his mind on the day of the Wall Street crash in October 1929, when he and other journalists in New York were being reassured by Thomas W. Lamont, the acting head of the banking house of J. P. Morgan, that all would be well, although 'there had been a little distress selling on the stock exchange'. Claud would also quote with approval his former boss, the *Times* Washington correspondent Sir Wilmott Lewis, who told him that 'every government will do as much harm as it can and as much good as it must'.[4]

I used to think these cavalier dismissals of governments as malignant, incompetent liars were too sweeping to be convincing, but I have changed my mind since seeing Donald Trump take office in the US, the ascendancy of Boris Johnson and Liz Truss in Britain, and Vladimir Putin in Russia launching his war in Ukraine. Claud, while fully agreeing with Lewis's dictum, emphasised the latter's use of the word 'must', saying that while governments might be vicious, they lacked fixity of purpose, and that if the right kind of pressure was exerted on them, they would prove more malleable than they pretended.

Political leaders, autocratic and democratic, are acutely sensitive to pinprick criticism and can be prodded into self-destructive overreaction. Claud's copious MI5 file contains many furious memos from high-ranking officials at the heart of government complaining of revelations in *The Week* – and vainly demanding that something be done about its editor, though invariably they wanted somebody else to do the dirty work. When an important British minister and arch-appeaser, soon to be foreign secretary, Lord Halifax, saw Hitler and his propaganda chief, Joseph Goebbels, in late 1937, the Nazi leaders complained vigorously about British press criticism, timid and episodic though that had been. Despots are no less sensitive today: recall that, according to the CIA, in 2018 Saudi crown prince Mohammed bin Salman sent a death squad to kill and dismember the mildly dissenting Saudi journalist Jamal Khashoggi. Democratic regimes can be equally vengeful. The British government has imprisoned the WikiLeaks founder, Julian Assange, in the Belmarsh maximum-security prison since 2019 pending possible extradition to the US for publishing a hoard of not very highly classified US diplomatic and military cables.

Claud was modest about the achievements of *The Week*, though proud that it had exerted considerable influence on public opinion at a crucial moment in European history. He recognised that circumstances were in its favour: there was a giant vacuum of information about matters of war and peace; scoops about these vital issues would attract a pool of influential, politically engaged readers; divided elites would leak secrets to him. This formula worked well up to about 1940, but not, as he realised retrospectively, after the war had got fully underway. He saw his newsletter as but one means of harrying the authorities and was keen to mobilise the broadest-possible coalition, so resistance would not be confined to a core of radical activists. At the same time, he believed that a committed energetic core, in this case the Communists, was essential for any resistance that hoped to win.

Claud could justly claim that he had shown that radical insurgent journalism was possible, but his career demonstrates how difficult it is to fight this sort of campaign successfully. Over the years, few other publications like *The Week* have been launched, and fewer still have been successful. The publication that most resembles *The Week* (and, according to its long-time editor Richard Ingrams, is based in part on the same formula) is *Private Eye*, for which Claud wrote for many years and which continues to flourish.

Yet, despite the arrival of the internet, the information battlefield has seen no decisive shift towards democracy. Claud had taken advantage of the mimeograph to reach an audience numbering a few thousand at little cost, but the internet allows people to access an audience of millions for free. The old media monopolies in the print press, television and radio have been partly broken, though they still largely dictate the news agenda – even if their grip has loosened. The proliferation of online publications, as well as platforms like YouTube, Twitter (recently renamed X), blogs, podcasts and Substacks, means a vast increase in the number of people who are, so to speak, in the news business. In theory, there ought to be lots of publications like *The Week*, but evidently the balance of media power has not swung as far as optimists expected – though this might happen in future.

This is because traditional news outlets and news providers have colonised the online space, drowning out critics and other providers of information. Governments have much expanded their own propaganda efforts – though 'propaganda' is a word they avoid – and, in much of the world, online critics are pursued and punished just as brutally as print journalists ever were. The volume of information available to the public has greatly increased, but its quality far less so, while in some areas it is much reduced. The non-metropolitan press in the US and UK is a shadow of what it used to be. Advertising revenues are syphoned off to internet platforms like Twitter/X and Meta, leading to fewer journalists and a general deskilling of news-gathering operations as newsrooms shrink or disappear. Not all the change has been bad, however, as events like the murder of George Floyd by police in Minneapolis in 2020 and the destruction caused by the Israeli bombardment of Gaza in 2023–4 are now instantly communicated to the world. But the collection and distribution of more complex information, particularly if it is critical of government or departs from conventional wisdom, is almost as difficult as it has ever been and subject to the same obstacles.

Claud identified some of these obstacles in the 1930s, but many of them are still scarcely recognised today. At the time, his views were often denounced as heretical or overly cynical or were misunderstood. He made the point that journalism is much more judgemental than most non-journalists realise: news outlets may claim to report only the facts, but, given the infinite number of facts in the universe, the journalist or news organisation must use their best or biased judgement to select those facts they believe significant enough to constitute news. This should be fairly obvious, but Claud found himself criticised for supposedly saying that a journalist was free to make up stories. In reality it is 'selectivity', not the 'fake facts' denounced by Donald Trump, which is at the heart of media bias. In an early issue of *The Week*, Claud made another important point: in their pursuit of the largest-possible audience, newspapers – and the same is even more true of television and radio – must dilute or boil down complicated events so their oversimplified version is distorted or rendered meaningless.

Journalism is a much-misunderstood profession. In some ways it is easy to be a journalist, but it is very difficult to be a

good one. Most movies about journalists are hopelessly misleading, as true to reality as Western movies are to the real life
of cowboys, or detective fiction to that of criminal investigation.
Many of the obstacles facing Claud when he was producing his
anti-Nazi newsletter in an attic in London in the 1930s are the
same as those facing somebody today producing their podcast,
in which they promise to tell people significant information
that they did not know before. Most news in the media comes
from governments and officially sanctioned sources, so publishing it poses no problem. But finding out information that
powerful institutions and people do not want publicised is far
more difficult than it looks. Unless they are under pressure
from those with legal powers to put them in prison, few people
impart information damaging to themselves or their interests.
What they say to damage others will be partisan and unlikely
to be wholly true. Many will refuse to speak at all, and none
will blub and confess their sins. Iconic journalistic scoops like
Watergate, as portrayed in *All the President's Men*, depended
on the journalists accessing secondary sources such as prosecu-
tors, judges and the FBI to discover information. Famous lines
from the movie, such as 'follow the money,' sound plausible to
a non-journalist, until they consider how very unlikely it is
that a bank will voluntarily disclose financial information
about their clients.

Claud was an excellent reporter. He needed to be because the
type of journalism he pioneered would not have worked without
professional skills of a high order. Small publications like *The
Week* have no influence and seldom survive long unless they
really do deliver the informational goods in the shape of exclu-
sives that are significant and true. I used to wonder what would
have happened to Claud had he stayed at the *Times* and not
gone back to Berlin; in fact, this would have been disastrous for
him because the paper became the foremost advocate of appeasement, censoring news likely to be offensive to the Nazis.
Journalists often dream of resigning from their jobs on a point
of principle, freeing them to say what they want. However, very
few do so, because they fear unemployment and know that alternative employers will be wary of people known to cause trouble.

Claud was much admired by colleagues for having left a stellar career at the *Times*, but few followed his example.

Launching his own publishing venture took daring and determination, but it only succeeded because Claud regularly unearthed confidential information and revealed genuine secrets. He searched out people who might feel it in their interests to make public what others want to conceal. Sources might be the French foreign ministry, a dissident Whitehall official, or a British or foreign journalist unable to get a story into their own newspaper because of editorial and proprietorial bias or disinterest. It was helpful for him that the two biggest international stories were Nazi Germany and the Great Depression, both of which he knew a great deal about because he had recently worked in Germany and the US. He realised that knowing a confidential piece of information is only half the job; the other, possibly more challenging half is persuading the public that it is something that they ought to care about. Claud was conscious of the need to dramatise his scoops to maximise public interest and the likelihood that they would be picked up by the rest of the press. His most influential story was unmasking the highly connected and powerful circle of appeasers, but the first two times he wrote about them, his story 'made about as loud a bang as a crumpet falling on a carpet'.[5] But when he wrote about the group a third time in a sharper tone, this time calling them the Cliveden Set, his story suddenly took off and was endlessly repeated around the world.

Claud was untiringly combative, never admitting defeat and convinced that, even if the powers that be were momentarily victorious, their excesses might be curbed and their self-confidence punctured if they knew that they were in for a fight. Never a knight errant, he was a man who considered seriously the practicalities of beating back arbitrary power, whatever its origin. Escalating crises in the 2020s have a frightening resemblance to the savage turmoil in the 1930s, making Claud's suspicion of established authorities and the need to resist them feel ever more justified by the calamitous course of current events.

Acknowledgements

I have been collecting materials for this book for twenty years though without a fixed idea about when I would sit down to write it. My father, Claud Cockburn, wrote much about his life, but I gradually came to appreciate just how much he had omitted as I discovered a wide variety of unpublished sources, from the papers of his first wife in the US to the files of MI5, the British security service. I came to understand him better as a person, political radical and journalistic innovator.

I have received generous help from many people and institutions during my research. My gratitude is all the greater because they provided me with essential information at a time when they were partially shut down at the height of the Covid-19 pandemic.

I am particularly grateful to the Schlesinger Library at the Harvard Radcliffe Institution in Cambridge, Massachusetts, for overcoming these difficulties in sending me copies of the Hope Hale Davis Papers. Despite similar restrictions in the UK, Nick Mays, archivist at News UK, located and enabled me to examine relevant correspondence from the *Times* archives.

Crucial also to this book was access to Claud's MI5 file which I requested from the security services at the beginning of my research and is now in the National Archives at Kew. I transcribed important documents at the Russian State Archive for Social and Political History in Moscow. Thanks to both.

I am truly grateful to Célestine Fünfgeld for expert research during which she successfully identified the people whom Claud knew and was strongly influenced by in Vienna and Berlin in the 1920s.

My task was made much easier by the Netherlands-based Brill making available in 2021 over 600 issues of *The Week* published between 1933–46. The Marx Memorial Library kindly allowed me to look at copies of the *Daily Worker* for the relevant period. Some material in the book previously appeared in the Independent and the *London Review of Books*. Thanks to both.

Many thanks also to Simon Blundell, the librarian at the Reform Club, who speedily produced difficult-to-find books and documents with his customary efficiency.

Many thanks are due to Lesley Koulouris, archivist at Berkhamsted School, for providing materials on Claud's school days. Peter Monteith, archivist at Keble College, Oxford, found useful information about his time as an undergraduate there.

I am as always grateful to my literary agents Sophie Lambert of C&W and Anna Stein of CAA/ICM.

My wife Jan Montefiore played a decisive role by urging me to get started on the book. She read and commented on each draft chapter as it was written, as well as sharing her profound knowledge of the literature of the period. She found several important documents by and about Claud. I cannot thank her enough.

I

'This Small Monstrosity'

Claud Cockburn [author's photo]

In July 1932, Claud Cockburn resigned, at the age of twenty-eight, as a correspondent of the *Times* of London in New York, where he had worked for three years, explaining that he could no longer live with the newspaper's conservative politics. The tone of his letter to the editor of the *Times*, Geoffrey Dawson, expressing his determination to go, shows his anguish over his decision. 'I do not do so either easily or lightly,' he wrote of his impending departure, but he intended to do things which would be 'a long distance on the other side of the political fence from the Times',[1] adding that he was leaving the best newspaper in the world, for which he had greatly enjoyed working.

Dawson wrote back saying that he was 'really distressed by your news – and also a little mystified', since he did not believe that Claud's differences with the *Times* were so deep as to necessitate his departure. '*The Times* sits so firmly on the political fence that you will have to become a Die-hard [Conservative] or a Communist to get very far away from it,' he wrote, noting that 'your work in the States has been an unqualified success, and I repeat that I am distressed by the thought that it is coming to an end'.[2]

Claud's decision to bring a premature end to his flourishing career at the *Times* was propelled by his conviction that Europe was sliding swiftly into a catastrophic crisis. The Weimar Republic in Germany was in inexorable decline and already appeared likely to be replaced by a far-right militarised regime. He had left Berlin three years earlier on a promise from the *Times* to send him as a foreign correspondent to the United States, where he wanted to see if American capitalism had truly discovered the solution to the world's social and economic ills.

Within three months of his arrival, he witnessed the Great Crash of 1929, which by 1932 had produced a calamitous depression resulting in 12 million Americans without a job and hungry people fighting for scraps of discarded food at the back doors of luxury hotels. Disastrous though the economic crisis in the US might be, Claud knew that its impact was far worse in Germany and Central Europe, which he had got to know intimately since his diplomat father, Henry Cockburn, had been stationed in Hungary in the early 1920s.

Claud spoke fluent German and, while in Berlin, had socialised with a circle of radical, politically engaged people from all over central Europe, many of whom were Jewish. As well as receiving news in America from these old friends in Berlin and Vienna about the startling rise of the Nazis, he had a well-informed contact close to hand: Wolfgang zu Putlitz, a fiercely anti-Nazi Prussian aristocrat in the German foreign ministry, whom he had known well in Berlin and was now a diplomat at the German embassy in Washington. 'With Germany lurching towards a calamity,' Claud wrote, 'he had the air of a man attending a non-stop performance of *Gotterdammerung*' with 'his profound Prussian sense of doom, his Teutonic taste for disaster'.[3] In the event, his apocalyptic outlook turned out to be all too prescient.

Convinced that disaster was impending in Germany, and thereafter in all of Central Europe, Claud hoped to walk straight out of the *Times* office in New York and go directly back. Instead, he discovered that he had too little money in the bank to fund his European travels, forcing him to sign a contract with a publisher to write a quick, anonymous 'insider' book on Washington politics for $1,500 (£600–700), with the manuscript to be submitted in just six weeks' time. Rushing down to Washington at the height of a hot summer, he produced a 268-page book called *High Low Washington by 30–32*, which is surprisingly readable given the speed at which it was written. One chapter relates how a single but very able American journalist, Oswald Schuette, had defeated a vastly powerful commercial enterprise, the Radio Trust, in a prolonged information war by using innovative journalistic methods. It was a David and Goliath story and one which stuck with him in the coming months.

Once he was paid for his book, Claud took a berth on a ship called the SS *Dunquerque* sailing from New York to the French port of Le Havre. So great was his enthusiasm to be back on European soil that he jumped from the deck of the ship to the ground as it docked at Le Havre, hoping to avoid a tedious wait at French customs and immigration. In the event, he sprained his ankle badly enough to force him to stay in Le Havre for several days, a delay during which he encountered some French dockers who said they were going to a conference against war and fascism to be held in Amsterdam on 27–28 August. Going along with them as a sympathetic foreign journalist, he believed he was getting a swift insight into the way Europe had radicalised under the impact of the economic crisis. The special train carrying delegates to the conference, its carriages daubed with anti-war and anti-fascist slogans, was greeted enthusiastically as it passed through France and the Low Countries by men on their way to early morning shifts at their factories, who dropped 'their bicycles, came swarming over the railway embankments and rushed on to the line singing and cheering and waving red flags'.[4]

After the conference, Claud travelled on to Paris, Budapest and Vienna, where he got the same sense of deep economic ruin and frantic political turmoil. From Vienna, he wrote to his newlywed wife, the US-based journalist Hope Hale, that the schools and hospitals in the city were shut because of lack of fuel while beggars filled the streets. 'They stand with their hands clasped in a theatrical way and beg or come into cafes and stand silently beside one's table,' he wrote. 'In the Grand Hotel the barman has a pile of coins to give them as they come in, in order to prevent them worrying the guests.'[5]

He planned to spend the winter in Berlin, where he arrived in late autumn to find the city had utterly transformed since he had lived there a few years earlier. He had always found the German capital a menacing place, even in the more relaxed years before the Great Depression, but it had become a great deal worse. 'In Berlin, you always felt the deluge was just around the corner,' he reflected later.[6]

During what were to be the last days of Weimar, Claud found that, whatever false optimism German leaders of the left and right might express in public, they all privately expected disaster, which they thought impossible to prevent. 'Thence to Berlin,' he wrote in a long letter to Hope, giving a vivid description of what he saw when he got there. Contrasting the Berlin of 1929 with that of 1932, he found that

> the sole visible sign of activity is war propaganda: huge exhibitions of 'the Front', soldier figures standing in a real-life size trench playing with a dummy machinegun ... and the last time I was there it was the week of the publication of [Erich Maria] Remarque's *All Quiet on the Western Front*. These three years have changed so much that it is difficult to imagine that this is something one is really seeing, and not a sort of preview of something one dreamed would happen way back in those cotton wool and rose petal days of 1929 before the beginning of this blood and iron decade that is here now.

The Nazi triumph was just over the horizon, but already the mood in Berlin was despairing. 'The town is enveloped in an air of melancholy so extreme and so excruciating and so theatrically complete as to be almost indecent,' he wrote.

> The leaves fall off the trees, the ground turns yellow with the falling leaves among the mud, the water rats and the toads still play in the Tiergarten, and at the corners of all the streets the Nazis and the Communists stand with their collection boxes crying for funds to all the passers-by and rattle their boxes, a noise you hear all over Berlin; and the beggars are there too and there too the hospitals are closing down and the war is being prepared and everything that used to be Europe is dying very very quickly.[7]

This lamentation was written by Claud several months before Hitler became German chancellor in late January 1933, but he correctly forecast the direction of events. As Hitler's takeover of power became imminent, an exodus began of those the Nazis deemed enemies to be eliminated. Friends warned Claud that he was on a Nazi blacklist as an associate of anti-Nazis and Communists, and was at risk of becoming a minor victim of the new regime. 'Storm Troopers were slashing and smashing their way up and down the Kurfuerstendamm [the main avenue in Berlin city centre] and there were beatings and unequal battles in the city streets,' he wrote.[8] He reflected that, though he expected that the Foreign Office and his former employers at the *Times* might protest if he was beaten to death by Storm Troopers, this would not do him a lot of good.

When he told friends that, as a British passport holder, he had every right to stay in Germany, he was answered by a caustic American journalist who quoted to him the rhyme about William Gay, 'who died asserting his rights of way / He was right, dead right as he sped along / but he's just as dead as if he'd been wrong.' Impressed by this mordant advice, Claud took a train to Vienna twenty-four hours before Hitler took over.[9]

◄◊►

At the *Times*, a year earlier, it had appeared to him absurd to spend his time writing about transitory events in New York, Washington and Chicago when Europe was at a turning point in history. Since then, he had witnessed Hitler take power, and it seemed a grossly inadequate response to remain an observer of world-shaking events and do nothing to oppose the Nazis and their allies.

In Vienna, he was struck by how little the world had taken on board the savage violence of the new German regime. Reacting to Hitler taking power, the mainline British and American press were feeble, grossly underplaying the importance of what had just happened. The *Times* praised Hitler's 'moderation and common sense', while Dawson, the editor, reassured readers that the Nazi leaders' aggressive speeches were solely for home consumption and that people should not worry about German militarism.[10]

On 31 January, the day after Hitler became chancellor, the *New York Times* told its readers about the strong domestic opposition that Hitler would face 'if he sought to translate the wild and whirling words of his campaign speeches into political action'. With a shocking lack of prescience, the paper foresaw a 'tamed' Hitler, adding that 'we may look for some such transformation when a radical demagogue fights his way into responsible office'.[11]

Claud found these misjudgements about the Nazis depressing, but he realised that they created a giant vacuum of information that he could seek to fill. He was convinced, moreover, that he had an original idea about how this could be done effectively by somebody like himself without resources. He intended to start a kind of journalistic guerrilla campaign that might even up the odds in any information war between himself and a far-richer and better-equipped opponent.

Before leaving Berlin for Vienna, he already had a half-formulated plan which had been 'buzzing' in his mind. He was confident it would work because he had seen something like it bring down a mighty commercial power in the US shortly before he left for Europe. The story of what had happened is the subject of the longest chapter in *High Low Washington*, in which Claud gives a detailed account of Oswald Schuette's one-man assault on the Radio Trust, as mentioned above.

Schuette was a former journalist on the *Chicago Daily News* based in Washington. Claud knew him personally and respected him professionally. Schuette had harassed, exposed and discredited the Radio Trust, which was owned by some of the biggest companies in America, who had built up near monopoly control of the American radio and telecommunications industry. In 1932, partly as an outcome of Schuette's campaign, the trust was broken up under the anti-trust legislation for operating a monopoly.

It was a genuine victory of the little guy and, as such, fascinated Claud, inspiring him to wonder if he could use the same tactics to fight political powers in Europe who thought themselves invulnerable. A cheap mimeograph was all Schuette had needed to send out a stream of critical but well-informed news bulletins about any action by the Radio Trust over a period of years. His information was accurate, fresh and newsworthy, and directed primarily at the great numbers of newspaper and radio offices in Washington. He wanted to influence the journalistic opinion-formers and, through them, shape public opinion.

When the lawyers and PR men of the trust tried to counter-attack, they simply gave his stories publicity and traction. Schuette's approach sounded easy, but it required a skilled professional journalist to make it work by dispatching newsworthy information packaged so it was attractive to journalists, who needed to be convinced that it was relevant and true. In a chapter in his book (which is indeed titled 'David and Goliath'), Claud lauded 'the humble mimeograph machine' as 'one of the few weapons which gives small and comparatively poor organisations a sporting chance in a scrap with large and wealthy ones'. The latter might still be sitting pretty, but 'not nearly so pretty as they would be sitting were it not for the mimeograph machine'.[12]

A second instance of a publication, this time a newsletter, punching much above its weight came to Claud's attention soon after his return to Berlin. It was a subscription-only mimeographed newsletter put out weekly by the office of General Kurt von Schleicher, a dubious right-wing military politician who briefly preceded Hitler as German chancellor. In the furious crises of 1932–3, von Schleicher's newsletter was considered 'a must-read' by politicians, businessmen, foreign diplomats and journalists in the capital. In conditions of permanent turmoil, none could afford to miss 'insider' news unobtainable elsewhere.

In the long term, the publication did not do von Schleicher much good, since he was murdered by the Nazis in the Night of the Long Knives in 1934. Claud noted, however, that while the newsletter was being published 'in terms of influence, one reader of Schleicher's sheet was, on an average, worth about five thousand of one of the daily newspapers'.

Claud spoke of *Le Canard Enchaîné* as a further influence because of its willingness to publish anything, however scandalous and regardless of the legal consequences. But Claud's instinct was always to attack, so he did not really need anything to spur him on.[13]

By combining these three approaches in a newsletter, Claud believed that he could do significant damage to those who considered themselves invulnerable to press criticism. His newsletter, called *The Week*, was based in London and was written wholly by himself. He wanted to publish the first issue an unrealistic two or three weeks after he arrived back in London, and he was scathing about what he considered the dilatory habits of the English. He knew a great deal about Central European and American politics, but he had only spent a few months in England over the previous six years. In the event, it was fully six weeks after Claud left Austria – and eight weeks after Hitler had come to power – that the first issue of *The Week* was posted to would-be subscribers on 29 March 1933.

Claud often told funny stories about how he had borrowed forty pounds from a novelist friend he had known at Oxford who had been vegetating in Hertfordshire. He rented a one-room office on the seventh floor of 34 Victoria Street, near Westminster Abbey (a site now occupied by New Scotland Yard). He secured the essential mimeograph machine on hire-purchase in order to save money and to possess no saleable assets to be seized by a successful litigant. Costs were low because he himself was paid no salary and survived on a trickle of twelve-shilling postal orders from early subscribers. There were to be no editorial board, lawyers, advertisers or shareholders, all of whom he thought might urge caution or otherwise interfere. Even so, he had to fend off well-meant offers of assistance because, as he put it, 'I had to keep firmly in mind that what we were running was a pirate craft and we could not burden ourselves with conventional navigators and mates, however skilled and knowledgeable.' The only skipper of this craft as it steered into stormy waters was going to be himself.[14]

He promised readers that they would read information not available elsewhere – and he did everything to encourage a sense of confidentiality. Printed in messy brown ink and sent in sealed buff envelopes, the newsletter was, so Claud claimed with some pride, 'not merely noticeable, it was unquestionably the nastiest looking bit of work that ever dropped on to a breakfast table'.

Unfortunately, he had used an out-of-date list of potential subscribers, many of whom had died or changed their opinions. The result was dismal: 'The number of paying customers secured by that first circularisation was seven,' he recalled. Just seven.[15]

The first issue of *The Week* is written in the authoritative style of a Foreign Office memorandum, but, in contrast to Foreign Office mandarins, Claud assumes that all governments and political players are motivated by Realpolitik or are generally up to no good. The lead article is a meaty read about 'plots and counterplots' revolving around a plan for diplomatic cooperation between Germany, France, Italy and Britain. It presumes that all countries are in 'the opening moves in a new phase of the present pre-war situation in Europe'.

From the early thirties, a constant theme of *The Week* was the inevitability of military conflict since the Nazis took power. An issue of the newsletter on 11 October 1933 gives details of a split within the cabinet about supporting France in its opposition to German rearmament. Describing the line-up, Claud says that the Foreign Office, Admiralty and War Office, in addition to a large section of the Conservative Party, wanted to take a tough line against Hitler and Germany. He goes on to say that the 'snag in the way of this policy is [Ramsay] MacDonald, Prime Minister, who is known to hanker after a policy of extending a friendly hand to Nazi Germany, and permitting German rearmament'.

MI5 reacted with alarm to what was evidently a high-level leak. They drew attention in particular to a sentence in the article stating that MacDonald 'was in a minority of one in a discussion on German armaments which took place at a Cabinet meeting on the morning of October 9th'. The MI5 official writing a memo on the leak needed to know from other parts of government if this information was correct; if so, he writes, 'we shall obviously have to intensify our enquiries about its source'. The same officer says firmly that steps should be taken 'to restrain Cockburn' from detailing the policy positions of the different departments of government – though how this was to be done he does not say.[16]

Readers were given graphic descriptions of the sadistic brutality of the Nazis inflicted on Jews and on many others they demonised as pariahs. On 8 June 1933, *The Week* gave details of the 'unreported case' of a Jewish businessman resident in Vienna named Salomon Dukler, a sixty-one-year-old Austrian subject, who had travelled from Vienna to visit a property he owned in a northern district of Berlin. 'On the ground floor of the building owned by him are a café and a number of rooms used as meeting places by Nazi storm troopers of the district.' Dukler went inside the building to discuss some alterations with a tenant called Wahrman, who also appears to have been Jewish. The newsletter described what happened next:

> Dukler then walked out onto the street. This was soon after five-thirty in the afternoon. Two Nazi stormtroopers came out of the café and spoke to him. They told him that Schetler, manager of the café, wanted to pay direct to him his share of the rent. Dukler went in with them to the café. He was there seized by half a dozen Nazis and dragged down to the basement. They then began to beat him and went on for six hours, working in one hour shifts, two men at a time. Apart from the beating his teeth were knocked out and 450 marks which he had in his pocket

were taken from him, and he was forced at intervals to sign cheques in favour of the Nazis. Towards midnight they gave him a [paper?] to sign, which affirmed that he would rather 'poison a German worker than employ one'. Dukler refused to sign the document. They then offered him the choice between signing it and drinking his own urine. So he did the latter. Wahrman, Dukler's tenant, who had meantime been beaten in another room, and the two men were thrown out onto the street together.[17]

It is possible that Dukler's Austrian nationality saved him from being beaten to death, since the incident took place three years before the Anschluss between Germany and Austria.

Claud was especially well informed about the intentions of the German government in 1933 because it still contained conservative and anti-Nazi officials with whom he was in covert contact. In one article titled 'Financial Pogrom', *The Week* described how the Nazis were planning the seizure of Jewish property by expropriation and forced loans. One idea they were discussing was to decree the return of Jews to Germany from abroad within a short period of time, and that 'failure to comply with this order would be followed by the confiscation of property'. In another ploy to ruin them financially, Jews still resident in Germany would be ordered to contribute to a so-called patriotic loan – a sum paid by an individual, determined by the amount they paid in income tax in 1931.[18]

Many of the stories appearing in *The Week* during its first months were genuine scoops, but its audience was small and not many people saw them. However, one who did was the prime minister, Ramsay MacDonald, whose political skin was notoriously thin and to whom some well-wisher had shown the newsletter. MacDonald was outraged at its jocular dismissal of his favoured project for ending the Great Depression and curbing international discord.

The saviour was to be a World Economic Conference, attended by senior leaders from Britain, Germany, Italy, Japan and the United States among many others, which began in the Geological Museum in London on 12 June.[19] World statesmen solemnly pledged economic cooperation, but *The Week* commented rudely that everybody from bankers on Leadenhall Street in the City of London to diplomats at the Afghan embassy knew that the conference was dead on its feet before it began.

Comically oversensitive to such pinprick attacks from even the most obscure publication, MacDonald called an off-the-record press conference in the crypt of the museum. Claud's description of the scene in his memoirs is a typical example of his mocking self-confident style: 'He [MacDonald] said he had a private warning to utter,' wrote Claud.

> Foreign and diplomatic correspondents from all over the world jostled past mementoes of the Ice Age to hear him. For as a warning-utterer he was really tip-top. In his unique style, sugges- tive of soup being brewed on a foggy Sunday evening in the West Highlands, he said that what we saw on every hand was plotting and conspiracy . . . and here in his hand was a case in point . . . Everybody pushed and stared and what he had in his hand was that issue of *The Week*.

To Claud's gratification, MacDonald called on all to ignore such false prophecies of disaster, thereby making the attendant jour- nalists, politicians, diplomats – the very people whom Claud hoped would make up his pool of influential readers – aware for the first time of the existence of *The Week*.[20]

Within a couple of years, it was well enough established for Claud to give a whoop of triumph: 'This small monstrosity', he wrote, 'was one of the half-dozen British publications most often quoted in the press of the entire world.'[21]

How far was this claim of wide-ranging influence justified? Politicians at all times downplay the degree to which their views are affected by media coverage, while the press itself seldom admits that another publication is the ultimate source of its information, particularly if the news outlet in question is an upstart newsletter with radical opinions. Yet there exists con- vincing contemporary evidence of the impact of Claud and *The Week* on decision makers – notably politicians, civil service mandarins and security chiefs at the heart of government – in the twenty-six bulky folders that MI5 built up on Claud and the activities of what he termed 'his pirate craft'.[22]

The folders give a detailed account of Claud's professional and personal life between 1933 and 1953. Memos to and from officials list his contacts, possible sources of information, copies of letters opened at the post office, transcripts of phone calls, and reports by policemen who followed him around. At a more senior level, officers sought to create a picture of his career past and present, interviewing former colleagues on the *Times* in London, Berlin and New York. Agents listed by MI5 as 'casuals' clambered up the rickety stairs to his office in Victoria Street in a bid to pump him – or, since he was frequently out, his two assistants – about the workings of the newsletter.[23]

The intelligence document in the folders predating *The Week* dates from 1924, when he and Graham Greene, then both students at Oxford, paid an illicit visit to the occupied Rhineland and drew the attention of military intelligence officers to themselves by failing to get permission to go there from the French and British authorities. But serious Security Service interest in Claud only begins nine years later, in 1933.[24]

Generally speaking, MI5 officers were complimentary about Claud's professional abilities. Summing up the MI5 attitude, an officer wrote in January 1934, 'I think it is only reasonable to state that COCKBURN is a man whose intelligence and capability, combined with his left wing tendencies and unscrupulous nature, make him a formidable factor with which to reckon.'[25] Another investigator said, 'I am informed that so much is thought of the ability of F. Claud COCKBURN that he could return to the staff of the "Times" any day he wished, if he would keep his work to the desired policy of this newspaper.' As for *The Week* itself, the same MI5 officer wrote that it 'is a curious farrago of would-be clever cynical inside information, mainly on foreign affairs. Sometimes COCKBURN seems to have been singularly well-informed on matters of a confidential Government nature, but so far it has not been possible to establish how far this may be due to some leakage, or to intelligent anticipation.'[26] Sir Vernon Kell, the founder and head of MI5, wrote discouragingly to the Committee of Imperial Defence, the main military planning body, saying that Cockburn 'has a very great variety of sources from whom he obtains his information, and we are endeavouring to keep some sort of check on his activities'.[27]

Government officials had become so accustomed to a compliant, spoon-fed press supportive of government policy that they expressed outraged surprise when anybody stepped out of line. Soon after the first appearance of *The Week*, a Foreign Office official rang MI5 to complain, not so much that the newsletter's facts were wrong – he said that they were for the most part correct – but to voice astonishment that 'Cockburn appeared to be getting information from someone in Government Departments, to which he should not have access'.[28]

Claud's affability tended to obscure his steeliness in pursuing his objectives. A perceptive guide to his personality at this time is Hope Hale, an American magazine editor in New York, whom he married in 1932, though he had already told her that he was planning to leave the *Times* and return to Europe, where he believed revolutionary change was underway. 'It was the way history was going he told me,' Hope recalled, 'and he wanted to play his part in it.'[29] 'What charmed me was his gaiety, his mischief, his wit,' she continued.[30]

> Though Claud took a genuine interest in other people, he could hardly enter a room before he became the centre of a group, listening and laughing. They would hear some comic tale such as his being swindled at age eighteen in a Budapest castle by a shady count teaching him Hungarian. Claud's sort of self-mocking humour required a special kind of assurance – maybe cultivated only in England.[31]

But later, when Hope and Claud were alone, he 'took off the concealing glasses' and said that something should be done about the disaster caused by the Great Depression. Hope was impressed by his revolutionary fervour, which 'made him irresistible – knowing that within the frivolity and fun was what he called "un homme serieux"'.[32]

He was, indeed, a highly serious man wholly absorbed in politics who was well suited to what he called 'a blood and iron' decade. Giving up a comfortable job at the *Times* to fight a one-man campaign against Hitler, the Nazis and the powers that be took determination of a high order. Asked why *The Week* had not had more emulators, Claud replied that 'to employ *The Week* formula you need to be more committed, more starry-eyed and reckless than most people want to be'.[33] The fierce political struggles that gained full force in 1933 – combined with the self-censorship and misjudgements of a partisan press – provided the ideal environment for his kind of journalism. He wrote that 'the smug smog with which the press of that time enveloped the political realities of the moment were even thicker than I had anticipated'.[34] They were ideal conditions, when, even if he made only a little noise, 'a squeak could sound like a scream'.[35]

2

The Limits of Diplomacy

Henry Cockburn house fortified with sandbags during siege of Peking 1900 [author]

Claud was born in the British Legation in Peking (Beijing) on 12 July 1904, the son of Henry Cockburn, a British diplomat who lived for a quarter of a century in China. He married Elizabeth Stevenson in 1899 during an infrequent visit to Britain, and they returned to China the following year in time for the Boxer Rebellion and the fifty-five-day siege of the Legation Quarter in Beijing in the summer of 1900. Their house was in the front line, a photograph taken during the siege showing it to have suffered some damage during the fighting, though this was caused more by amateur firefighters drawn from the diplomatic staff of the legations than by rebel action.

'Great destruction has been wrought on this house by parties of would-be friends,' wrote a foreigner missionary who had taken refuge in the Cockburn's dining room. The firefighters 'tore in and in their panic, simply cleared the house of everything, recklessly tearing down pictures and hangings . . . much was broken and lost'. Immediately outside the house, the garden had been turned into a deep pit as its soil was removed to fill sandbags.[1] A messenger Henry tried to send out of the city was captured by the rebels, who crucified him. Henry later told Claud that this was the worst moment of the siege for him.[2] The incident is not mentioned by Henry in letters to his mother and his brother Frank, a banker in Canada, though they look as if they were written to reassure and play down the danger. In one letter sent on 13 June, however, as the Boxers streamed into the city, Henry says that he was trying 'to obtain the release of a Chinaman, shut up in a Police station, to protect him from an anti-foreign crowd. I have never heard what happened to the man, but no doubt he was killed.'[3]

In 1880, at the age of twenty-one, Henry had arrived in China as a consular official, and he would spend the next twenty-five years there. His request for a pension on retiring from the Foreign Office in 1909 says that he started as a 'student interpreter on 30 March 1880 with an annual salary of £200'. Fluent in Chinese, he served as British vice consul in a string of cities, such as Chungking on the upper Yangtze, where he saw only half a dozen Europeans in four years – none of whom were, he remarked to Claud with relief, 'unduly obtrusive'. Isolation did not worry him, and, as a member of the consular service, Henry did not move from country to country like a regular diplomat, eventually earning the nickname 'China Harry' among friends in England. Cut off in these far-flung outposts, he decided important questions himself, without interference from superiors who were too far away or too indifferent to pay much attention to what he did.

In 1896, on becoming Chinese secretary, he joined the Foreign Office, dealing with Chinese-language matters, at the British Legation in Beijing. He knew many leading political figures in China, including the Empress Dowager, though he had a lower opinion of her than most, saying that she showed 'amiability verging on weakness'.[4]

Until a year or more after Claud's birth, his father had enjoyed a solid but scarcely meteoric diplomatic career in China. He had no doubts about the British Empire being a force for good, though he would on occasion deride the personalities and forces – political, financial, commercial – controlling the imperial machine as 'comical, subjects for savage ribaldry. Or pathetic. Or sordid'. But of the empire itself, he was a full supporter, maintaining that to condemn it because of the failings of the individuals in charge was like criticising a great musical symphony on the grounds that 'the composer took dope and the conductor lived off the immoral earnings of women'.[5]

On the day Claud was born, the Japanese blew up the Russian flagship *Petropavlovsk* at the height of the Russo-Japanese War in 1904–5, the outcome of which was to affect significantly the lives of Henry, Elizabeth and their newborn son. Within months, Henry was appointed the British minister in Korea, a difficult posting because Japan was exploiting its victory over Russia fully to occupy the country. When his parents left Beijing for Seoul, two-year-old Claud was sent back to Britain, accompanied only by a Chinese amah, or nanny, with whom he went to stay with his grandmother in Scotland.[6]

Henry arrived in Seoul at the moment Japan was in the process of occupation, in the wake of its victory. In the next couple years, Henry was to get a close-up view of the British and Japanese empires at work and become a significant player in a rancorous dispute between them. What occurred revolved around the 'rendition' – Henry used the word in the modern post-9/11 sense of the detention of a political dissident with the implication that he is to be mistreated and tortured – of a Korean journalist opposed to the Japanese occupation. The story of this minor crisis foreshadows and confirms Claud's thesis that a radical journalist running a small publication can impede, harass and prod into an overreaction a much-greater power, which in this case was the Japanese Empire.[7] The episode also reveals that Henry, who was by far the greatest influence on Claud growing up, was the kind of independent-minded High Tory, with an overriding objection to injustice, whom his son always liked.

Henry's residence was a handsome brick building in the centre of Seoul, not far from the gaudy royal palace where he presented his credentials to the Korean emperor. Britain had swiftly recognised Japan's enhanced power in the Far East since it needed good relations with Tokyo in order to enable the Royal Navy to concentrate its warships in European waters to confront the growing threat from Germany. Henry's own title of 'minister' was downgraded to 'consul-general', but he did not express any objection to this in his first dispatches to the Foreign Office, to whom he continued to report directly. Seeing Korea purely in terms of geopolitics, he spoke of it as 'a pawn in a game of chess that has been the centre of interest solely by reason of its position relative to the pieces of the great powers'.

The abdication of the Korean emperor, forced by Japan, provoked an uprising in 1907 that lasted four years and left 17,000 dead. Henry's dispatches are coolly written non-partisan accounts of Japan's destruction of Korean independence, the resistance, the emperor's enforced abdication, the mutiny and dissolution of the Korean army, and the beginning of a ferocious guerrilla war. He could see that 'the continued military occupation of disturbed districts . . . has had the unfortunate result of further embittering the people against Japan'.

Ill-treatment had driven those who were formerly neutral into revolt. Koreans who worked for or cooperated with the Japanese were despised as traitors, worse than the Japanese themselves. 'As for the interpreters employed by the troops,' Henry wrote, 'they rely on the fact that no complaint can reach a Japanese officer's ears except through themselves, and harass, bully and rob the people with impunity.' But the Japanese military had not been 'indiscriminate[ly] laying waste the country and many of the houses and villages of which the destruction is laid to the account of Japanese troops were in fact burned by the insurgents as a punishment for harbouring the troops'.[8]

At the heart of Korean resistance, so the Japanese occupation authorities had convinced themselves, were two British-owned newspapers, which they very much wanted to close down; however, they could not do so, because Britain had extraterritorial rights in Korea under the terms of the Anglo-Japanese Alliance Treaty of 1905. The papers were the English-language *Korea Daily News* and the Korean *Taehan Maeil Sinbo*, both of which were owned by a British journalist, Ernest Bethell, who was a fierce critic of the occupation, and they were safely located on British property. Henry reluctantly began court proceedings against Bethell under pressure from Prince Ito, the former Japanese prime minister who was overseeing the occupation of Korea. Henry wrote a private letter to a Foreign Office official in London saying that he 'hated interference with free criticism being convinced that it generally did far less harm than good'.[9] He only acted more energetically when an American adviser to the Japanese authorities in Korea, Durham White Stevens, was assassinated in San Francisco in March 1908 by a Korean nationalist. Bethell's Korean paper reported the killing under the headline 'Particulars of the Attack upon the Scoundrel Stevens'.

Exultation over the murder was too much for Henry, who wrote that a parallel case would be if 'the assassination of a prominent Anglo-Indian official by a native of Bengal' had been praised as a patriotic act by the Bengali press.[10] He sentenced Bethell to three weeks in prison, to be served in Shanghai, and believed that he had gone a long way to meeting Japan's demand for Bethell's deportation. He also felt that they exaggerated the influence of Bethell's newspapers, which Henry saw as reflecting rather than provoking Korean anti-Japanese feeling.

But on 13 July, Japanese police lured the chief witness for Bethell's defence, a prominent Korean journalist called Yang Ki-Tak, from the safety of a British-owned property and arrested him. Henry wrote angrily that the 'police had made up their minds to punish Yang, and the higher authorities thought the information that might be obtained from him, if he were left sufficiently long at the mercy of the police, worth getting for political reasons'. In other words, he would be tortured into making a confession, 'but, if so, the police will certainly ensure by threats his silence on the subject if he is ever released from prison'. In any case, Henry pointed out, a Korean like Yang could be executed at any moment on charges of having contact with insurgents.[11]

Three weeks later, on 1 August, a visitor who saw Yang in prison said he was shocked to find him emaciated, sick and terrified of his guards. Confined to a filthy flea-ridden cell so crowded that he could not lie down, but with a ceiling so low that he could not stand upright, the visitor – so Henry reported to the Foreign Office – had been struck by Yang's skeleton-like appearance after only a few weeks and 'by the cowering timid air with which he looked nervously at prison officials before he answered the simplest inquiries'. At first, he said that he had nothing to complain of, but then whispered in a low, agitated voice, 'I can't breathe. I can't breathe. I can get no air.'[12]

The arrest, imprisonment and torture of the chief witness in a trial over which he had presided ended Henry's voluntary cooperation with Japanese officials, whose misbehaviour he described with growing outrage.[13] He compared the dimensions of the prison cell in which Yang was held unfavourably with those of the Black Hole of Calcutta, in which British captives had been confined during the Indian Mutiny. He wrote sarcastically that the only effect of his insistence that the British government was concerned about the torture of a prisoner was to convince the Japanese officials that 'if I persisted in dwelling on so trivial a side issue [as the torture of a suspect], it must be because I was inspired by an unfriendly wish to interpose obstacles in the Japanese path'.[14]

The case then took a bizarre turn. Henry's vigorous protests had had an impact: Prince Ito sent orders from Japan that Yang should be taken to hospital. Misunderstanding their instructions, the prison wardens released him instead, and he immediately fled back to safety at Bethell's newspaper office. The Japanese demanded his surrender, but Henry refused to comply. Newspapers in Japan attacked Henry as viscerally anti-Japanese and demanded his recall. Sir Claude MacDonald, the British ambassador in Tokyo, was sympathetic to the Japanese demand, saying that conditions in Korean prisons sounded no worse than those he had seen in British-controlled Egypt. Henry's dispatches began to carry a sense that he knew he was losing support in the Foreign Office, and this was indeed correct, with one senior official commenting in a minute that 'with a little goodwill and less heat on Cockburn's part', the confrontation with the Japanese could have been avoided.[15]

Henry wrote a telegram to MacDonald, entitled 'Rendition of Corean', warning that 'if it became known that we had handed over a prisoner to the Japanese & that he had subsequently been subjected to conditions similar to those which obtained in the case of Yang, the worst impression would be created'. He stalled for time, but to no avail.[16] On 20 August, Henry was directly ordered by the foreign secretary, Sir Edward Grey, to surrender Yang to the Japanese, and he grudgingly did so the following day. 'Had I seen him [Yang] in a hospital bed I should have said that he looked a very ill man,' he wrote pointedly in his report on the handover.[17] Henry's obduracy did, however, produce one positive result in that the Japanese had been embarrassed into promising Britain that Yang would have a fair trial. When it took place, he was found innocent and released.

This could have been small consolation to Henry, who had left Korea for England by the Trans-Siberian Railway on 15 September, writing to MacDonald to say that he felt let down by his superiors. 'Twice in the course of the case I was forced to do something I had formally refused to do,' he wrote.[18] Japanese newspapers claimed that he had been sacked for his refusal to give up Yang. This was denied by MacDonald, but he clearly blamed Henry for provoking the row and informed the Japanese, somewhat treacherously, that Henry was determined to resign once he got back to England.

Henry did so in the summer of 1909, but he made no mention in his letter of resignation of the Yang Ki-Tak affair, saying only that he wished to retire on a pension because of ill health brought on by his long service in China and Korea. He included in the letter a doctor's certificate saying that Henry was no longer able to discharge his official duties.

Had he had some form of psychological breakdown as a result of events in Korea? He wrote that it is with some sense of humiliation that one admits oneself to have broken down at an earlier than usual age, but I am, I think, justified in regarding the strain of my work at Peking between 1894 to 1898, and of the siege of the Legation in 1900, as having been of more than usual severity. My work in Korea was not light, but it would not have overtaxed my strength, as it did, if I had ever fully recovered from these earlier strains.[19]

The studied lack of reference to his row with the Japanese, which had produced a flood of Foreign Office documents, suggests that he wanted to avoid such a controversial subject. This was probably because he was keen to maximise his pension, which was all the more necessary since he had no job to go to.

In the event, none of those involved in the rendition of Yang prospered: Henry's diplomatic career was ended, Bethell died young in 1909, his early death attributed to excessive brandy-drinking and smoking. Great numbers of Koreans attended his funeral. Prince Ito was assassinated by a Korean nationalist the same year. The Japanese occupation took four years to catch up with Yang, whom they again imprisoned after a trial, in which his co-defendants said they had been hung by their thumbs from the ceiling, brutally beaten and burned with cigarettes until they confessed. Henry's successors as British consul-general in Seoul all cooperated assiduously with the Japanese authorities.

Henry never revealed to Claud precisely why he had abruptly left Korea and resigned from the Foreign Office. His silence was probably motivated by a mixture of official discretion and a feeling, as Claud grew up, that telling him about what his father had done in Korea, however commendable, would serve only to further fuel his son's growing hostility to the British Empire.

Back in Scotland, Claud was being brought up by his Chinese amah, who remained the main influence on his childhood at this time. The amah spoke no English and was unhappy – boys threw stones at her because of her strange appearance. She was from the Manchurian border and was frightened that she and Claud would be attacked by tigers when they walked in the hills. After his parents returned to Britain at the end of 1908, they discovered that he spoke only Chinese. To Claud's distress, they sent the much-loved amah back to China.

Claud's third wife, Patricia Arbuthnot, believed that he never forgave his mother for this. He recalled standing up in his bath and shouting at her in Chinese, which she did not understand: 'I wish you would go away to a far country.' He later forgot the language and had only shadowy memories of anything relating to China, though one night, just before he died in 1981, he spoke deliriously about Chinese pirates attacking the house and asking for his mother to tell Number One Houseboy something about firearms.[20]

Towards the end of 1908, his parents came into his life once again, following his father's retirement. 'Quite suddenly', wrote Claud, 'he announced he was weary of the whole business and retired, saying that at forty-nine it was high time to start leading an entirely new sort of life.'[21] Claud knew that his father's retirement was connected to his view that Britain's alliance with Japan in the Far East was a disastrous mistake. This was true in general terms, but Henry never explained the highly dramatic reason for his final departure from China.

The most immediate effect of Henry and Elizabeth's early return to England on Claud, now four years old, was that he – unlike many children of the empire – was not scarred by a lengthy separation from his parents at an early age. Rudyard Kipling, sent home from India to stay with unsympathetic foster parents, referred to this period of his own life as 'the House of Desolation'. Claud, on the contrary, was to spend more time with his father and mother than most children, and he always regarded his father with great affection and respect for his political insights, even when, as he grew older, they were diametrically opposite to his own. His mother Elizabeth and his elder sister Louise, who had been born a few months after the siege of Beijing, are shadowy figures in his autobiography, though it contains many anecdotes about his two uncles – Frank Cockburn, a Canadian banker, and Philip Stevenson, a half-pay major turned historical novelist. When Claud does talk about his mother, she is presented as somebody with an unremarkable personality and highly conventional opinions. His sister Louise moved to Canada when relatively young, and they largely lost touch.

Going by Henry's diplomatic cables and the accounts of people who met him in China, he was a highly educated and intelligent man of wide-ranging interests who spoke fluent Chinese and was very much at home in China. A Dutch diplomat, William Oudendyk, whom Henry befriended in Beijing in the 1890s, wrote of Henry that he 'had a very clear judgement, as well about men as about books and political events, and in everything he discovered a comical and often pathetic aspect which other people did not discern'.[22]

This sounds very much like Claud, who had a similar absorption in politics. Oudendyk remembered Henry in Beijing in 1895 discussing the prospects for war in Europe: 'I can still hear him saying that "should we ever have to fight against the German army, I should fix all my hopes on the Kaiser, he will be sure to mess things up for the Germans."'[23] Since this was largely what Kaiser Wilhelm II was to do before and after 1914, the Dutch diplomat was much impressed by Henry's prescience.

Claud had a happy childhood to all appearances, though he was dismissive of the belief that he and his family were living in the golden glow of Edwardian England, blind to the onrushing disaster of the First World War which was soon to engulf them. 'In our little house [in Tring, Hertfordshire]', Claud wrote in the first line of a three-volume memoir, 'the question was whether war would break out first, or the revolution.' His family was of the opinion that war was likely to come first and that it was at least a familiar evil, unlike revolution, which was unknown and possibly more dangerous.

In 1910, Henry told the six-year-old Claud to stop playing French against English with his tin soldiers and instead play English against Germans. This bothered Claud since one of the soldiers was a clearly identifiable Napoleon on a white horse and could not be credibly reassigned as the commander of the German army. Out for walks with Louise and the new nanny, who had replaced the amah, he worried about their lack of alertness to the threat of German cavalry charging out of the Chiltern Hills.[24]

Henry spent much of his life outside Britain and the boundaries of the British Empire, where he was wholly immersed in Chinese culture and society for decades. As a result, he had difficulty settling back into life in England, a country which, according to Claud, he did not much care for aside from the English countryside in spring. At the age of sixteen, Claud cross-questioned his father about his contradictory attitude to England and the British Empire:

'Were you always absolutely sure it was good thing to try to extend British power in China?' Claud asked.

'Absolutely.'

'But you don't much like English people.'

'Hang it, I like some English people.'

'Not many.'

'True.'

'You don't care for their attitude to life. You know they bore you to death. Secretly, everything they say seems to you platitudinous or else untrue.'

'A lot of Chinese are awfully silly, too,' replied Henry before changing the subject and suggesting a game of chess.[25]

Henry's dissatisfaction with life in England explains why the family moved restlessly from place to place, living in four or five different houses in the years before the outbreak of the war, by which time they had settled permanently in the village of Tring in Hertfordshire. Claud said that his father had later admitted to him that all these houses had a common fault: none of them were in the hills west of Beijing.[26]

Claud's intellectual closeness to his father differed markedly from the experience of most of his generation at Oxford, many of whom were alienated to a greater or lesser degree from their parents. In Claud's case the opposite was true, as his father treated him as his intellectual companion from an early age; this, in turn, may explain why Claud was so sympathetic to earlier generations of his family in Scotland.

3

'First Experiences in Revolution'

Claud aged 15 at Berkhamsted school; 2nd row from back, 7th from left [Berkhamsted School Archive]

Henry paid much attention to Claud's education, though he had reservations about the English public school system. His doubts concerned not its reputation for barrack-room discipline but what he saw as its lack of intellectual and moral rigour. The school he chose for Claud was Berkhamsted in Hertfordshire, in the market town of the same name, twenty-six miles northwest of London. Contemporary accounts suggest that it was a more civilised place than many public schools of the day, its standards raised by its high-minded, forceful and politically liberal headmaster, Charles Greene, the father of the novelist Graham Greene.

At the last moment, just before Claud entered the school at the age of nine in 1913, Henry was shocked to discover that the school's motto was 'Virtus laudata crescit' (Virtue grows with praise).[1] To most people this might appear a harmless piece of advice, but Henry disapproved of it strongly, feeling that it 'was virtually to flaunt a conviction that people cannot be expected to be any good *unless* they are patted on the back for it'.[2]

Claud started as a day-boy in the Preparatory Section at Berkhamsted and stayed at the school for nine years, until he went up to Keble College Oxford at the age of eighteen in 1922. He later became a boarder, but Tring is only six miles from Berkhamsted, so he was not separated from his parents for long periods. Suspecting laxity in the school's academic standards, Henry coached Claud in Latin for two hours a day in term time and for one hour a day in the holidays. The school said encouragingly that Latin was not hard to learn, but Henry insisted to Claud that it was, on the contrary, an extremely difficult language to learn which required intense concentration and hard work.

This attitude might have repelled many children, but Claud found his hours of study 'happily astringent' and 'agreeably challenging'.[3] It is not clear how far this personal tuition by his father was interrupted when Henry returned to government service at the start of the war. He told people that he was working in the Censorship Department, and his obituary in the *Times* says the same thing, but Claud believed he was engaged in 'some hush-hush job', the nature of which his son never discovered.[4]

In pressing Claud to work harder, Henry was not motivated solely by high-mindedness. Claud recalled a conversation with his father soon after 1914, when he was ten or eleven years old. He had proudly said that he had come second out of fifteen in his Latin class three weeks running, though most of the boys were older than himself. 'But why not be top?' Henry asked him. 'If you can be second, you can be first. This war is going to make things unpleasant for any one of our sort, who doesn't get to the top and stay there all the time. Don't take your pace from other people. I doubt if the people at the school realise what things are really like.'[5]

Claud enjoyed academic study at school, saying that he found it so stimulating that what was described as 'work' was more like an entrancing game. Not many schoolchildren give such high marks to their teachers. Outside the classroom, he was less enthusiastic about the rigorously enforced asexual morality and the emphasis on 'keenness' in sports and general behaviour. 'Offenders against the moral tone, when detected, were expelled two by two,' he recalled. 'But there were few such, if only for the reason that there simply was not time for anything of that kind, at least not among the boarders of whom, after a few years as a day boy, I became one.'[6]

One boy who was spotted by a master kissing a girl in a public park was expelled the next day.[7] Convinced that school-boys, if left alone and unoccupied for more than a few minutes, would get up to vicious mischief, the school authorities filled their time with compulsory communal activities. In summer there was cricket, played on a field half a mile from the school which could only be reached at a brisk jog-trot. In spring and winter, cricket was replaced by football, running and the Officers' Training Corps (OTC). Berkhamsted school records show that Claud was in the Lowers House football team.[8] Only in the OTC is he recorded as playing an active part, becoming a corporal and later an officer. He wrote: 'The thing seemed to make sense. It was realistic. You would be out one day on a field exercise firing blank ammunition under command of a prefect who was also your platoon commander, and a few weeks or months later on, you would hear that he had been killed in France.'[9]

By closely observing the timing of roll-calls, Claud avoided the cricket pitch and went for long walks in the Hertfordshire countryside. He discovered a way to disappear by crawling through a hole he had found in the ceiling of a classroom that led into its roof space. Since it was a new classroom, nobody suspected that such a hole could exist. Once inside his hideout, he lay on the wooden beams and safely read Edward Gibbon, Lord Macaulay and the poems of Robert Browning. He even sought to teach himself German, which was not on the school curriculum, learning to read it with some proficiency; however, since there was nobody to teach him pronunciation, his version of German bore no relation to the real pronunciation of the language, such that he was fluent but entirely unintelligible.[10]

Another escape from the tedious routine of school roll-calls and compulsory games came about because his headmaster, Charles Greene, was a passionate chess player and Claud was deemed to be the best chess player in the school. When the urge to play the game overcame Greene, Claud would be summoned to his study, where he would sit safely for hours beside the fire, 'listening contentedly to the imperious but temporarily innocuous jangle of bells summoning people to get on with something or other and the shouts of prefects driving others along cold corridors without'.[11]

Charles Greene – referred, though never to his face, as 'Charles' by the schoolboys – was the headmaster of Berkhamsted between 1910 and 1927, a period which includes the entire nine years when Claud was there. Greene had a powerful effect on everybody he met, but his influence on Claud was all the greater because Greene had become a friend of Henry, despite the latter being a fervent imperialist and Greene a committed supporter of the Liberal Party.

Of Greene, Claud recalled, 'He was a man of powerful and vivid reactions . . . Certain events, sometimes important, sometimes quite trivial, seemed to strike his mind with the heat and force of a branding iron.' History lessons to the sixth form were sonorous commentaries on the current state of affairs, which Greene believed to be heading towards general ruin. Wherever he looked, he saw signposts, from the days of Pericles in ancient Athens to the Boer War, pointing inexorably towards disaster: 'For Charles Greene was in the widest, as well as the party-political, sense of the word, a Liberal, and in the crack-up of Liberalism he saw the mark of doom.'[12]

In the very early days of the war, Henry may have been correct in telling Claud that nobody at Berkhamsted, neither teachers nor pupils, fully understood the depth of the calamity that was about to engulf them. But within a year or so, they would know all too well about the mass slaughter on the Western Front. When the fighting ended in 1918, no less than 230 former schoolboys from Berkhamsted had been killed, and many more wounded.[13] One boy who did go straight from school to France but survived was Cecil Hodges, who later described the grim mood among the older boys as they awaited the military call-up. He recollected 'a period at Berkhamsted (2 to 3 years or so) of unrelieved suspense and oppression' during which the soldiers-to-be were warned by grown-ups never to allow their sense of dread 'to diminish the will to win'.[14]

Claud was only fourteen years old when the war ended and was too young to feel threatened by conscription, but he witnessed the shattering impact of the conflict on Charles Greene: 'Most of the sixth form was wiped out year after year, and he'd sit there teaching the sixth form, then they would be called up and 80 per cent of them would be killed . . . it must have been an appalling experience for a man of his great liberal mind.' Militarism was on the rise everywhere. Claud recalled one day when a distraught Greene

came to our house and he said 'The most appalling thing had happened.' He had visited the playing fields where the school OTC was training and heard the Sergeant Major speaking to the recruits, saying 'well now when the enemy come out of trenches to surrender and raise their hands, remember not to take your fingers off [the trigger of] your machine guns.' Charles said: 'My God – we must all protest against the army becoming as barbaric as those fellows.'[15]

Just how far the mood of the times was out of keeping with Greene's own beliefs was made spectacularly clear on 11 November 1918, when the Armistice was signed with Germany. Claud played a small but crucial part in the dramatic events of that day in Berkhamsted, a role of which he may not have been especially proud, as he scarcely mentions it in his autobiography. That afternoon, he had covertly thrown the keys of the main gate of the school out of an upstairs window to a soldier waiting below. This allowed soldiers being trained around Berkhamsted town later to break into the school and thrash it in retaliation for what appeared to them to be Greene's unpatriotic and anti-war refusal to call a school holiday to celebrate the Allied victory.

In reality Greene's reasons for not declaring a school holiday, as was happening all over Britain, were by no means a sign of his opposition to the war, but he failed to explain them adequately to his pupils, the oldest of whom were overjoyed to have escaped death in the trenches, as were the soldiers doing their training in the Berkhamsted area.

Schoolboys and soldiers were both mistaken about the headmaster's motives. Greene in fact supported the war, but he was acutely aware of its hideous cost to Britain and to its educated elite in terms of dead and wounded. The names of the hundreds of dead from the school were commemorated by plaques outside the school chapel, while a further 1,145 former pupils remained on active duty in the armed forces. The end of the butchery might have persuaded Greene to declare the expected holiday, but he had reached a radically different decision about how victory should best be celebrated.

He had time to think about what to do because the news that the German kaiser Wilhelm II and Crown Prince Ruprecht had abdicated reached Berkhamsted on Sunday, 10 November, and the announcement of the end of the war was imminent. When this happened at 11:00 a.m. the following day, Greene announced it to staff and pupils, who sang 'God Save the King' before dispersing. He did not call a holiday but instead instructed everyone to go on working as if this were a normal day. His argument was that with so many dead – 880,000 British forces had been killed in the conflict – the survivors had to work even harder to make best use of the victory for the good of civilisation and they could not afford to take holidays. 'We must go on,' he said. 'Now is the time for effort.'

His decision, however reasonable in the abstract, was so entirely contrary to the patriotic fervour of the day that it provoked an almost-instantaneous uprising. Explaining this in an interview sixty years later, Claud told Norman Sherry, the author of the magisterial biography *The Life of Graham Greene*, that, deeply though he admired Charles Greene, he could understand the anger of the prefects and senior boys at not being allowed to celebrate victory. He pointed out they had been living in expectation of death or injury in the near future, 'so they didn't take much interest in the preservation of civilisation or the school spirit and they got pretty rough'.

The prefects, normally in charge of keeping tight discipline in Berkhamsted, had conspired with men from the Inns of Court OTC to break into the school. It is worth citing Claud's account of the uprising since it gives a tangible sense of the rapidly unfolding events:

> We were all sitting at prep in the Great Hall at about 7pm. So suddenly all these drunken troops and women came surging in and were planning to throw Charles Greene into the canal . . . and Greene and the second master Cox appeared at the end of that little passage, and defended the door, and Greene was persuaded to retire to his study. Cox stood at the door, and drunken troops joined in with the students, and we surged out of the school, and marched through the streets of Berkhamsted, and I can remember to this day walking down Berkhamsted High Street and I took off my shoes in order to beat on the drum with them. We then occupied the local cinema and we sprang onto the stage and sang songs and yelled and shouted. And at last, the troops retired, and we, rather bedraggled, returned after this enormous elation, this tremendous night, and suddenly realised that we had to face reality. And that reality was Charles Greene who was sitting at the big desk in the Great Hall, and said 'you're expelled, you're expelled' one after another. He expelled 122 of us.[16]

The rioters went to bed deeply worried. Claud was particularly anxious because he knew that his father would be furious if he were expelled. The following morning, he and the other expellees were brought back to the Great Hall and given a lecture by Greene, his denunciation of their action delivered with all the force and rolling periods of which his Victorian rhetoric was capable.

He linked the previous day's riot to the revolutionary upsurge spreading everywhere since the Bolshevik Revolution in 1917: 'This is one more exhibition of the spirit of Bolshevism which is spreading across Europe. Over there in Moscow, there sits Lenin, there sits Trotsky, there they are. The spirit of Bolshevism and atheism is creeping across Europe. It is breaking out all over. Look at Lenin, look at Trotsky and look at you.'

Fortunately for his by now thoroughly rattled listeners, Greene had expelled more of his pupils than he could really afford to do in one go, so all were reinstated aside from two, whom, Claud recalled, had 'tried to get the soldiers to break into Charles Greene's study and tear up his books – a really rather shitty thing to do'.[17]

After the Armistice Day riot, Claud spent nearly another four years at Berkhamsted. Charles Greene evidently did not hold his involvement in it against him, perhaps because of the extraordinary nature of the day and because so many others were involved. Claud said sixty years later that 'it was my first experience in revolution'.[18]

Of what quality was the education Claud received at Berkhamsted? By the time he left Berkhamsted he was cultured and well read, so the general level of teaching must have been good. An unrevealing certificate from the Oxford and Cambridge Schools Certificate Board in July 1919 says he had passed with credit in Latin, Greek, French and history.[19] A report for the school term ending on 21 December 1920 is good but not spectacularly so, listing him as coming fourth out of sixteen in Classical vi A. Of Claud's Latin and Greek. It says that he 'is quick and appreciative, but must not be led away from thoroughness by the facility with which he can turn out work'.[20]

Far more revealing about Claud's level of intellectual development is a handwritten magazine called *The Illiterary Digest*, published in October 1919 when he was fifteen.[21] The masthead of a surviving copy says it is a bi-monthly and 'the Magazine of the Sixths and VAs', in other words of the sixth and the upper fifth form. Going by his age, Claud would probably have been in the fifth form at the time, making him younger than other contributors. What makes the magazine so interesting is that he said later that he had started 'two school newspapers both of which were suppressed' and, given some of its content, this is most likely one of them.[22]

Two articles in the magazine are signed 'F. C. Cockburn', one of them a short story called 'The Vision', written in the style of Robert Louis Stevenson, but it is wordy and a bit dull. Much better is a series of verse parodies entitled 'The Poets and the Gnat', in which six famed poets – Tennyson, Coleridge, Wordsworth, Whitman, Macaulay and Swinburne – are imagined sleeping in the same bedroom, which is invaded by a gnat. Awakened by the sound of his buzzing, each poet writes a verse in their own style describing their attempts to deal with the gnat. The parodies are sophisticated and amusing, the best being about Macaulay who finally squashes the gnat with a railway guide:

> And nearer yet and nearer
> I brought that Railway Guide,
> And then – the yellow binding upper,
> The massive volume slid and slipped,
> With agile thumb I nipped
> And so, the creature died.

What got the magazine banned was most likely an anonymous gossip column written in Claud's handwriting which includes a sharply worded criticism of Charles Greene's performance during the annual speech day, known as Founders' Day. 'We hope', the item reads, 'that nobody noticed the unfortunate incident during the speeches. Our revered headmaster adopting his usual exalted tone told us dramatically how the school had flung open its doors to the boys from the streets etc etc. Two minutes later we were told "We have to do it. We get paid for it. That's all."' Claud also commented on the second-rate quality of the school prizes.

Not every boy at Berkhamsted had such happy memories of it as Claud. The only other pupil at the school whom Claud refers to by name in his memoirs, and who was to remain his friend for life, was Graham Greene, Charles's fourth child. Born in 1904 and Claud's exact contemporary, he described his eight terms as a boarder at St John's House at Berkhamsted as a time of undiluted misery. Bullied because of his ambivalent status as the son of the headmaster, he was friendless and depressed. Having attempting suicide by different means such as drinking cleaning fluid, hay fever drops and, finally, by swallowing twenty aspirins, he ran away from school. His protest worked surprisingly well, since his family reacted by sending him to stay with a psychoanalyst in London. His spirits much restored by this, he returned to Berkhamsted in 1921, where 'instead of those petty gangsters of St John's there were Eric Guest (later a distinguished Metropolitan magistrate), Claud Cockburn and Peter Quennell'. Graham and Quennell took riding lessons to avoid 'the loathsome O.T.C.', which Claud took seriously and enjoyed.[23] He relates how Graham's familiarity with the works of Sigmund Freud, thanks to his sojourn with the psychoanalyst, led to him listening with extreme interest to other members of the Greene family relating their dreams at breakfast – a common-enough practice at the time. 'He would leave the bacon cooling on his plate as he listened with the fascination of a secret detective,' recalls Claud. '"It's amazing," said Graham, "what those dreams disclose. It's startling – simply startling," and at the thought of it gave a low whistle.'[24]

In 1922, Claud took his Oxford scholarship examination, not caring which college he went to, so long as he went there immediately and thus got away from school.[25] Knowing how short his father was of money, he applied for the Field Marshall Gomm classical scholarship, worth £100.[26] He was sitting on the terrace of the Gellert Hotel in Budapest drinking iced beer when a telegram came from Keble College, Oxford, asking the question: 'Are you member Church of England?' Realising he must have won the scholarship, he was worried that he might not be a properly signed-up member of the Anglican church. Despondent at the possibility of being tripped up at the last moment by this requirement, he took the telegram to his father, who asked, 'Had I, for example, been received into the Roman Catholic or Mohammedan church? Since most of my ideas at that time seemed to him strange and even perverse, he would not have been surprised to hear that I had secretly become a Buddhist.' Reassured by Henry that early baptism into the Church of England meant membership for life, a much-relieved Claud sent a telegram to Keble simply saying, 'Yes'.[27]

4

'Budapest Rather Than Berkhamstead'

Budapest in time of civil war [wiki commons]

Soon after Claud arrived at Keble College, Oxford, in October 1922, his cousin Evelyn Waugh – like Claud, a great-grandson of Lord Henry Cockburn, the Scottish author and judge – came to see him.[1] Waugh says he made the visit only because of his strong sense of family loyalty. 'I went dutifully to call with small expectation of finding anyone very agreeable, for I found most of my mother's family a dull lot,' he wrote. 'I found a tall, spectacled young man with the air of Budapest rather than

Berkhamsted. His father had been there for the last two years on diplomatic business and Claud was already captivated by the absurdities of Central Europe.'[2]

Claud confirmed this account many years later, saying that Waugh 'dubbed me "mad" because I lived, except during Oxford terms, in Budapest'. It was not so much Claud being in Hungary that his cousin found extraordinary, but that he 'took the politics of Central Europe seriously'. For Waugh, England was the touchstone for reality. Claud recalls, 'He said to me, puzzled that "you talk as though all that were quite real to you."'[3]

Waugh was correct in seeing that Claud's time in Hungary, and in other countries in Central Europe which had been on the losing side in the First World War, had had a profound influence on his personality and politics. From the age of sixteen, his experiences differed radically from those of his contemporaries at Berkhamsted and later at Oxford. He felt that what was happened in Budapest, Vienna and Berlin was 'more real' than 'the artificiality' of England.[4]

Claud made his first visit to Hungary in 1920 after Henry had been unexpectedly offered a diplomatic posting there. After returning to government service during the war, Henry retired for a second time at the end of it, but then found himself acutely embarrassed by the sharp post-war rise in the cost of living. Fortuitously, he was offered a job by a friend on an inter-allied mission known as the Clearing House, dealing with the finances of war-shattered Hungary.[5] Claud quotes Henry asking his friend if the fact of him knowing almost nothing about Hungary and absolutely nothing about finance might pose an obstacle to him taking the post. The friend replied 'that they had had a man doing this job who knew all about Hungary and a lot about finance, but he had been seen picking his teeth with a tram ticket in the lounge of the Hungarian Hotel and was regarded as socially impossible'. Henry said that, if such was the case, he was prepared to accept the job offer, and, after buying a Hungarian grammar manual and a short book on finance, he took the Orient Express to Budapest, while Claud became a full-time boarder for his last two years at Berkhamsted.[6]

Hungary had been severely affected by the First World War; however, as in much of Central and Eastern Europe, the fighting did not end in 1918 but produced other equally ferocious conflicts. The job offered to Henry was a minor consequence of the Treaty of Trianon, signed at Versailles on 4 June 1920, which spelled out the full extent of Hungary's defeat.

As the great ethnic jigsaw puzzle of nationalities making up the Austro-Hungarian Empire broke apart into hostile fragments, Hungary became a rump state, losing two-thirds of its territory and population. Instead of the previous population of 21 million, most of whom had been non-Hungarians, the new state had a population of 7.5 million, with 3.3 million Hungarians left as minorities in neighbouring countries. Not only was the new state far smaller in geographical size than the old one, but it was under the tutelage of the victors, with its army reduced to 35,000 men and foreign commissions, such as the one for which Henry was working, supervising different aspects of the settlement enshrined in the treaty.[7]

Hungarians portrayed themselves as the victims of a vindictive peace, but this was not as unjust as they pretended. The Hungarians had been co-partners with the Austrian Germans as rulers of the Austro-Hungarian Empire, dominating subject races from Croatia to Transylvania. As the empire collapsed in 1918, long-repressed ethnic and social forces exploded. From the moment Claud first set foot in Central Europe, he was under pressure from Hungarians, Austrians and Germans to see them as victims of an unjust peace.

Revolution and counter-revolution were still in the air. Béla Kun had briefly established a Communist government in Budapest in 1919. Red Terror was followed by White Terror. Hungary's half million Jews were subjected to persecution and pogroms. When Claud first arrived at Budapest station from England, he was met by a member of the staff of the luxurious Gellert Hotel, where his family was staying, who stopped their car on a bridge over the Danube. 'We got out of the car', wrote Claud, 'and what he wanted to show me was a place beside the piles on the Pest side of the bridge, where he himself personally, he avowed, had seen the bodies of at least 300 Reds, who had fought for

Bela Kun and Communism in Hungary, floating against the piles after being shot or driven at bayonet-point into the river by officers of the counter-revolution.'[8] This had happened the previous year.

One motive for Henry and his family's move from placid Hertfordshire to chaotic and violent Hungary was money. On arriving in Bucharest, they temporarily took a suite of rooms in the Gellert, while they searched for a reasonably cheap house in the outskirts of the city. Henry argued that less impressive accommodation might reflect poorly on British prestige, expensive though it might be. Failing to find the ideal house, the hotel became their permanent address. 'We lived in that enormous suite in the Gellert approximately eighteen months,' Claud recalled, 'at the end of which it turned out that, so far from any money being saved . . . we were actually spending more money than we had.' They moved upstairs to a cheaper suite, but since this was smaller and more cramped than the old one, they took several additional rooms. This was to be their home for the next eighteen months, so the final cost was more than they would have paid if they had stayed in the suite they had originally occupied.[9]

Budapest was an extraordinarily exciting place for a boy who had been living a placid life in an English village or a public school. The Hungarian capital 'was a battlefield where everyone has come to a bad end, where all the heroes are dead and all the great causes betrayed'.[10] As for the public mood, people were 'frightened – frightened of being arrested, frightened of being murdered, frightened of being just ruined'.[11] A young man called Von Tanos was hired to teach Claud German and Hungarian five days a week. The family never knew much about him, his own stories of his origin changing by the day, other than that he was probably the offspring of a Hungarian aristocratic family down on its luck. 'He must have been some sort of liar and was not a very good teacher,' Claud wrote, but he was an anglophile, entranced by the idea of a mythical England where the upper classes were effortlessly wealthy and the lower orders respectful and compliant.

Claud sat in cafés in Budapest with Von Tanos and sympathised strongly with him over the tribulations of the Hungarians.

After drinking a great deal of wine over lunch, Von Tanos liked to read to Claud passages from Oswald Spengler's *Der Untergang des Abendlandes – The Decline of the West –* published in 1918. The book appeared to give comforting reasons rooted in history for the disastrous outcome of the war without blaming anybody in particular. The book sat on a shelf beside Claud's bed in the Gellert along with John Maynard Keynes's *Economic Consequences of the Peace,* the great liberal argument for a moderate peace with Germany and its allies.

Many others from Britain and other victorious countries were to become disillusioned with the outcome of the war in the coming years, but for Claud this disillusionment came earlier and went deeper. 'No doubt', he explained, 'this reaction was strongest among people who, like myself, lived in Central Europe at the time and were exposed to the well-organised lamentations of Hungarian landowner, German steel barons in the Ruhr, and ulcerated international bankers who declared that the break-up of the Austro-Hungarian Empire . . . had made profitable business virtually impossible.'[12] People like Claud ceased believing that Britain had fought the kaiser and his regime because of 'the Belgian atrocities and the torpedoing of innocent passenger ships'. Instead, they abruptly converted to the belief that power-hungry imperialist leaders were 'revengefully strangling the new German democracy, ruining the gay Viennese and depriving the good-natured Hungarians – who, as everybody knew, had really been on our side all along – of reasonable living space'.[13]

Claud's subsequent description of his sympathy for the defeated nations is self-mocking in tone, but at the time his views provoked furious rows with his father, who had never believed the Allies' war propaganda about fighting for democracy and self-determination – and was surprised that anyone else had been so naive as to do so. 'During the war itself he had never for moment imagined that the battles were being waged in the interests of democracy or civilization or even freedom,' recalled Claud. 'He found quite adequate inspiration in the conviction that we were fighting to prevent the German Empire doing us down.'

As for the awfulness of the Great War itself, Henry, who had plenty of experience of wars in the Far East, thought it not much more dreadful than other wars – aside from its scale and length. To Claud and other young men, this sounded like the sort of cynicism that had destroyed their world, an impression reinforced by Henry saying that people were exaggerating the uniqueness of the First World War, which seemed to him neither more nor less horrific than any other war.[14]

Family arguments became so bitter that Claud's mother Elizabeth – whom he seldom mentions in his writings and speaks of as a quietly conventional person – tried to make the peace between her husband and son. 'My mother,' said Claud, 'who liked everyone to have nice feelings, used to explain and try to excuse my rude outbursts against Western policy and Western diplomacy and my emotional paeans on behalf of the nobility and the heroism of the former enemy as being motivated simply by a natural and creditable sympathy for the fallen and the underdog.'[15] Looking back many years later, Claud felt that it would have been good had what his mother said been entirely true, but 'there was a good deal of hate as well as love in this attitude' of the young, like himself, who blamed the 'cynical old men' for tearing the world apart.

Claud later came to feel more sympathy for his father's point of view, self-criticising people, like himself and the liberal economist John Maynard Keynes, who too readily accepted the propaganda claims of the defeated. 'The curious alliance', he wrote, 'between the British liberal thinker [Keynes] and the most extreme of Central European Nationalists who cheerfully would have chopped his ears off had they seen the slightest profit to themselves in so doing, was one of the grotesque ironies of the period, but it was an irony which escaped people like myself.'[16]

On the other hand, by recognising by the end of the 1920s that he had been over-influenced by the fake claims to victimhood of Central European nationalists, Claud inoculated himself against similar claims made in the 1930s by the Nazis and the Italian fascists. He came to agree with his father that most of the uplifting things that governments say about why they go to war should be ignored as propaganda and that war itself is always a savage mess. In the event, it was Waugh who turned out to be wrong and Claud right about the 'absurdities of Central Europe' being a more accurate guide than peaceful England to a murderous future for everybody.

Arriving in Oxford in October 1922, Claud found it to be one of the few places where it was just possible to imagine that the First World War had not taken place. Former soldiers who became undergraduates soon after they left the trenches in 1918 had by this time mostly departed.

During his first days at Keble, Claud and Evelyn Waugh met and would spend much time together. With his mixture of gloom and exuberance, Claud found Waugh 'immediately attractive and stimulating ... with his eager, challenging, yet bewildered stare'.[17] Waugh, who had been there for a year already, 'introduced [Claud] to the Hypocrites' [Club], 'which he [later] described as a 'noisy, alcohol-soaked rat warren by the river', a description to which Waugh took offence. Writing with some venom, he said that Claud was 'as noisy and alcohol-soaked as any of the rats and soon became a fast friend of Hamish [Lennox], Christopher Hollis and all the "offal"-eaters'.

The 'offal-eaters' reference is to the dozen or so of Waugh's friends, whose collective nickname it was, who met regularly to eat and drink in his room at Hertford.[18] In fact, Claud was less condemnatory of the Hypocrites' Club than Waugh implies, saying that some might see it as a centre for civilised and literary conversation. 'I realized,' he wrote, 'not for the first time, that every story can be told two ways.'[19]

Claud found that his tutors were comically and unapologetically behind the times, impervious to any idea that had not been around for at least two hundred years. When he mentioned any concept of more recent origin to his philosophy tutor, the latter would invariably say, 'I think you'll find that it's pretty well been exploded.' Irked by this evasiveness, Claud describes bringing the tutor an important new book on philosophy just published that he knew the man had not read. In his old age, Claud remembered this as being Ludwig Wittgenstein's

Tractatus Logico-Philosophicus, the renowned philosophic work published in German in 1921 and in English the following year.[20] The tutor took the book, only to return it after a few hours, saying, 'I rather gather that the man is soon to be exploded.'[21]

More generally, the tutors Claud met at Oxford may have been moribund, but during the first half of the 1920s the university was to produce more notable writers – mostly novelists but also historians, journalists and critics – than in any period before or since. The novelists included Graham Greene, Evelyn Waugh, Anthony Powell, Henry Yorke, L. P. Hartley and Henry Green. Men of letters included Harold Acton, Cyril Connolly, Peter Quennell, John Betjeman and Robert Byron. They did not belong to any single intellectual movement, though they were often derided by more philistine undergraduates as decadent modernists and aesthetes. By all accounts, the university as a teaching institution had little to do with this surge in literary achievement.

Most members of this disparate intellectual group were intelligent, gregarious and well educated, drinking heavily but doing little academic work at Oxford until panic set in in their final year. The explanation for their non-stop socialising was most probably that – as with other less intellectual undergraduates – they were young men shifting abruptly from an adolescence subjected to the infantilising routines of public school life to the largely unrestricted freedom and near-adult life of the university. Over-strict the public schools may have been, but their teaching was usually of high quality and the work much harder than at university, where the tutors were frequently as mediocre and hidebound as Claud described them and the undergraduates could get away with doing little prescribed academic work.

An important difference between university life then, compared to sixty years later, was that undergraduates lived in an almost exclusively male world. Waugh estimated that, though there was much talk about sex, 'fewer than ten per cent of my contemporaries had experience of heterosexual intercourse'.[22] Graham Greene made a similar comment, saying: 'We lived in those days continuously with sexual experience we had never known; we talked, we dreamt, we read, but it was always there.'[23] This sexual inexperience was probably not quite so true of Claud, since he was spending part of each year in the less inhibited atmosphere of Budapest and Vienna.[24]

Instead, there was drinking – mainly at the Hypocrites' Club, occupying two rooms and kitchen above a bicycle shop at 31 St Aldates, until it was suppressed in 1924. Members marked its end with a funeral dinner in a hotel, and leading members had driven riotously back to Oxford in a glass hearse.[25] 'We enjoyed not only drink but drunkenness,' said Waugh. 'There was a drinking set and I was of it. Most of my friendships were made in our cups.'[26]

The gargantuan consumption of alcohol was astonishing, and it was not confined to the Hypocrites. Graham Greene at Balliol belonged to a different set from Waugh, but during one term he 'went to bed drunk every night and began drinking again immediately I woke'.[27] Asked about this in a television interview years later, Claud said that if he had not noticed Greene's drunkenness, it was because he himself 'was equally drunk'. Speaking to Norman Sherry, Greene's biographer, he recalled, 'I got up fairly early, 8 a.m. I would then drink a large sherry glass of neat whisky before breakfast and . . . drink heavily throughout the day . . . God the amount of liquor one took on board.'[28] He remained a hard drinker all his life, a point mentioned frequently and sometimes censoriously in MI5 and police reports. He became and remained a heavy smoker.

Claud edited the student magazine *Isis* and wrote a column for a local paper in Oxford in exchange for small sums of money. He speaks of his political activities as coming a distinct second to having a good time and, if possible, finding somebody else to pay for it. He was secretary, at different times, of the two different factions of the Liberal Party, whose university branch was split between the adherents of Lloyd George and Herbert Asquith. 'Lloyd George', Claud said, 'like so many clever old men thought that younger men, particularly young upper-class men, were fools.' He funded a club of sympathetic Liberals called the New Reform, but his generous subsidy was spent on expensive champagne which was sold to members at below cost price.[29] Later, after the Hypocrites was suppressed, the New

Reform became a place of refuge for former members.[30] At another moment, Claud and Graham joined the miniscule local Communist Party, motivated – according to Graham's account – by the far-fetched idea of getting free trips to Moscow and Leningrad, which never happened because their mercenary motives were soon detected and their membership lapsed.[31]

At the end of 1923, Claud's and Graham's second year at Oxford, they staged an undergraduate exploit, and then, a few months later, took part in a much more serious and potentially dangerous adventure. The first escapade happened just before Christmas in 1923, when they dressed as tramps and rented a barrel organ, which they took to Berkhamsted and played outside the houses of people who had known them since childhood, but without being recognised. They had agreed to take no money with them and live off their earnings, which turned out to be meagre. They soon found that it was only the poor who gave them anything.[32] They stayed out three nights, at first trying to sleep in a frozen field and then taking refuge in a half-built house.

Graham later wrote a description of their weird adventure that gives its flavour, which he said remained fresh in his memory after fifty years.[33] He reflected that it was the last time that he could recall 'a Claud frightened, and a Claud disguised'. His account is worth quoting at length:

> The first night we spent in a half-built house in a field outside Boxmoor – a drear December lodging, with a wind biting at us through the empty window spaces, so that we rose while it was still dark to escape the cold and found ourselves pursued the length of a long hedge by an invisible figure who coughed at us from the black field. Then – I can swear it – Claud as well as myself experienced fear until he realised that it was a cow which coughed. As for the disguise, while we passed through the town of Berkhamsted, where we were both known, we thought it better to wear Christmas masks, and these masks brought the tour to a premature close, each of us became so enraged by the other's false face. I know nothing of how I looked, but Claud's long lantern face was hidden under the swollen pink cheeks of

Billy Bunter. The mask wore a perpetual toffee-fed grin, so that Claud's serious running commentary on his life and times irritated me profoundly. Billy Bunter had no business to hold views about [German foreign minister Gustav] Stresemann's darker side, and I began to contradict every one of them behind my equally misleading mask, so that we would almost certainly have come to blows if we had not slipped in time behind a hedge at the entrance of Tring, taken off our false faces and changed our clothes. Then we abandoned the organ and parted, not quite such good friends for a while as we had been.[34]

Graham, in his later writings, liked to join up the dots between the experiences of youth and the actions of the mature adult. In this case, he suggested that the episode with the barrel organ taught Claud never again to wear a mask to conceal his true identity and his intentions, though this seems to rather force the evidence.

The escapade with the barrel organ does show an adolescent taste for mischief-making and cocking a snook at their elders. There was nothing very strange in this student jape, except their determination in carrying it out. Their next adventure, a few months later, was much more grown up and was a foretaste for the sort of activities that Claud and Graham were to carry out for the rest of their lives.

5

'A Damned Odd Sort of Englishman'

A French soldier menaces a civilian in the occupied Rhineland [wiki commons]

In April 1924 a British military intelligence officer in the Rhineland – German territory occupied by the British, French and Belgian armies – was perplexed by the contents of a copy of an intercepted German government letter.[1] It revealed that two nineteen-year-old students at Oxford University, Claud Cockburn and Graham Greene, were undertaking an illicit trip to the Ruhr, occupied by France and Belgium in 1923 because of Germany's non-payment of reparations for the First World War. The two young men planned to investigate atrocities inflicted by the French occupiers and their German separatist proxies in what came to be called the 'Revolver Republic'.

Claud was already sympathetic to people from the defeated powers, whom he viewed as victims of collective punishment unjustly inflicted by the victorious Western allies. Graham was outraged by an account he had read of French and Separatist atrocities in British historian Stephen Moss's book *Defeat*, which included an eyewitness description of a German policeman being beaten to death with lead pipes by Separatists. 'I was easily aroused to indignation by cruelties not my own,' wrote Graham by way of explaining the motives for their expedition.[2] 'We decided to do something about it,' recalled Claud. 'When you say to Graham, "let's go somewhere," and you mean next month, he means tomorrow afternoon.'[3] For two young students with no money to contemplate such a risky journey showed self-confidence and political engagement carried to the point of knight errantry on behalf of those suffering injustice. 'Graham is a real campaigner for the underdog,' said Claud. 'If a man was having a raw deal, Graham would honestly rush out into the street and get killed.' Much the same was to be said of Claud himself, though in his account of their journey he portrayed himself as the cautious one of the pair.

They had no money to pay for their travels, but they acted with impressive speed to secure funding. Claud wrote articles to raise small sums, while Graham, 'on a blind and impudent off-chance', wrote to the German embassy in London saying that he and Claud might write articles sympathetic to the German position on the French-led occupation if the embassy helped finance them in getting to the Ruhr and provide introductions for them once they got there. The request for a subsidy was taken seriously by diplomats at the embassy, possibly influenced by Graham's Balliol College address, who provided twenty-five pounds in cash.[4] Graham's father Charles, who was still headmaster at Berkhamsted, was worried about his son accepting money from the German government and offered to pay for the trip himself. 'I knew that he could ill-afford his generosity, so I turned down the offer,' wrote Graham.

He interpreted German suspicions that their communications were being intercepted by the British authorities as paranoia, but their fears turned out to be entirely correct. A telegram marked 'Secret' sent by a Captain Miller, apparently in military intelligence, dated 10 April 1924, survives in the National Archives at Kew. A file contains a translation of a German Foreign Office paper sent from Berlin to Cologne telling the authorities there to give all assistance to the two young visitors 'in word and deed'.[5]

Miller was aware that they had not obtained the necessary documents to visit occupied territory. He asked London for information about the travellers, which was duly sent to him, presumably drawing on the details supplied by them for their passport applications. Claud's description reads: 'Height 6ft. 2 ins.; eyes brown, hair brown; wears spectacles.' Confirming Claud's and Graham's beliefs, often expressed in their later writings about the ineptitude of intelligence services, the memo confuses Graham Greene with his cousin Tooter Greene, who was the same age as Graham. An undergraduate at St John's, Cambridge, Tooter had joined the trip because he spoke German, though Claud insisted that he could speak it 'damn near as well as Tooter'.

Tooter says that there was a craze for Limericks at the time and remembered one composed by Claud as they travelled between the cities on the Rhine. Claud often made up Limericks in later years, but this is the first one to be recorded. It reads:

> While in a boat with Eva
> She went into a sexual fever
> She opened her thighs
> And to my surprise
> A man on a bank called, 'Beaver!'

Tooter emphasised that they were all very young at the time, but, despite their age, they were resolute and efficient in carrying through their rather dangerous plan. Claud and Graham picked up their letter of introduction in Cologne, unaware that it had already been copied and translated by British military intelligence.

They did not like all the Germans to whom they were introduced. Graham describes a 'Dr Henning, who owned a great dye factory outside Cologne and gave us a gargantuan feast in Leverkusen, while he talked glibly of Germany's starvation'.

They visited Bonn, Trier, Mainz and Essen, where the factory workers were on strike and they were mistaken for detested French officials overseeing the occupation. 'In the evening we went to a cabaret where we were even more unwelcome,' Graham wrote to his mother, 'and a rather fat naked woman did a symbolic dance of Germany in chains, ending up of course with her breaking her fetters.'[6] In an interview half a century later Claud gave a vivid picture of their time in Essen:

> It was a very dangerous place, the French trigger-happy, and the thugs from the separatists and so on. My plan was to stay in the hotel, examine the situation and in broad daylight go out and see what was going on. Not so Graham – 'it's at night things happen' – and so, against my will, we set out. We walked through the streets of Essen and under some awful railway bridge. It looked like some recipe for murder, shots going off at intervals. I suggested that it was more prudent to survive and get back home with our story, but it was no use. I think Graham had a pistol so we trekked on under endless railway bridges and underpasses and God knows what and I was scared shitless. Graham striding boldly along, oblivious to danger.[7]

In Heidelberg, outside they occupied zone, they met a man who ran death squads operating against alleged collaborators with the French or the Separatists. He would kidnap his victims and bring them back to Germany for trial for high treason. Graham may have been more conscious of the dangers than Claud imagined, since he says that 'we flirted with fear' and remembered how they started to plan a novel in the manner of John Buchan.

They never wrote the book, though Graham did write at least one piece sympathetic to the Germans in the Ruhr, and their accounts in letters and interviews are atmospheric.[8] Momentarily, Graham even considered going back to Germany and becoming a sort of secret agent for the anti-occupation Germans, though such ideas lapsed when the French withdrew from the Ruhr in 1925. Neither Claud nor Graham expressed any regrets over their visit, which was quite an accomplishment for young men with no resources. Describing it decades later, they both sound a little defensive, as if they recognised that many of the German nationalists they met at the time later became firm supporters of Hitler.

As Claud approached his last year at Oxford, he was faced by the question of how to pay off his debts to shopkeepers and tradesmen in the city, and the important longer-term question of what he would do once he left the university in 1926. The two problems were interrelated because he needed a job to satisfy his creditors, as he himself explained:

> By this time my debts were relatively enormous – enormous that is in relation to any prospect there seemed to be of ever meeting them. They seemed to rise uncontrollably like flood water, without any reference to my effort to increase my income. For a while, I edited the Oxford University weekly paper *The Isis*, I wrote a weekly column during term time for one of the Oxford city papers, and occasionally I sold articles or a short story elsewhere. None of it seemed to make any difference.[9]

Whatever decision Claud took about his future was given greater urgency because his father had again retired after the Clearing House in Budapest, for which he had been working, finished its work. It had long since become obvious that hopes of living more cheaply in Hungary than in Hertfordshire were illusory, and his parents had returned to Tring. They put polite pressure on Claud to decide what he was going to do in life, one suggestion being that he should follow his father into the Foreign Office.

As with many undergraduates leaving university, he found that the very idea of irrevocably choosing a career gave him an acute sense of claustrophobia.[10] Casting around for an occupation that might allow him to postpone choosing what job he would do, he learned that Queen's College, Oxford, offered a travelling fellowship, named after a wealthy donor called Laming, which was open to anybody gaining first- or second-class honours degree. The fellowships, which were particularly suitable for those intending to enter the Foreign Office, offered £250 a year to a graduate to enable him to live in one or more foreign countries for two years.

Claud knew that in most parts of modern Europe this sum would scarcely keep a person in cigarettes, but he believed he knew a number of places where a student without financial obligations to anyone but himself could live in comfort and freedom on that amount.[11] Above all else, the fellowship would enable him to return to Central Europe, for which he felt an intense longing. 'The valley of the Danube', he wrote, 'was the first area in which I had ever felt immediately and completely at home, not after months or even days of living there but immediately – within an hour.'[12]

Dismayed by Claud's decision, Henry argued that he might not get one of the four fellowships on offer annually, as some of the brightest undergraduates in the university were also candidates. Since the examination for the fellowships would not take place until the spring of 1927, and Claud was leaving Keble the previous summer, what was he going to live on in the interim? 'For two days', he recalled, 'the whole project of the fellowship filled my father with gloom and foreboding. On the third day, he suddenly remarked characteristically, that "I've been thinking this thing over and it seems to me that if this is what you want to do, the best thing to do is to do it."'[13]

Claud may have wavered over what he should do, but once he had decided to try for the Queen's fellowship, he was wholly determined that he would get it. To do so he needed at least a second-class honours degree in *literae humaniores*, commonly known as 'Greats', a four-year course focused on classical culture with an emphasis on the study of original texts in Latin and Greek. The course was divided into two parts, the first over five terms and known as 'Mods', concentrating on Latin and Greek as languages; the second, over seven terms, was broader in its themes and involved the in-depth study of ancient literature and history.

As Claud had done almost no academic work over the previous two years, he needed to study to make up for this and obtain the right degree. 'I found myself compelled to get up at six-thirty to start reading', he wrote, 'to read intensively for most of the day and to dose myself with caffeine tablets so as to keep awake and working until two or three in the morning.'[14] In the event, this self-imposed cramming succeeded, and, in the second of the final examinations in June 1926, he got the necessary second in Classics that he required.[15]

He still had to pass the examination for the Queen's fellowship in a little over six months' time, for which a good command of modern languages was essential for aspiring diplomats (though other professions were not excluded). The founder of the fellowships had wanted to raise what he considered to be the inadequate language abilities of British embassies, but candidates needed to show that they already possessed some linguistic skills.

To do this successfully, Claud believed that he needed to improve his French, and the best way to do this quickly was to live in France. He had gloomy visions of rival candidates burnishing their language skills at expensive finishing schools in Tours and Hanover that he could not afford. He learned, however, of a village, which he does not name, in the Cevennes in southern France where he might survive with minimal resources. 'Since somewhere around ten shillings a week was all I could afford', he wrote, 'it was necessary for me to find the cheapest place in France.' The village he found was 'strung out, gaunt and beautiful, between the rocks and the broad pebbly beaches of the Gard, with bad roads and a railway line that went nowhere else, attracted no tourists from anywhere outside the immediate area and existed in frozen or torrid isolation in winter or summer, hardly aware of what was happening to the cost of living'.[16]

He was to spend some months in this impoverished village, which he always spoke of with great affection, saying that it was full of people whose lives had somehow not amounted to very much. The greatest grievance was the outcome of the First World War eight years earlier, which had supposedly ended in a glorious French victory but had done the villagers little practical good. Living *en pension* in the dismal local hotel, Claud was told that history had once again played France a dirty trick: life would stay the same, the British would once again betray the French, and Germany would not pay for its defeat.

Poverty ensured Claud's integration into village life; he even briefly filled in at the local tax office while the official nominally in charge pursued a love affair in a neighbouring department.[17] He worried that an Englishman distributing and stamping official tax forms might stoke ill feeling among locals, but his tax collector friend told him reassuringly that 'they all think that if you are English at all you are a damned odd sort of Englishman'.[18]

From the Cevennes, Claud took a train to Vienna with the intention of improving his German but found he could not afford the right kind of language instructor. He moved on to Luxembourg for a couple of weeks, where both French and German were spoken and which he believed to be the cheapest place in Europe.

He then returned home to Tring, leading Evelyn Waugh, who was teaching at Aston Clinton school close by, to write jubilantly in his diary on 25 November 1926 that 'to my real delight Claud has come back to Tring for some little while'. He walked over to talk to Claud for several hours over lunch and then tea, after which he 'returned [to Aston Clinton] much stimulated'.

For the six weeks before the examination, Claud moved to a flat in Bloomsbury, but it proved so cold in the London winter that he had to take refuge in the nearby Warren Street Tube station. Sitting on a bench, he read his books in comparative warmth and was touched when the station staff quietly installed a light bulb of greater strength to make it easier for him to study.

On the day of the examination, he thought apprehensively that the other competitors looked 'horribly intelligent'. He was nevertheless confident that he could win a fellowship if his near down-and-out appearance did not discredit him in the eyes of the provost and dons of Queen's College, who were conducting final interviews. His description of this testing interview is a good example of Claud's anecdotal style, full of amusing but convincing details:

An attempt was made to give this interview something of the character of an informal social occasion. One was expected to sit at ease in a comfortable chair and was offered sherry. When I sit at ease I like to cross the calf of one leg over the knee of the other, but unfortunately in the course of my wanderings my shoe leather had worn through utterly and where the soles of my shoes should have been only my socks were visible. Indeed, having had to walk some distance from my rooms in the college to the place where the interview took place, I could not be sure if my exhausted socks had not given way too, leaving the bare flesh showing. In any case, either socks or flesh would create an abominable impression, so that throughout the conversation I had to sit rigidly in an entirely unnatural position trying to remember, while chatting in an easy manner, to keep my feet flat on the carpet. Also I am in the habit of gesticulating a good deal when I talk; but since the cuffs of my shirt were almost spectacularly frayed and had to be kept out of sight, this habit too had to be abandoned for the duration of the interview, and I sat hunched like some semi-petrified gargoyle. My hands gripping my wrists so as to display neither the frayed cuffs or even to suggest to the minds of the examiners that the cuffs could not be shown.

Nor did his trials end with his successful effort to hide his ragged clothing, because he revealed that he had been in Luxembourg. 'And what did you gather of conditions there?', the provost asked him. Claud spoke knowledgably about the operations of the International Steel Cartel that had its headquarters in Luxembourg and the impact of the recent decision by Luxembourg to link its currency to the belga rather than the franc. 'Meaty stuff, I secretly opined, after only a fortnight in the country,' he wrote.

'The provost tapped the table impatiently and his expression was that of a man who does not relish having his time wasted by chit-chat about trivialities. "Yes, yes, yes," he said, "very interesting, no doubt, but what I would really like to know is what you gathered about the varying systems of land tenure in the north and south parts of the Grand Duchy?"'

Having won a fellowship, Claud fended off a concerted attack by his Oxford creditors by pledging half his fellowship money to pay off the bank overdraft which he had to take out. Complicated manoeuvres like these to avoid being submerged by debts and penury are a repeated theme in Claud's writings and the topic of numerous, and often very funny, anecdotes such as his raggedness at the crucial Queen's College interview.

Yet the gaiety with which he described these financial problems understate the anxiety they caused him at the time. Friends too often concluded that he simply had a cavalier attitude to money, or they compared him to Charles Dickens's Mr Micawber in his perennial optimism about 'something turning up'. He himself attributed his lack of respect for money to the influence of living in Central Europe at a time when hyper-inflation could halve the currency's purchasing-power between breakfast and lunch. Yet he was scarcely alone among his generation at Oxford in coming from a family hard hit by the wartime rise in the cost of living. W. H. Auden, who was part of the undergraduate generation that followed Claud's, says that 'no college scholarship was sufficient to live on without parental support'.[19] In the post-war years, Evelyn Waugh's and Graham Greene's fathers, both holding solid professional jobs, had similar money problems. Henry Cockburn had only his pension and could give only minimum financial support to Claud, while Keble College has an item in its records under Claud's name which simply says 'Dues unpaid'.[20]

Before leaving Oxford, Claud visited his Keble College tutor, with whom he had had little contact as an undergraduate. The tutor was a man who normally shunned other humans, in so far as possible, especially if there was the slightest chance of any display of emotion such as might occur on the departing of one of his students. Groping for words appropriate to the occasion, the tutor told Claud that while hitherto his 'life has been neatly crisscrossed by school terms, university terms and vacations . . . now you are going down from Oxford and you have well, one may say that you have a straight run to the grave'.[21]

His own ideas about his future career had not jelled, but journalism appeared to be one option. He had not mentioned this half-formed ambition to the Queen's examiners because 'there were bound to be several among examiners who would instinctively feel that the fewer British journalists there were running about the world the better'. But, as he wavered between Vienna and Berlin as his destinations, a friend told him that he knew the *Times* correspondent in Berlin and would provide Claud with a letter of introduction. Later this turned out to be less use than expected, but 'by that time, I was there [in Berlin] and the smell of Central Europe had a new tang to it'.[22]

Claud's return to Central Europe marked a new chapter in his life, but it was not the only one. His father Henry, to whom he was so close, died on 19 March 1927, just before he departed for Germany. 'China Harry died,' Waugh wrote in his diary on Sunday 27 March. 'On Wednesday Claud came to London and I spent the evening with him. China H seems to have made a characteristic death – reading Ludwig's William II and making characteristic remarks about himself. Mrs Harry is going to be rather poor but Claud has his fellowship all right.'[23]

6

'Of Course, You Will Write for the Paper'

Disastrous flood in Saxony was Claud's first scoop [wiki commons]

On his first day in Berlin, Claud made the disconcerting discovery that the *Times* correspondent to whom he had a letter of introduction – his main reason for choosing Berlin over Vienna as a place to live – had left the city. Obtaining the name and telephone number of his successor, he rang him up at 8:30 a.m., believing that the early hour might give an impression of alertness to a potential employer – 'not one of these slouching Oxford decadents'. He realised later that this approach could have proved disastrous to his chances of employment because the correspondent, Norman Ebbutt, had only just gone to bed after an all-night party.

Fortunately, Claud found Ebbutt to be 'a man of warm-hearted goodness and this he displayed immediately, pretending that it was time for him to get up and behaving in general as though I really was an old friend'.[1] By all accounts, Ebbutt, who had been deputy correspondent in Berlin since 1925 and chief correspondent since 1927, was an exceptionally knowledgeable and intelligent man.[2] Speaking of their first encounter, Claud recalled,

> He even pretended to believe that I might actually be of use to him in *The Times* office in Unter den Linden. With extraordinary tact he somehow managed to suggest that I might be doing him positively a favour by coming and 'helping'. He must have known that he, of course, would have to spend hours teaching me to do things he could have done himself in a tenth of the time.[3]

Claud was downplaying his potential usefulness. Ebbutt evidently liked him from the start, but he also understood the benefit of having a highly educated German-speaking assistant working for him for nothing. As his first task, Claud read a sample of the thirty or forty German morning and evening newspapers which appeared daily, a time-consuming but essential chore in any foreign newspaper bureau, which cannot be done without complete fluency in the local language.[4] Having somebody like Claud, who was familiar with the politics of Central Europe, volunteering to do this job unpaid was a major 'help' for an overworked correspondent wary of missing a story.

Evidence of the good impression Claud made on Ebbutt can be found in the MI5 files on Claud, which contain a report of what Ebbutt told a British intelligence officer in an interview some years later. By then Claud was notorious as a dangerous radical, hostile to the government of the day, yet Ebbutt did not hesitate to express high admiration for his former protégé as a professional journalist, explaining that he had 'discovered Cockburn in 1926 [in fact it was the following year], and was so impressed by his brilliant intelligence that he appointed him to his staff'.⁵ This overstated Claud's initial status, but confirms Ebbutt's favourable opinion of him.

Word of his presence reached the *Times* in London, which wrote to Ebbutt saying that while it had no objection to Claud learning about journalism in their office, he must on no account be allowed to write anything for the paper. Ebbutt, who was ten years older than Claud and a veteran of the *Times* since 1914, aside from a break for war service as a naval lieutenant, was experienced in the ways of newspapers and ignored this instruction, though he would scarcely have done so unless he had confidence in Claud's abilities. Since all stories appearing in the *Times* were anonymous, editors in London did not know the identity of the author.

'Of course, you will write for the paper', Claud quotes Ebbutt as saying, 'and we will get as many pieces of yours in as we can, although naturally it will be necessary to pretend that I have sent them.'

'But suppose they are no good?' Claud asked.

'In that case we shall not send them.'

'But suppose they find out that I have sent them.'

'It will do a lot of good,' said Ebbutt, understanding the hunger of a good newspaper for accurate eyewitness reporting, which usually overcomes all other obstacles in the news business.⁶ For Claud an advantage of being loosely and unofficially attached to the *Times* was that it automatically elevated his status in Berlin, giving him access to the upper strata of German political life – something that otherwise would have been impossible for a twenty-three year old just out of university.⁷

In his attitude to the *Times*, where Claud was soon ensconced, he was both impressed and amused by its own exalted sense of its moral and political standing. Viewed abroad as an august counterpart to the British government, its correspondents enjoyed a quasi-diplomatic position which brought with it the expectation that they would behave with suitable decorum. In illustration of this, Claud told the story of one part-time correspondent for the *Times* in Latin America who attended official gatherings of diplomats and local grandees with a woman whom everybody was prepared to pretend was his wife.

Unfortunately, the man was of painfully high principles and felt it necessary to explain publicly that he and the woman were not, for various good reasons, married. At the same time, he insisted that unless she was invited to these functions as if she really were his wife, the correspondent would feel compelled to make a row and otherwise disrupt the proceedings. The British Legation in the country in question wrote to the Foreign Office, which in turn wrote to the *Times* requesting that the man be asked to avoid these embarrassing contretemps by saying that the girlfriend was his wife, or at least cease to deny it, or perhaps even leave her at home. As requested, the *Times* wrote a mildly admonitory letter making these suggestions, but the correspondent rejected them. 'He simply wrote that she was his wife in the eyes of God,' Claud's informant sighed, but surely 'he couldn't expect the *Times* to see eye to eye with God, could he?'

Once having got his foot in the door, Claud's daily presence in the paper's office soon came to seem natural and he was well positioned to take another step in his journalistic career. On daily newspapers there is invariably more news than reporters available to report it, so somebody in the office, possessing a modicum of journalistic talent, is likely to be pushed into service in an emergency. In Claud's case his opportunity came fast, but it took energy and initiative to take advantage of it.

In May 1927 a discursive piece in Claud's style appeared in the *Times* about the political stances of different German newspapers towards British foreign policy.[8] He found it informative to wade through the local press but hankered for 'straightforward journalistic occasions' to report. One such was the arrival at Berlin's Templehof Airport of two American pilots, Clarence Chamberlain and Charles Levine, who had flown the Atlantic soon after Charles Lindbergh had done so. The Berlin police had manhandled journalists covering their arrival, leaving Claud with a black eye and a bruised jaw.[9]

He does not appear to have written anything about the minor riot, but in early July Ebbutt went on leave for a couple of weeks, his place temporarily taken by a correspondent called Barker. Claud was in the office on the night of 9 July when news began to appear in the German papers about a disastrous flash flood in southern Saxony, on the border with Czechoslovakia. 'Barker and I', Claud wrote, 'both had the curious impression that something rum, and possibly sensational, had taken place in the mountains down there beyond Dresden.' Since Claud was not on the staff, and possibly nothing serious had occurred, Barker felt that he could not give Claud any of the *Times* money to travel to Saxony to find out what had really happened. But he suggested that if Claud could go there at his own expense, it might be worth his while to do so. 'I could raise only enough to travel fourth class', wrote Claud, 'in a series of trains which moved all night at the speed of city trams.'[10]

When he arrived at dawn on 10 July in the highlands below the Eastern Ore Mountains in Saxony, he discovered that the catastrophe – caused by rainstorms turning mild-looking mountain streams into destructive torrents – was on a far-greater scale than anybody in Berlin had realised. Rising swiftly above the banks of the little rivers, the floodwaters had torn through pretty Saxon villages, drowning more than 110 people who had been trapped in their houses.

Looking around, Claud noted with some professional satisfaction that he was the only foreign journalist present and would scoop all competitors back in Britain. He does not say how he transmitted the story so quickly, but he must have spoken about it to others because a résumé of his career by the *World's Press News* in 1935 says that 'after a cloudburst had killed 120 people in Saxony, Cockburn, heavily caked in mud talked the headwaiter at principal hotel in Dresden into giving him three-quarters of an hour phone call to the Berlin *Times* office with the only eyewitness account of disaster'.[11]

Claud's story, which appeared in the *Times* the following morning, described the shattered villages and contained interviews with inhabitants who had escaped the raging waters. His text has the graphic, though slightly disjointed feel of a reporter with a scoop hastily dictating copy from scribbled notes over the phone to meet a fast-approaching deadline. The dateline was from the stricken village of Berggiesshubel on 10 July and is accredited to 'a Special Correspondent'. The article describes how a prolonged cloudburst had dumped vast quantities of water into streams that ultimately flow into the Elbe River. Squeezed into narrow valleys, the floodwaters carried 'uprooted trees, which smashed whatever came in their way, or caught in the arches of bridges'. The bridges turned into dams, forcing the water to rise up the sides of the valleys and sweeping away people as it broke through the walls of buildings and tore up railway tracks.

Claud reported the devastating flood in Berggiesshubel, which had left ninety-three people dead and obliterated the main street, burying it under three or four feet of mud. The fronts of houses had been torn off so that 'in the upper rooms one can still see clothes and pictures hanging on the walls'. As he walked through what remained of the village, he saw 'the ruins of a house which has collapsed, and beyond that, rising out of the other wreckage, a pile of uprooted trees, bricks, broken beams, iron girders, in the middle of which a big motor-lorry lies on its side embedded in the mud'. Some forty-two people had saved their lives by taking refuge on the top floor of a hotel. When it had threatened to collapse, 'they managed to hack a hole with axes in the roof of a more solid building adjoining the hotel and with ropes made from sheets lowered themselves into this new place of refuge'.[12]

Houses built further up the sides of the narrow pine-tree covered valley suffered less damage, but 'a woman described to me how their inhabitants had to sit helpless in the darkness and listen to the screams for help from their less fortunate neighbours nearer the river'. In the village of Glashütte, passengers on a train barely had time to flee before its coaches were battered to pieces by a mass of floating trees. In his memoirs, written a quarter of a century later, Claud could still recall the impression made on him by the power of the floodwaters. 'Half a mile of that little valley smelled of death,' he wrote. 'There were corpses in the mud and in one house the table in an upper back room had been laid for breakfast. In several other houses canaries were singing or moping in their cages.' He says he omitted mention of the canaries in his *Times* story, because he feared that 'the canary angle' was too much of a cliché in newspaper disaster reporting. 'I suppose that the trouble is', he wrote, 'that life is a good deal cornier than it ought for . . . there really were canaries in the wrecked village in Saxony.'[13]

No other paper in London had a correspondent on the spot reporting the disaster. Nothing makes newspaper editors look more favourably on a young reporter than a scoop that rival news outlets do not have.[14] By his dash on night trains to Saxony, Claud won himself credit back in London, which had already suggested that he return to England to work on one of their provincial newspapers, before moving on to the *Times* proper.[15] He turned this offer down because he was repelled by the idea of swapping Berlin for Nottingham or Newcastle. He rejected two improved job offers, one to go straight to the Foreign Room in London and even one to stay as assistant correspondent in Berlin, a job he thought might be too restrictive. He was worried that these rejections might strangle his budding but very recent friendship with the *Times*, but Ebbutt told him that the powers on the paper had been impressed by his originality in turning them down, something that no aspiring journalist had done for years.

Given the trouble he had taken to get himself back to Central Europe, his decision not to return to England was scarcely surprising. The death of his much-loved father in March made England seem 'more distasteful, more drearily alien to me than ever'.[16] The very thought of 'immuring myself in a regular job' gave him a sense of claustrophobia.

Claud was swiftly making himself at home in Berlin, living at first in an apartment on Bismarckstrasse, romantically attracted by the name of the highway that somebody told him stretched from Amsterdam to Moscow. A few weeks later, he moved to a large second-floor apartment on the Kurfürstendamm, an avenue some deemed to be the Champs-Élysées of Berlin. His apartment was palatial in size, so much so that people scarcely noticed that the rooms were filled with mountains of furniture covered in dust sheets. The owners had departed suddenly for what neighbours suspected were scandalous reasons, though Claud doubted if anybody knew the real cause of their flight. Whatever their motive, they had been prepared to let the flat cheaply to anybody who would look after it and guard their furniture.[17]

Soon after moving in, Claud met the owner of a nearby book-shop, Herr Uhlmann, whom he portrays as a prototype Berlin fascist. 'I had never liked him,' Claud wrote, 'but I had liked to be with him because he seemed to combine so many of the char-acteristics of the Berliner – including the fact that he had been born in Breslau.' Uhlmann identified himself self-consciously with the city and its inhabitants, whom he portrayed as smarter, more cynical, more ruthless and faster moving than other people. Lauding the hugeness, harshness and roaring pace of Berlin, Uhlmann was 'ashamed of nothing, because the only qualities he would have been ashamed of would have been slowness in thought or action, gentleness or sentimentality, and since he lived in Berlin he could not believe any of these weaknesses could have been his'.[18]

Not everybody in Berlin suffered from this confrontational, militarised mentality, as Claud discovered to his surprise in a chance encounter with the Berlin police:

I had been visited at the flat by a policeman who had cross-questioned me about my friends or acquaintances in countries other than Germany and showed particular interest in the ques-tion of what kind of correspondence I had with them – did they write to me often and so on. I was indignant at this question but also nervous, because I thought it indicated that they took me for a spy and might upset all my plans by expelling me from Germany. Herr Uhlmann listened to my account and was visibly pleased. The episode, he thought, was typical of the intrusive efficiency of the Berlin police. I went on to tell him that the policeman had finally asked me to accompany him to the police station to interview his superior officer. There seemed to be nothing else to do and I went with him in a high degree of alarm and exasperation, expecting to be interrogated violently by some brutish Prussian officer type.

When I got there the superior officer was a Prussian all right but in appearance and manner resembled rather a small farmer of the North German Plain than a city police officer. He had long yellow moustaches and gentle blue eyes, and when the policeman had reported to him on our conversation, he said apologetically that he was very sorry to have bothered me but the fact was that he had a small nephew who was a keen stamp collector and was at the moment in the tuberculosis ward of a sanatorium. He, the officer, had promised to do everything in his power to add to the boy's collection of foreign stamps, and had taken the liberty of asking for my cooperation.[19]

Though only a twenty-three-year-old apprentice journalist on the *Times*, the prestige of the paper was such that it gave him entrée to the German diplomatic and political worlds. His access was furthered by Ebbutt, whose protégé he had become and for whom he expressed admiration and affection, describing him as intelligent, courageous and a man of goodwill, who even believed that one day he might go 'to the British Embassy in the Wilhelm-strasse and find out what the policy of the British Foreign Office was, and perhaps that would turn out to be intelligent and courageous'.[20]

Claud's own political beliefs at this time differed little from those of Ebbutt, which he describes as those of a 'left-wing Liberal, which meant, at any rate in his case, that he hoped for the best in everyone'. He brought Claud with him to drink beer with the foreign minister, Gustav Stresemann, in the garden of the foreign ministry. Stresemann, foreign minister from 1925 to 1929, stabilised Germany's relations with Britain, France and America, while recognising the Soviet Union.[21] 'Personally, I found him [Stresemann] entertaining so long as you did not believe in him,' wrote Claud.

He was one of those Germans who had, at a fairly early date, discovered that the way to get away with being a good German was to pretend to be a good European. He had a wonderful act in which he pretended to be not only fat, which he was, but good-hearted and a little muzzy with beer into the bargain. In reality, he was as quick and sharp as a buzz saw, and if being a sharp fast-moving buzz saw was not enough, he would hit you from behind with a hammer.[22]

It was while watching Stresemann in action – sitting under a plum tree in the foreign ministry's garden – that Claud began seriously to doubt that 'my warm-hearted enthusiasm on behalf of the victims of the World War, my romantic belief in the nationalist movements of Central Europe (nationalist even when they were disguised as the resurgence of Central European democracy) and my conviction that the Treaty of Versailles had been a disastrous diplomatic crime really covered all the facts'. He did not have an all-out biblical conversion from his old certitudes but described himself as being more like a Victorian clergyman worried by doubts about the Book of Genesis.

Viewed from Budapest or Oxford, Stresemann and Central European politicians like him had appeared to be just the kind of liberal-minded democratic patriots who deserved support against the hostility of bitter old men in Paris and London who had won the war. Up close, Claud started to have a more negative impression – that 'if this was the kind of old boy I had been feeling sorry for and enthusiastic about all this time, I probably had been making a mistake'.[23]

Eager though Claud had been to insert himself into the *Times*'s Berlin office early in 1927, by the end of the year he had become wary of taking a full-time job there. He had recently sold a few articles and short stories to German and American newspapers and magazines, one of which was published by a celebrated New York–based literary magazine called *The Dial*, which was then at the peak of its success. Among other masterpieces, it had published W. B. Yeats's 'The Second Coming' and the first American edition of T. S. Eliot's 'The Waste Land'. The twice-yearly magazine, edited since 1925 by Marianne Moore, attracted an impressive line-up of contributors, from William Carlos Williams and Ezra Pound to E. E. Cummings and Thomas Mann. Its January–June 1928 edition printed a sixteen-page short story by Claud, which he most likely wrote no later than the summer or early autumn of 1927.[24] Called 'You Have to Be Careful', it is the third item in the magazine, coming after part of Ezra Pound's 'Canto XXVII' and a less than enthusiastic essay by T. S. Eliot on Pound. Claud's story is set in Luxembourg eight years after the end of the World War, which was the period in 1926 when he had lived there briefly in order to improve his conversational German in preparation for the Queen's travelling fellowship examination.

The short story is an accomplished work in terms of literary skill and sensitivity to German attitudes to the First World War and all that followed. Its originality and subtlety explain why Marianne Moore, celebrated for her acute editorial judgement, decided to run a piece from an unknown writer just out of university alongside Pound and Eliot.[25]

The story is told from the point of view of Mr Gregory, a polite and apparently naive English student with similarities to Claud, who is seeking to improve his German after leaving Vienna, which he had found too expensive. The narrative opens with Mr Gregory writing a letter home, having spent the morning walking about the streets of the city. He says that the people are 'placid and confident', adding that there is something to be said for living in a country like Luxembourg, which was politically *entre les deux* between Germany and France. 'Perhaps', he writes, 'because it is a capital and yet such a very small one, everything has a miniature air, as though one could lift up a roof here and there, and peep, without disturbing them, at the lives inside of these people.' He goes into a café where he asks the husband and wife running it if he can take a room. The man, Herr Fleck, is initially unenthusiastic:

> His voice gave a melancholy appearance to the small brown room with a half-dozen oblong tables, and pale-coloured bottles on a shelf, and a mechanical piano. His wife had been looking at Mr Gregory, and when he looked at her he saw that she thought him funny and interesting and quite harmless. Also he wore gold rimmed spectacles which made such people think that he was 'solide'.

Frau Fleck sends Mr Gregory off to the railway station to pick up his suitcase, suggesting that he find Gustav Engel, the taxi-driver son of friends of the Flecks, to carry it. 'He'll know where to bring it,' she says. 'You have to be careful nowadays. It wouldn't be nice if a thief were to run off with it.' Distrust of everybody and everything is the constant refrain of the characters in the story, all of whose lives have been diminished or crushed by the outcome of the war.

Once the Engels family had lived in Munich, but they left because of the 'war, and the inflation time, and the revolutions, and no money'. Anxiety bred of uncertainty overshadows the lives of the petit bourgeois Germans who, for one reason or another, have ended up in Luxembourg. Yet the tone of the story is buoyant, even light hearted, rather than tragic. This is not to say that the tragedy is not clearly stated: 'My two brothers were killed and that killed my mother and her dying killed my old father,' says Herr Fleck. 'The war's done for our lives. We shan't really see the end of this war. Our children; grandchildren more likely.'

Potentially comic scenes are never played for laughs. After Mr Gregory takes a room and joins the Flecks for a meal, Herr Fleck serves him with a giant plate of porridge. 'Just look at it,' he says. 'I know what the English like. I worked for eight years in the Hotel Adlon in Berlin, and while I was there, I remember well that the English Lord Kitchener stayed there, and every day, every day, every day he ate porridge. The English all eat porridge.' Mr Gregory says the porridge is good, partly because it is, and partly because 'he liked to be cheerful and friendly and "get on with people"'.

He advertises for somebody to converse with him in German and is inundated by offers from people eager to earn a little extra money. He finally chooses a former Prussian officer, Von Uhl, with whom he goes on long walks and who tells him what appear to be fabulous tales of his prowess in war and achievements in peace. But later he shows Mr Gregory his eighteen military medals, suggesting that at least some of his tales are not fantasy. But he has come down in the world, leading him and his sick wife to take refuge in Luxembourg, where she stays with her father, who does not like Von Uhl. He lives in a neat little bed-sit along with one good suit and a tie press. When he and Mr Gregory go for walks or visit a cinema or a café, Von Uhl leaves messages saying where he can be found in case his wife's illness gets worse.

As he is a Prussian, the Flecks (who come from Alsace) and the Engels (who are from south Germany) do not like him, criticising, on his first appearance in the café, 'the way he came in and clicked his heels – all that Kaiser stuff'. The playing out of the animosity between the different kinds of German is one of the tensions of the story. Yet none of the characters are caricatures or act stereotypically. The Flecks and the Engels may be right in believing that there is something dodgy about Von Uhl, but it is never made clear how far he is a fake or how much, if anything, of what he says is untrue.

On a snowy evening, Mr Gregory and Von Uhl are sitting in the café when the Prussian infuriates the others by playing military and patriotic German music on the mechanical piano. Furious, they kick and tug at the piano until it breaks 'with a tinkle, tinkle and a little bang'. But just as a fight appears about to begin, Von Uhl is called away by a messenger saying his wife is again sick. The story ends with Frau Engel worrying about what will happen to her son Gustav: 'The poor boy', she says. 'So tired, he gets, driving his motor car all the time. What is to become of him? I ask myself, I ask everyone, I ask God, what I say, is to become of him? Such a fine young man.'

The art of the short story lies in brevity and implication – the narrative skills of suggesting things without spelling them out, telling enough for an alert reader to sense the things that are not said. This is a very different style of writing from journalism, which, broadly speaking, aims to tell the reader significant facts, with an emphasis on describing action rather than character. Claud's piece in *The Dial* shows an understanding of the techniques of short story writing, possibly under the influence of Rudyard Kipling, whom Claud greatly admired.[26]

The story also anticipates the novel *Goodbye to Berlin* by Christopher Isherwood, published nine years later in 1937, which is likewise a portrait of Germany and Germans during the Weimar period. The resemblances and differences between their stories are illuminating. Claud writes about hard-up German petit bourgeois and their fears, while Isherwood's characters are exotic and louche, with prostitutes and rent boys playing a central role. Isherwood later criticised himself for glamourising the Berlin underworld, saying that the real monster had been himself for battening on people who sold their bodies for sex because they were poor and desperate.[27]

7

Love and
Revolutionary Politics

Berlin during the Weimar Republic [wiki commons]

Claud had two love affairs in Berlin, one short and frivolous, but the second a serious passion that was to influence him for the rest of his life. He met the first girlfriend, whom he calls 'Atlanta', soon after he arrived in Berlin in the early spring of 1927. Describing her, he says that she could 'make you laugh a lot if you didn't much mind what you were laughing at, and her appearance certainly took one's mind off one's work'.

At first sight, she looked like Hollywood's idea of an exotic foreign beauty from a ruined aristocratic family, running wild because she keeps asking herself, what does life hold but sensual pleasure? In Atlanta's case, the cinematic fantasy was largely correct, since she was the daughter of a Hungarian count who, fearful of peasant revolution during the war, had unwisely sold his land and invested the proceeds in industrial enterprises in Austria, which all went bankrupt in 1918. Having failed to recoup his losses through shady currency deals and facing criminal prosecution, he fled to Bucharest, where he shot himself.

Atlanta's mother continued to live in Vienna, from where she sent her daughter letters rebuking her for not finding a rich lover. On Atlanta showing these to Claud, he remarked that, given his penury, 'you had better not mention me'. But it turned out that Atlanta had already done so, reassuring her mother that Claud was the great-grandson of a lord and, though momentarily impoverished, would shortly become foreign editor of the *Times*.[1]

At many levels, political and personal, the couple were incompatible since Atlanta was an arch-reactionary, her opinions reflecting those of the elderly Austro-Hungarian generals and younger currency speculators, whom she met at her mother's house in Vienna. Aside from her reactionary extremism, Atlanta had an unnerving taste for provoking or concocting melodramatic, emotional scenes, such as the one that largely ended their relationship. 'We began to bore each other rather,' wrote Claud, 'and, in what I am sure she felt was a praiseworthy attempt to liven things up, she persuaded me to leave Berlin in the middle of the night without waiting to notify *The Times* office and go with her on a trip to Salzburg.'[2]

On arriving there, Claud discovered that her real purpose was to arrange an 'amusing' encounter between himself and a former boyfriend of hers, who had been saying that he could not live without her. After much shouting and tears in the apartment in Salzburg, the former lover produced a pistol and fired two shots into a piano. 'We returned to Berlin the same day, both of us in a bad temper, I at having been dragged from my work for the purpose of being involved in this foolish scene and Atlanta because the scene itself had been unsatisfactory – a let-down.' Claud told Ebbutt about what had happened, who replied with some amusement that while Claud must of course please himself, and that he did not want to interfere in his private life but if there was anything in the way of gunfire in the *Times* office, it would probably adversely affect his standing with the paper.

Though her affair with Claud had petered out and she was about to return to Vienna, Atlanta asked him at the last moment to escort her to a party at the Kaiserhof Hotel in Berlin. Accidentally present, he immediately felt at home at this gathering of sophisticated and cosmopolitan people from all over Central Europe. Many were also Jewish. Not necessarily revolutionary or even progressive in their view of life and politics, Claud describes the milieu as including 'Viennese bankers, the diplomats suspected of undue brilliance by their Foreign Offices, the industrialist suspected of improper relations with socialist politicians, and the socialist politicians suspected of improper relations with industrialists, the painters, film directors, publishers, writers, dancers and musicians'.[3]

In the course of the evening, Claud learned that the Kaiserhof party was being given by a wealthy Austrian woman holding progressive views, with a rich banker for a husband, who presided over 'a perambulating salon that functioned sometimes in Berlin, sometimes in her house in Vienna, and sometimes in a huge chalet by a lake which she owned in the Austrian alps'.[4] He recognised, however, that for all the diversity of their opinions, the underlying assumptions of this 'set' or 'circle' about the way the world worked differed radically from those he had hitherto encountered among Oxford liberals, Hungarian nationalists or foreign journalists in Berlin.

Atlanta tried to drag him away from the party, saying, 'These people are all damned Reds.'

'Nonsense, they can't be,' Claud responded, looking around at a throng of white shirts and bare shoulders and pointing out to her well-known diplomats and bankers, whose politics was unlikely to be Red.

'I don't care,' said Atlanta. 'They all talk like Reds. And I despise intellectuals. Take me away.'

He refused to go, and she departed by herself to make her way back to Vienna. Claud never saw Atlanta again. He stayed on at the party, entranced and excited by the people he was meeting, and by the time he went home in the early spring dawn, he was feeling that he 'had stepped across an unseen ditch – dug perhaps partly by some unseen influence of my father and partly by older, subtler influences and accidents – to meet a Europe with which I had never made contact before'.[5]

The vibrant yet fragile culture with which Claud bonded so swiftly and emphatically was centred in Weimar Germany and post-war Austria. It flourished briefly but intensely in the fifteen years between the end of the First World War in 1918 and the Nazi seizure of power in 1933. 'When we think of Weimar', writes the historian Peter Gay in his book *Weimar Culture*, 'we think of modernity in art, literature, and thought; we think of the rebellion of sons against fathers, Dadaists against art, Berliners against beefy philistinism, libertines against old fashioned moralists.'[6] Politically, Weimar was an era in which the transformative forces were not only the defeat of the Germany and Austro-Hungary, but the victory of the Bolsheviks and the rise of Communism.

Claud was circumspect in giving details of the circle he encountered at the Kaiserhof, probably because many of those present were vulnerable as Jews, socialists or Communists, or simply for having values and holding beliefs diametrically opposed to those of the Nazis. Nor did the danger to members of the 'set' entirely evaporate after 1945 in the turmoil of post-war Europe. Claud refers to the presiding figure at the Kaiserhof as 'the baroness', but she was almost certainly a remarkable woman named Eugenie 'Genia' Schwarzwald, a Jewish philanthropist, educational reformer and salon host who lived in Austria. Her husband was Hermann Schwarzwald, president of the Anglo-Österreichische Bank in Vienna. In the 1920s, Eugenie was to establish a *Künstlerkolonie* (artists' retreat) in a former hotel at the Grundlsee, to which she would invite artists and friends to spend the summer. She was famous for bringing together people from varying political allegiances and class backgrounds. Moreover, Eugenie was involved in philanthropic projects in Germany as well as Austria, which explains why she was holding the charitable event in Berlin that Claud had chance to attend.

Aside from her educational and social projects, Eugenie had a talent for organising cooperatives to help the poor, more especially during the First World War, when she set up cooperative kitchens (no alcohol, vegetarian menu), orphanages, recreational facilities, and convalescent homes in the countryside outside of Vienna. After the war, she did the same in Berlin, making her 'one of the most popular women in Berlin'. Though she and her husband were rich, they could not have funded all these schemes, so she fundraised internationally and ran a taxi company and vegetable farm on the side.

A woman of great practical energy, Eugenie established the Chalet (or Villa) 'Seeblick' at the Grundlsee in 1920 in a former hotel, which she converted into a place for artists and intellectuals to enjoy the beautiful surroundings, albeit without alcohol – a prohibition whose success varied.[7] Claud, who was not much given to recreation and certainly not to abstinence from alcohol, recollected 'canoeing or boating on the icy blue waters of the Grundlsee, climbing to high places to see the shining or shadowy panorama of the Alps, chattering lazily under the fruit trees with fellow guests or walking over the grassy hills by moonlight to drink freshly distilled plum brandy in the kitchens of upland farms'.[8]

On the night in Berlin when Claud discovered the Schwarzwald circle, he says that, having seen the last of Atlanta, 'I was already a little in love again.'[9] He calls the woman who attracted him 'Madam T', who would be his girlfriend until he left Europe for New York in 1929 and remained in touch with him well into the thirties. He gives few clues as to her real name and identity, but Hope Hale, the American journalist whom he was to marry in New York in 1932, has a section titled 'Claud and Berta' in an unpublished manuscript, which she had once intended to turn into an extended article or book about herself and Claud. In it she writes that when Claud first went to Berlin,

> Berta had taught him what it was to love a woman. She had also taught him about politics; she and her friends had turned him to the left. All the years he was in Germany on that first job for *The Times* she had been important to him, and he had been deeply grateful to her. But she may well have been afraid of his other side – his light-heartedness – afraid that it would let him go cheerfully on from her to the next love.[10]

Hope does not give Berta's second name, but Claud says that she was 'the exceptionally beautiful daughter of an upper-class Austro-Hungarian family', with a melodramatic backstory. Married in her teens to a man who became an army officer during the First World War, she had a lover with whom she planned to live in Switzerland. But the lover was shot dead by her husband in a Munich hotel in 1915, and he got off scot-free after a trial because of wartime conditions.

Radicalised by war and her own grim experience, Berta played a prominent role in the 'revolutionary youth movements of Vienna' in 1917–19 as the Austro-Hungarian Empire collapsed. As revolutionary fervour ebbed, she 'became involved in some quarrel . . . with the Communist party leadership', following which she left revolutionary politics in 'disillusion'.[11]

The scandal over the murder of Berta's lover appears not to have been reported by contemporary German newspapers, but Claud's short account of her revolutionary career is an exact fit with that of Berta Pölz, whom contemporary newspapers report as setting up revolutionary organisations in Vienna between 1917 and 1920. They confirm Claud's reference to a 'quarrel' between her and the Communist Party leading to her exit from revolutionary politics, apparently because she thought the party not revolutionary enough.

Though evidence for Berta Pölz being Madame T is fragmentary, it is persuasive: four members of the Schwarzwald's circle – Egon Erwin Kisch, Karl Frank, Siegfried Bernfeld, Paul Lazarsfeld – were in the same revolutionary youth group as Berta Pölz in Vienna in 1918.[12] She and Kisch, later an intimate friend of Claud, established a short-lived revolutionary group called Federation of Revolutionary Socialists 'International' (FRSI) on 28 November 1918. Berta is no longer mentioned in newspapers after 1920, which suggests that she had dropped out of political engagement.

When Claud met her in 1927, she had returned to painting, which she had abandoned during the war and the revolutionary upsurge that followed.[13] She painted a portrait of Claud at this time, which Hope, who saw a photograph of it, says showed his 'full lips, high forehead, resting on his almost abnormally flexible bent-back fingers; but the deep shadows below the even line of brow gave his eyes an unlikely soulfulness. Berta had left out his wit and gaiety, his mischief.'[14]

Berta had a strong political influence on Claud, but she was scarcely alone. Among his new circle of friends was Dr Bertold Wiesner, a Jewish Austrian biologist three years older than Claud who would become well known for his pioneering research into human fertility and the diagnosis of pregnancy. Wiesner took up an academic post at Edinburgh University in 1927, but he and Berta were Claud's guides into radical culture in Berlin. Hope described Wiesner as 'a handsome, red-cheeked Austrian' who 'had an almost childlike quality due partly to his simplified English'.[15]

Wiesner was to achieve posthumous fame when it emerged that he was the biological father of 600 children conceived from his anonymously donated sperm, used by his wife, Mary Barton, at her fertility clinic in London.[16]

Claud's social circle was older than him – between twenty-five and forty-five years of age – meaning that all of them had been inescapably involved in the social upheavals of the years after 1916, at an age when they were still young enough to adjust themselves to these new conditions. The Russian Revolution and Communism were dominant features of the political landscape, regardless of whether they opposed or supported them, in a way that was certainly not true in Britain. Claud found that his own views of divisions between nationalities rather than social classes being the driving force of history, fostered by Berkhamsted and Oxford, sounded bizarre to them: 'Perhaps', he asked Berta, 'they think I am merely idiotic?'

'No, no,' she replied. 'They expect anything of an Englishman.'

Reluctantly, since he expected to be bored or repelled by the contents, he bought in Vienna a copy of Vladimir Lenin and Grigory Zinoviev's collected pamphlets called *Against the Stream*. He found the Bolshevik classics full of contempt for the notions he had grown up with and hitherto taken for granted. 'I found them shocking, repugnant, alien,' he wrote. 'They pricked and tickled like a hair shirt. They seemed to generate an intolerable heat.' He was not instantly converted to Communist beliefs, or even persuaded that these revolutionaries were on the right lines, but his instinctive hostility to the powers that be was finding a new focus. Over the following year, he read Karl Marx's *Das Kapital*, the *Eighteenth Brumaire, Civil War in France* and Lenin's *State and Revolution*, being particularly impressed by Nikolai Bukharin's *Historical Materialism*.

While impressed by these socialist classics, Claud also read books claiming that the post-war boom in the United States proved that Marx, Lenin and Bukharin had taken a gigantic wrong turn and were talking nonsense. No revolution was necessary, as the American version of capitalism would generate prosperity for all. 'The United States hung over my thoughts like an enormous question mark,' Claud said. 'I felt that I should never be able to make up my mind about anything unless I went there and saw for myself.'[17]

Needs must. Having rebuffed the *Times* offer of regular employment, he was surviving on meagre instalments from his Queen's travelling fellowship, supplemented by even smaller freelance earnings. His poverty became especially acute during Christmas 1927, when Berta had gone to Vienna, leaving behind a dog given to her by Dr Wiesner for him to look after. He ended up sharing the dog's Christmas dinner, consisting of scraps given to him for free by a kindly local butcher.

So long as Claud had an income from his fellowship dribbling in, he could keep a certain distance from the *Times*, for whom he was writing an occasional special article and a monthly half column on the Berlin theatre.[18] Before taking this on, he had only watched two plays in his life – one of them *Twelfth Night*, which he had seen on a school trip from Berkhamsted, and the other a matinee performance at a theatre in Shaftesbury Avenue when sheltering from the rain.

On moving to Paris in the autumn of 1928, presumably a condition of his fellowship, he continued to write theatre reviews, which were by now more sophisticated and acerbic, even provoking one actress to spit at him in a café.[19] He scraped around for money, sending a letter on 28 October 1928 pressing the Paris office to reimburse him for money he had spent on theatre tickets. He rented a studio which he says was more like a hovel, with nothing to recommend it except an 'almost ridiculously sublime' view across the rooftops of Paris.[20] He slept on a bed 'made of a couple of packing cases and the mattress of straw, and snow drove in through the walls and the roof to make wet heaps on the bare boards of the floor'.[21]

He kept alive by consuming potato soup and leeks, acquiring a lifetime distaste for both, and then made the demoralising discovery in the early spring of 1929 that he had received the last instalment of money from the Queen's fellowship. In these dismal circumstances, he wrote to the *Times* explaining that, since he had now finished his fellowship, he 'would like to work as a *Times* correspondent, provided, however, that I could do so in New York'. Given his rather desperate circumstances, such a request took some nerve. Much to his relief, the editor, Geoffrey Dawson, immediately dispatched a reassuring telegram reading: 'Have no fear for tomorrow. Return at once. Job waiting.'[22]

After joining the paper as a sub-editor on 17 April 1929, Claud was paid seven guineas a week. Prior to departing for New York, he spent several months in the Foreign Editorial Room of the *Times* building in Printing House Square, near Blackfriars Bridge in the City of London. He was impressed and amused by the time-consuming concern of the sub-editors for accuracy, such as which of the eleven possible ways of spelling of 'Kuala Lumpur' should receive the paper's imprimatur. He was awed by the intellectual calibre of his fellow sub-editors, one of whom until recently had been C. K. Scott Moncrieff, the translator of Proust's *À la recherche du Temps Perdu*. Having worked as a foreign correspondent, Claud shared some of their prejudices against London-based sub-editors, writing that 'all foreign correspondents believe subeditors to be malevolent troglodytes, happiest when casually massacring the most significant lines of an informed, well-balanced dispatch. Subeditors believe foreign correspondents to be flibbertigibbets, uselessly squandering enormous expense accounts, lazy and verbose, and saved from making fools of themselves in print only by the vigilance of the staff in the Foreign Room.'[23]

Worried that the promise of a job in New York had come unstuck and fearing that he might instead find himself packed off to Newcastle, Claud found sub-editing increasingly tedious. During this fraught waiting period, he played a game invented by other bored sub-editors, which was to write the dullest headline actually to appear in print. 'I won it only once', he claimed, 'with a headline which announced: "Small Earthquake in Chile. Not many dead." '[24] The story achieved much notoriety when published in his memoirs and appeared in dictionaries of quotations, but, despite assiduous efforts by staff at the *Times*, they failed to locate the famous headline.

Dawson was friendly and approachable but skilfully elusive about Claud's appointment. Claud need not, in fact, have been so anxious: his career was being distantly but powerfully supported by Sir Campbell Stuart, a director of the paper who had played a key role in its sale to the Astor family on the death of Lord Northcliffe in 1922. Sir Campbell was a friend of Claud's uncle Frank, both Canadian financiers, and, since the death of his father, uncle Frank was the family member to whom he felt closest and treated as a confidante.

Visiting Sir Campbell, who lived with his mother in a suite at the top of the Hyde Park Hotel, to find out about the unnerving delay, Claud learned that this was caused by fear on the part of the senior editors at the possible bad reaction to his appointment as an assistant correspondent to the highly distinguished and experienced senior correspondent in New York, Louis Hinrichs. It turned out, however, when Claud went to see Hinrichs, who was passing through London, that Hinrichs was just as frightened by the 'high priests' at the *Times* as they were of him. 'I wish', he confessed to Claud as they drove to Printing House Square, 'one could simply telephone them to say that everything is all right and I hope to see you in New York. The *Times* frankly terrifies me.'[25]

On 30 July, Claud received a formal contract appointing him assistant correspondent in New York at an annual salary of £750 and £250 expenses.[26]

8

'The Word "Panic" Is Not to Be Used'

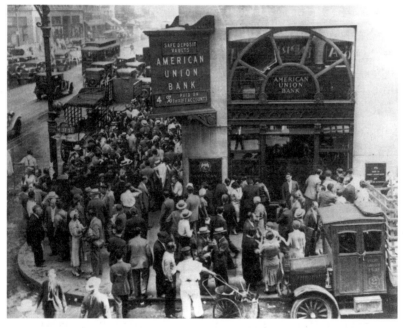

Desperate customers outside a failing bank in the US during the Wall Street Crash [wiki commons]

Claud liked New York immediately, saying that nothing had prepared him for 'the brilliance of the light – after all, the place is on the same latitude as Naples – [turning] even the white skyscrapers into precipices of colour'.[1] He found Americans sociable and spontaneous, more to his taste than English reticence, though he suspected that their reputation for frenetic energy was much exaggerated. As for their mood in the summer of 1929, when stock prices were still rising explosively, he discovered as soon as he had stepped off the boat from Southampton that nothing blighted a conversation more quickly than speaking lightly of the boom.

He experienced the same negative reaction to any hint of doubt, whether he was speaking to a taxi driver on the street in Lower Manhattan or a society hostess in her mansion in the East Sixties or on Long Island. 'You could talk about prohibition', he wrote, 'or Hemingway, or air conditioning, or music, or horses, but in the end you had to talk about the stock market and that was when the conversation became serious. Unless you understood this . . . you caused that shadow to fall. There was a *mystique* about the market.'

Claud compared confessing to doubts about this inspiring vision as like making a vulgar or ironic reference to the pope in the house of devout Roman Catholics.[2] Yet he did not, at the time or subsequently, view the great bull market of the late 1920s in the United States as a sign of American greed or that Americans were any more materialistic than other peoples. He saw it rather as evidence that Americans were readier than most people in the world to believe in miracles – and the booming stock market was one of them. In such an atmosphere, close to that of a religious revivalist meeting, Claud felt a certain loneliness as a European quietly sceptical about the permanence of this golden road to wealth and happiness. Knowing that his reservations might get him labelled as an anarchist, or at best a malign influence, he wrote, 'I kept my doubts pretty carefully under wraps, especially as they did not after all arise from any expert assessment of the immediate factors in the situation but simply from the "academic" theories of the Marxist and Leninist writers whom I had studied in the apartment on the Kufurstendamm and my studio in Paris.'[3]

He was especially keen not to share his observations – and particularly not the ideological reasons for them – with Louis Hinrichs, for whose knowledge of the American business and financial scene he had immense respect. During the first months after Claud arrived in New York, Hinrichs took him around

Wall Street introducing his new assistant correspondent to well-informed people who worked in 'this powerful, towering village, the activities of whose inhabitants could tilt whole nations'.[4]

One day, as they were walking from one office to another establishing these useful contacts, Hinrichs stopped suddenly, as he was accustomed to do when he wanted to make a profound statement. 'All the same, Claud, I don't really believe it,' he said, before explaining in detail why he thought that the great bull market might turn out to be a monstrous delusion, greatly damaging to America. Claud was astonished by these doubts, hearing his own half-formed opinions, based on the writings of anti-capitalist revolutionaries, confirmed by a conservatively minded expert with deep knowledge of the American economy.

Startled by Hinrich's words, Claud replied: 'Then you mean that you believe that the capitalist system won't work?' But he swiftly realised that Hinrichs meant nothing of the sort, since he believed that there was no alternative to capitalism, which he saw not as a distinct system but simply as the way the world worked, for good or ill. 'He knew the form book and he went by it,' wrote Claud, 'and he could see nothing in the history of American development to suggest that on behalf of the American Joshua of 1929, the Lord God was going to suspend the laws of economics.'[5]

Despite his apprenticeship in journalism in Berlin, Claud was conscious of his deficiencies as a professional journalist writing for a daily newspaper. He was even uncertain about how he should transmit his copy to Printing House Square in London. After writing his first hand-written dispatch for the *Times*, he gave it to a Western Union cable operator, who looked at it in disbelief. Claud learned that all dispatches had to be in typescript. Left with no choice but to use a typewriter for the first time, he painfully pounded out his 600-word article, which arrived in London only just before the deadline.

He also had a lack of confidence in his journalistic expertise. 'At the time, I wrote slowly and my style was erratic,' he recalled.

Echoes of prize essays floated about in it like icebergs; or else literary flying fish which ought to have been in some quite other story got loose; and sometimes there were doldrums where I was unconsciously imitating a man trying to write a suitable piece for the *Times*. Sometimes it was quite difficult to see what the piece was about because a shadowy figure kept jumping up between the piece and the reader shouting 'See me write a piece.' All these phenomena had to be looked out for, corrected or torn out.[6]

His confession of journalistic amateurism sounds excessive and is contradicted by the determination of the *Times* editors – who would have read his pieces from Germany – to give him a staff job. On the other hand, Claud had very high standards, seeing journalism as a branch of writing just as difficult to master as writing a novel, short story or a poem. He stressed the importance of 'style', by which he meant not literary flourishes but the art of arranging and presenting facts in a way that will have the maximum informative and persuasive impact on the reader's mind.

During Claud's first three months in New York, Wall Street had been occasionally hit by squalls, but they passed and were succeeded by rallies and even higher prices. As with other financial bubbles, the boom was self-sustained so long as investors remained convinced that the shares that they bought today – regardless of their intrinsic worth – would always be bought by somebody else for more money tomorrow.

This confidence began to evaporate on 24 October, which turned out to be the first day of the Great Depression. From that day, a collapse in share prices became inescapable. On what came to be known as Black Thursday, Claud felt 'that nip in the emotional air which you get on the day after a big air raid when people grasped that the bombers really did get through last night and may do so again today'.[7] Prices temporarily went into freefall, so the ticker tape recording the drop was soon several hours out of date. 'By eleven o'clock the market had degenerated into a wild, mad scramble to sell,' wrote the economist J. K. Galbraith. 'By eleven-thirty the market had surrendered to blind relentless fear.'[8]

Nobody understood the significance of what was happening at the time, though Claud believed that Hinrichs might have been an exception. Claud says that he himself certainly did not, but nobody watching the ticker tape that day foresaw that what they were witnessing was the start of a road that would lead to economic devastation that 'looked very much like the most lurid predictions of Marx and Lenin'.[9] Claud wondered aloud what could reverse the tidal wave of bad news. He was reminded of the story about the enthusiastic American who took his phlegmatic English friend to see Niagara Falls.

'Isn't that amazing', exclaimed the American. 'Look at that vast mass of water dashing over that enormous cliff.'

'But what', asked the Englishman, 'is to stop it?'

Claud says that he only first sensed how bad things were when Hinrichs said to him in a low voice: 'Remember, when we're writing this story, the word panic is not to be used.'[10]

Claud and Hinrichs hurried to a hastily called press conference at the offices of J. P. Morgan & Company at 23 Wall Street which was intended to reassure the market. They heard Thomas W. Lamont, a senior partner of Morgan's, make one of the greatest understatements of all time, saying that 'there has been a little distress selling on the Stock Market' but that this was 'susceptible to betterment'.[11] His phoney overconfidence proved spectacularly counterproductive. 'Silver-haired Mr Lamont', recalled Claud, 'received us with a manner so reassuring that, upon me and many others, it had the same effect as Hinrichs' warning against the use of the word "panic".'[12]

Like a man on the stage of a burning theatre telling the audience that there is no need for alarm, Lamont 'made soft, soothing gesticulations with his pince-nez as softly, gently, almost stammeringly, he deprecated anything in the nature of sensationalism'. Claud says that such ominous blandness should have immediately reminded him of the old journalistic advice 'to believe nothing until it has been officially denied'.[13] In fact, this only became a widely quoted adage in this form after he published it in his memoir in 1956.

This did not stop clear signs of panic among investors at a lunch the same day with Edgar Speyer, a multimillionaire patron of the arts and a grandee on Wall Street. The atmosphere in the house was normally one of decorous calm, the talk being about art rather than the state of the stock market. Yet, as Claud sat down for lunch with the Speyers and four guests, they heard strange noises on the other side of the dining room door leading to the kitchen. Claud guessed that it might have been caused by children playing or a large dog getting loose. The he saw the door handle turning slowly in one direction and then in the other – as if somebody was undecided about entering the dining room. When two manservants came into the dining room to serve the food, Claud glimpsed, through the open door, four or five agitated-looking staff at the end of the corridor.

The mystery was only resolved when an embarrassed-looking butler came into the room and asked to speak privately to Sir Edgar. Astonished by the request, he followed the butler out of the room, returning shortly afterwards to explain that his domestic staff were all heavy investors in the stock market and had access to a ticker tape machine. 'The staff saw their savings going down in chaos', wrote Claud, and 'since they were certainly operating on margin, they might already have been wiped out.'[14]

And at the very moment that this was happening, they were having to serve saddle of lamb and pompano to their employer – said to be one of the shrewdest financiers in New York. They absolutely insisted that, regardless of propriety, he come at once to the kitchen, study the situation, make telephone calls if necessary and advise them what to do for the best.[15] In the event, however, neither Speyer's nor anybody else's business acumen would be sufficient in the coming months to prevent the stock market crash deepening and provoking an economic depression of unprecedented severity.

As the crash turned into a cataclysm, Claud found the unhappiness of his friends and acquaintances in New York, all affected by the disaster in a way that he was not, ever more difficult to bear. He was, in these circumstances, both pleased and alarmed to be told by the *Times* to go at once to Washington to fill in for their vastly experienced correspondent, Willmott Lewis, who had suddenly been summoned to attend a conference in London.[16] Taking the train from New York, Claud reached Washington on

24 December 1929, arriving at Lewis's house, where he was to stay, to find him giving a party.

Before going to bed hours later, he found Lewis still up, writing down notes about his conversations with highly informed guests. 'There are millions of pieces in the jigsaw,' he said to Claud. 'At any moment, you may unexpectedly find that you have picked up the one you need.'[17] Claud had met many impressive guests in the course of the evening, but none were as impressive as Lewis himself. His first encounter with Lewis lasted only forty-eight hours, but during that time he successfully boosted Claud's faltering self-confidence, taking it for granted that an inexperienced journalist, less than six months in America, could manage fine on his own. Before departing for London, he also gave what Claud said were the two best pieces of advice about journalism that he received in his life.

'I think it well', said Lewis, 'to remember that when writing for the newspapers, we are working for an elderly lady in Hastings who has two cats of which she is passionately fond. Unless our stuff can successfully compete for her interest with those cats, it is no good.' The second piece of advice, imparted by Lewis as he clambered into a taxi on his way to England, was 'Don't be nervous. Remember old boy whatever happens, you are right and London is wrong.'[18]

Lewis was very much Claud's type of person and became the most important of his mentors on the *Times*. He enjoyed the jocular cynicism of Lewis's bon mots about people and politics in Washington, such as: 'In fairness to Senator Cole Blease, it must be said that he has the unique distinction of combining in his sole person all the disadvantages attaching to the democratic form of government.' 'One should perhaps avoid being hypercritical of acts of high policy. Take the charitable view, bearing in mind that every government will do as much harm as it can and as much good as it must.' 'He is one of those American politicians who believe that the women of his country are more virtuous and its diplomats more stupid than those of any other. Since he is wrong on both these counts, it is reasonable to assume that he is wrong on every other too.'

Claud was drawn to people who had led lives full of adventure and melodrama, similar to his own. This was certainly true of Lewis. Born in Cardiff in 1877, the son of a coal shipper, he was educated in Eastbourne, Heidelberg and the Sorbonne, and spoke fluent German and French, but, having failed to get a job on a mainline newspaper in London, he had gone on the stage. He had belonged to a troupe of actors in the provincial theatre in East-bourne, on the southeast coast of England, which had led him to acquire 'a kind of barnstorming fruitiness and floridity of tone and gesture which sometimes disconcerted the stolid'. He had returned to journalism and moved to China, where he became editor of the *North China Daily News* and covered the Boxer Rebellion when Claud's father Henry had been besieged in the Legation Quarter. Going to Japan in 1903, he covered the Russo-Japanese war, then made a brief foray to start a business in San Francisco. After that business failed, he returned to the Far East to edit the *Manila Times* in the Philippines between 1911 and 1917. He then went back to Europe to handle publicity for the American army in France during the war, then reported on the Versailles peace conference in 1919,[19] before being hired by Lord Northcliffe, the owner of the *Times*, to be the paper's correspond-ent in Washington – a position he held from 1920 until 1948.

Another aspect of Lewis's career which must have resonated with Claud, after his recent hardships in Berlin and Paris, was its precipitous ups and downs. 'The advantage', he told Claud, 'of having spent a good deal of one's early life on – not to put too fine a point of it – the bum, is that one learns not to take a square meal entirely for granted.' He said that once, having had nothing for four days in London, he had found just enough money in the lining of a trouser pocket to buy a tin of meat, only to find, on opening it, that it was hopelessly maggot ridden. 'It is a good thing', he said, 'to remember that, however nicely we may be doing, to millions and millions of people all over the world privations and disappointments of that kind are happen-ing all the time.'[20]

Working from Lewis's house in Washington, it took Claud several weeks to discover, accidentally, that the *Times* had an office in the Press Building that he had not been told about.

Having obtained the office key, he was appalled to find the floor littered with urgent telegrams and letters from London demanding reports on a variety of stories. Since some of these peremptory requests dated from after he had taken charge, he feared he had committed a disastrous blunder by inadvertently ignoring them. Only on the return of Lewis to Washington did he tell Claud that he routinely ignored such cables.

Not every article that Claud wrote passed the test of competing successfully with the two much-loved cats for the attention of the elderly lady in Hastings. Sometime after Lewis's return from England, Claud submitted to him a two-column piece of which he was especially proud. Lewis read it twice with close attention, nodding appreciatively as he did so. Then, holding it between his finger and thumb, he said: 'Old boy, this piece is not only informed but erudite. Its material is solid and accurately observed, its style polished – and, in my estimation, witty. In fact, it is everything which one imagines to oneself an article in the *Times* should be. Yet I'm afraid – my instinct tells me that' – he opened his fingers and thumb and the pages dropped into the wastepaper basket – 'I'm afraid the cats will have it.'[21]

Claud was eager to find stories far from New York and Washington that might allow him to write about the rest of America, which was reeling under the impact of the Great Crash. He found a hook for such a story with the murder of Jake Lingle, a crime reporter on the *Chicago Tribune* who was shot dead by a single gunman in a street on 9 June 1930. It was supposed at first that Lingle was a journalistic martyr, murdered in order to prevent him exposing gangsters. But it soon emerged that he was more than half gangster himself, living astonishingly well on his sixty-five-dollar-a-week reporter's salary (Al Capone had even given him a diamond-studded belt buckle). Lingle had in fact been earning a fortune as the linkman between the Chicago police and organised crime, acting as the conduit for protection money paid by criminals and shady businessmen to the police department.[22]

Nevertheless, the killing created a political furore not just in Chicago but nationwide, providing Claud with a good reason to go to Illinois to interview the crime boss Al Capone. Hinrichs agreed that this was a splendid idea and was hesitant only because he knew that whenever the *Times* wrote about crime in America, it was bombarded by protests from the American embassy and pro-American friendship societies in London accusing it of promulgating the myth in Britain that the United States was populated solely by gangsters and hoodlums.[23] In the event, Claud received guarded permission to go ahead with the story in a telegram from Printing House Square which read: 'By all means Cockburn Chicago-wards. Welcome stories ex-Chicago not unduly emphasizing crime.'[24]

He got the interview with surprising ease through another well-connected Chicago crime reporter who knew Capone and read the *Times*'s message over the phone to the astonished arch-criminal, who may have been tempted by the opportunity to express his broader views on the state of America and the world. In the Lexington Hotel, where Capone had his headquarters, Claud thought that his office looked like that of a newly enriched millionaire – aside from the presence of a bodyguard with a submachine gun half hidden by a door. Aside from 'the jowly young murderer on the other side of his desk', Claud was intrigued by a number of solid silver finger bowls filled with roses on the desk, in which Capone repeatedly dipped his fingers to relieve nervous tension.[25]

Claud took an instant dislike to Capone as he proclaimed drearily conventional opinions. 'Oh, I hated him,' Claud told interviewer Fintan O'Toole fifty years later. 'He really was a nasty little brute. His office looked like the office of a rather crooked oil executive, but his behaviour was that of a fuddy-duddy bank manager.'[26] Capone said that had he not gone into the rackets, he would have been selling newspapers barefoot in the streets in Brooklyn.[27] Claud may have taken this as suggesting that Capone saw himself as the product of social deprivation, but he went on to give Claud a pretentious homily on the virtues of American capitalism. 'All my rackets', he asserted, 'are run on strictly American lines and they are going to stay that way.'[28]

Claud interpreted this as a reference to the influence of Sicilian gangsters whom Capone accused of going in 'for this black-hand stuff', which he considered un-business-like and archaic. 'Can you imagine', he said, 'people going in for all these blood feuds – some guy's grandfather was killed by some other guy's grandfather, and this guy thinks that is a good enough reason to kill the other.'[29] Claud might have been more sympathetic towards Capone had the gangster boss shown any sense of humour, but he did not laugh once during their meeting.

Claud made the surprising decision not to write up the interview, saying Capone was a murderous buffoon whose views he saw no reason to publicise and which were, in any case, worryingly similar to those in the *Times* leader columns. Asked about this, he said that he believed the *Times* would not have been 'best pleased to find itself seeing eye to eye with the most notorious gangster in Chicago'. Meanwhile, he had covered himself with the paper by writing a couple of readable pieces about Chicago, which they must have liked since they sent him a sizeable and much-needed bonus.[30]

9

With Hope

Unemployed queue for food during the Great Depression [wiki commons]

Some months after his interview with Capone, Claud met Hope Hale, a twenty-seven-year-old journalist originally from Iowa, who was managing and writing for magazines in New York. 'Claud and I had met in the Fall of 1930,' she says in an unpublished account of their relationship. 'We were brought together purposely at a lavish dinner party given by one of Claud's older colleagues . . . Claud and I discovered we were almost the same age, in our mid-twenties; he had published a story in the *Dial*, and my work had started [to] appear in the

New Yorker. Yet at first glance it's hard to see why our match-makers saw us as a match.'[1]

Both were sexually adventurous. Claud had had a long affair with Berta Pölz, while Hope had briefly been married. Speaking of herself and her young women friends in New York in the 1920s, she wrote that they risked getting pregnant, but this was a price that they paid 'as writers [who] represented the spirit of the twenties. We spent our days pursuing success and our nights pursuing what we thought of as experience.'[2]

She found Claud hugely attractive, though intellectually intimidating:

Tall and willowy with an Oxford stammer, he was already showing the talents that would make him an internationally enjoyed raconteur. While I, half educated, or maybe less than half, had to guess what he meant when he spoke of a 'double first'. Snatching my high school diploma, I had fled from Iowa, from my widowed teacher mother, her proud proper poverty and her overpowering religion. I was as naïve a rebel as my apple cheeked sturdy looks suggested.[3]

On the other hand, she was intelligent and wrote limpidly and sensitively, so her self-deprecating stress on her own lack of education and sophistication sound exaggerated. She was certainly fascinated, from the moment they met, by Claud's blend of mischievous humour and social warmth, combined with a private determination to change the world for the better. 'This made him irresistible,' she said, knowing that he was at bottom a very serious man. 'This gave our hours in bed a quality beyond comparison with my earlier quests for experience.'[4] Different though their national, political and cultural backgrounds might be, they 'were both New Yorkers now, and took to each other's exuberant quest for experience'.[5]

Yet that search was no longer focused primarily on liberation from the sexual and social norms of traditional American society. Hope emphasised her political naiveté, but she shared Claud's rebelliousness and his revulsion at the misery they saw all around them.

The financial crash on Wall Street was turning into an economic catastrophe that did not end until 1940. At first, the government did not even admit that there was a crisis, though 'unemployed men in Chicago had to fight one another for the first grab at the garbage cans put out the back of the great hotels because a full and proper system of unemployment relief would have been "socialistic" and above all would have been an admission of the existence of a crisis of scarcely believable proportions'.[6] By 1933 13 million Americans – a quarter of the workforce – would be out of a job.[7]

Claud, who had come to America to see if its version of capitalism made Karl Marx irrelevant and social revolution unnecessary, felt that these questions had been categorically answered in the negative. As he witnessed the onset of the Great Depression, he came to feel that the transformation of society was the only way forward. He was contemptuous of official speeches, dripping with false optimism, to which he was forced to listen in Washington.[8] He preferred those like the director of the Illinois Central Bank, whom he met in Chicago when there to interview Capone, who concluded their discussion about how commodity prices were affecting the economy of the Midwest by saying: 'Hell boy, the capitalist system is on the skids anyway. Let's go and get a drink.'[9]

'Gradually we discovered a more important bond,' Hope wrote.

> Under our excitement as we raced from work to speakeasy to party, we both felt a nagging discontent. The stock market had crashed, the Depression was deepening, Riverside Park [in Manhattan] was turning into a colony of shacks. Mortgages were foreclosing at the rate of a thousand a day. The architects who could have built houses were selling five-cent apples on the streets.[10]

Hope's brother, a chemist, wrote to her from Iowa to say that he had kept his job by taking a salary cut, but an unemployed colleague with a PhD had been reduced to scouring the local race track enclosure with his family after the last race, looking for 'lost coins, the rare bill dropped, and the even rarer uncashed winning ticket'.[11]

Hope says that Claud thought revolution inevitable. 'It was the way history was going, he told me, and he wanted to play his part in it. If he had been born a century earlier, he said, he would have been an empire builder.'[12] Claud says that he was by no means so certain about the imminence of revolution in America. 'I knew the United States pretty well by that time and I agreed with Mr Capone that the American system would get by for a lot longer than that.'[13]

Hope's sentence quoting Claud about the British Empire is interesting, suggesting the lingering influence of his father and grandfather, who saw the British Empire as a means by which they could, and should, shape the world for the better. 'I think that because of that background and partly because of my close-ness to my father, and his assumptions', he said in an interview many years later, 'it would have seemed absurd not to affect the world.'[14] Claud told Hope that he regarded his job on the *Times* as training for a career as a revolutionary activist – much though he enjoyed his work and liked his colleagues. She was greatly impressed by the way in which he was prepared to give up a glittering journalistic career 'with a smile, for the chancy life of a revolutionary'.[15]

But she was uneasily conscious that, just as Claud could move on from a good job more easily than others, he could also move on easily from a woman he liked, or even loved. In her papers, Hope kept an angry letter from Suzanne La Follette, a feminist and writer, with whom Claud had been living in New York until he met Hope. Undated but clearly written in late 1930, La Follette tells him that she was sending his belongings left in her apartment to the LaFayette Hotel, which was his pied-à-terre in New York. She asks him to come the following day to pick up anything else while she is at the office 'so there is no danger of running into me'. She goes on, with mounting fury, to say that though he had every opportunity to make 'a clean and decent getaway, you could have behaved so contemptibly'. As for his suggestion that they be friends in future, she rejects this as 'effrontery' designed to make him feel better about his bad behaviour. 'Never mind, you will [feel better about dumping her],' she concludes acidly.[16]

Deeply in love with Claud though she was, Hope was clear-sighted about their relationship. They had entered very much into each other's social worlds, and in her journal entry for 22 March 1931 she writes: 'Entertained Claud's cousin Alec Waugh [Evelyn's older brother] at breakfast with Claud and others; gin fizzes, kidneys and bacon, scrambled eggs, muffins, straw-berries and cream. Coffee.' On 7 May she writes that Claud has been in Washington for ten days 'but no letters'. She adds, 'I love Claud and he loves me but not enough.'[17]

By the end of 1931, Claud told Hope that he was planning to resign from the *Times* and return to Europe. Her response was a measure of her love for him and her self-reliance, wrapped up in revolutionary romanticism, which she believed might enable her to overcome all obstacles. She avoided trying to dissuade Claud from his revolutionary course, but she did decide that she wanted to have a baby by him, calling her plan 'Project Revolu-tionary Baby'.[18] She asked Claud to marry her for the sake of propriety. 'I was sure I could carry out the project alone,' she said, underestimating just how all-consuming it would be to look after a child alone while holding a full-time job.

She and Claud were married in New York on 19 February 1932, after a party given by Alec Waugh the previous night where Claud had repeated a toast he had learned from Paul Claudel, the French ambassador.

> In English, it said simply 'May it be to you like good bread.' In French, and in Claud's voice, it sounded lyrical. Good bread, he lovingly pointed out, was something of which a man would never tire. The real meaning may not have occurred to either of us; that a wife should be something a man went on consuming for his nourishment all their lives.

This may not be fair on Claud, since he had told Hope before the marriage that he was going back to Europe permanently. She was probably right in thinking she was more in love with him than he with her, and she semi-consciously hoped that the marriage might turn into something more than a bow to conventional morality. By the time he sailed for Europe on the SS *Dunquerque* in July 1932, she was pregnant and feeling his departure more than she had expected. Vague plans were made for her to join him in Europe at some later date, after the baby was born. 'Our parting was far more wrenching than we had planned', she wrote, 'but we told each other that the separation was not to be for long.'[19]

A baby girl, Claudia, was born in Presbyterian Hospital in New York on 11 February 1933, less than two weeks after Hitler had become German chancellor and Claud had fled from Berlin to escape the Nazis.

Claud's departure from the *Times* and return to Europe came because he had detailed information about the approaching calamity in Germany and Central Europe. He had remained in touch with Berta Pölz, Berthold Wiesner and the Schwarzwald circle in Vienna and Berlin. A highly informed source closer to hand was Wolfgang zu Putlitz, the young Prussian aristocrat in the German Foreign Service, whom Claud had got to know well when he was in Berlin in 1927–9 and who had become a third secretary at the German embassy in Washington.

Claud and Putlitz had seen much of each other in Berlin. He hinted to Claud, whom he was meeting for lunch or dinner a couple of times a week, either in the rooftop restaurant of the Washington Hotel or in bars by the Potomac, that he intended to take some sort of action. 'As the news from Germany grew worse, he became more and more restless,' Claud wrote. 'He considered that at any moment now the situation in Germany might reach a point where he would feel it essential for himself to return to his native land and "do what has to be done."'[20] It was not clear to Claud, and almost certainly not to Putlitz, what the latter intended to do at this time, but his anti-Nazi convictions would lead him a few years later to become British intelligence's most knowledgeable informant inside the German government, until he was unmasked and escaped to England in 1940.[21]

Doom-laden but accurate forebodings by Putlitz contributed to Claud's growing feeling that he was on the wrong side of the

Atlantic, while history was being made in Europe. Moreover, he did not believe that his editors back in London had really grasped the tremendous impact of the Great Depression in the US. When he wrote about Chicago in the summer of 1930, he later recalled, 'I became aware, really for the first time, that about fifty per cent of what seemed to me to be the truth about the situation in Chicago would certainly be unpalatable and perhaps in parts unintelligible to *The Times*.'[22]

Even so, resigning from a good job with what he still considered to be the best newspaper in the world in the middle of a depression – and without much idea of what he was going to do next – was not a decision easily made. Not all the correspondence between Claud and the *Times* about his resignation has survived, but three key letters between him and Dawson show how much Claud agonised over his departure, and why Dawson was not entirely convinced that Claud would really go. Claud's undated and emotional resignation letter must have been sent in November 1931, since Dawson's reply was dispatched later that month. They address each other by their surnames, suggesting that, since Claud was only a junior employee, that they had developed a fairly close friendship.

Dear Dawson,

I have delayed rather a long time in writing this letter because it is such a difficult and unpleasant letter to write. To cut a long story as short as possible, I have felt for some time and am now definitely at the conclusion that I must soon go to England to work there: work, too, rather a long distance on the other side of the political fence from *The Times*. If you know, as I hope you do, how enormously I have enjoyed my work here, you will know too that leaving it is not something I do either easily or lightly. For one thing, the more I see of other newspapers the more obvious it is that *The Times* is the best in the world: and incomparably the most agreeable to work for in every respect. Whatever I do now, and at the moment I do not know exactly what I shall do, I'm sure I shall not find anything so pleasant as my work for *The Times*.

However, there comes, I think, a point where not to act, or try to act more or less on ones [*sic*] political convictions becomes damaging to oneself in some way, and unfair also to one's employers – and so far as I am concerned I haven't any doubt that that point has come.

I am especially sorry that I now have to resign from *The Times* because it will [end] my association with [Wilmott] Lewis and [Louis] Hinrichs – either of whom alone even would be more in the way of good luck than any young correspondent has any right to expect.

I would like to thank you adequately for all the kindness and help you have given me. I should have answered long ago your kind letter of the early summer, but these ideas were in my head and I found it difficult to know what exactly to say. I can think of many kind things you have done for me but I should especially thank you for the telegram you once took the trouble to send to me in Vienna – where I was then penniless telling me that there was a job open for me.

I have of course told Lewis and Hinrichs what I am doing.

Yours
Claud Cockburn.[23]

The reply by Dawson to this letter is warm and conciliatory. Dated 15 November 1931, it says:

My Dear Cockburn,

I am really distressed by your news – and also a little mystified. There is no question of thinking you ungrateful. We all have to make up our minds from time to time whether we are following the best course or whether we had better change it. But I cannot quite understand – and must wait until I see you – what exactly it is that you want to do. *The Times* sits so firmly on the political fence that you will have to become a Die-hard or a Communist to get very far away from it.

There is nothing more to be said for the moment except to tell you how very sorry we shall all be to lose you. When I wrote to you some months ago it was really with the object of finding out whether you yourself wanted to change to England or some other part of the world. I do not know if I could have provided you with it, but I would have done my best. Your work in the States has been an unqualified success, and I repeat that I am distressed by the thought that it is coming to an end.

Let me know if you want to come to England.

Yours sincerely[24]

There was a final coda when Dawson and Deakin, the imperial and foreign news editor, came to New York, en route to an economic conference in Canada, for a final meeting with Claud. He quotes Dawson as saying that it 'does seem rather bad luck that you of all people should have gone red on us'. Wilmott Lewis, having invited himself to the meeting, warned that in future many young intelligent journalists whom the *Times* might hire would be Reds. 'Dawson', wrote Claud, 'who had put on his spectacles to watch the performance, now peered at Lewis over the top of them. He gave a small, acid-sounding laugh. "I am afraid", he said, "you have been talking too much to your ex-assistant." Then I knew that I had resigned at last.'[25]

As Claud travelled back to Berlin via Budapest and Vienna, his relationship with Hope showed immediate signs of strain. He spent a few days in the Austrian Alps with his former girlfriend Berta Pölz, writing to Hope that 'the country round Vienna is beautiful.[26] I stayed at a little hotel on the edge of town near Berta's apartment. We walked about the country and drank new wine in pubs and had a very good time.'[27] Hope said that this 'might seem innocuous enough . . . but I read between the lines', and her return letter evidently revealed her disquiet.[28]

Claud's response was scarcely reassuring: 'You imagine perhaps that if I do more than just whore around and fuck girls that I don't give a hoot about in a general way, then it becomes dangerous for you, but that is only because you underestimate what I think of you and how solidly I think and feel it.' Understandably unconvinced by this, Hope later wrote that she 'had tried to believe in this solidity . . . I prided myself on taking a modern view. In fact, some of my own past required it. But I remembered my first night with Claud and the change it had made in both of us. This is what people had meant when they shook their heads over our plans for a long separation.'[29]

10

The Week

Claud edits *The Week* [author]

After Claud returned to London from Vienna in mid-February 1933, his letters to Hope became less frequent. He was absorbed in launching *The Week*, the first issue of which would be published six weeks later, on 29 March.

Claud said that he knew almost nobody in England, having spent only a few months there during the previous six years. But this was not quite correct, as he still had friends from Oxford, among whom was Archie Harding, a rising figure at the BBC, with whom he stayed in Chelsea free of charge. Sympathetic to Claud's project, Harding put him in touch with Benvenuto 'Ben' Sheard, who had also been an undergraduate at Oxford at the same time as Claud. He was writing a novel in a cottage in Berkshire when Claud recruited him as the manager of the proposed newsletter. More essentially, Sheard produced the forty pounds necessary to pay the first instalment on the lease of an office high up in a building at 34 Victoria Street in Westminster.

A single room, it could only be reached by taking a shaky lift and then climbing a steep staircase which users complained was more like a stepladder.[1] A mimeograph was bought through hire-purchase, along with paper and ink. Harding's wife Crystal, whom Claud had imagined to be an apolitical socialite, surprised him by volunteering to work for free on the new venture. 'Until about this time her idea of a major event in Home Affairs had been the exclusion of some friend from the Royal Enclosure at Ascot,' he wrote. But he thought she was pretty, energetic, intelligent and loyal, with plenty of common sense, though she could not type and 'most of the people who dashed in and out of the attic in Victoria Street were as alien to her as if they had escaped from the Zoo'.[2]

The lack of resources was all too real, but Claud believed this would deter potential litigants who might see that, whatever the outcome of a court case, they were not going to get any money.[3] Claud refused to withdraw a story in the face of a threatened legal action, but would offer to write a second article based on fresh information supplied by the potential litigant showing that the original story was wrong. A further advantage of open indigence was that it reinforced the image of *The Week* as a David against Goliath or perhaps Robin Hood resisting some modern-day Sheriff of Nottingham.

The Week was designed as a one-man band in which all instruments could be played by Claud. It had no editorial board or other organisational impedimenta. He planned a publication, compact in opinion and style, targeting a limited but influential pool of politicians, journalists, diplomats, academics, financiers and businessmen, along with people appalled by the rise of fascism and the near collapse of capitalism. He was keen to avoid any departure from the simplicity of his original idea. 'Several times', he wrote, 'during that [first] six weeks, I had to tuck my idea under my arm and run with it to prevent it being suffocated by some well-intentioned conference or by a committee.'⁴

Several would-be helpers either misunderstood the nature of the project or turned out to be mad. One enthusiast from Vancouver talked for hours about getting advertising, which Claud did not want because he would have to water down the newsletter's content in order to please advertisers. 'He stayed with us', Claud wrote, 'throughout the launch of the paper and for three weeks after it had begun to come out, but then he went out of his mind just outside the Army and Navy stores where he knelt on the pavement one morning, addressing me as his Brother in the Sun.'⁵

A further mishap, gleefully recorded by MI5, was an early financial crisis brought on by Sheard suffering a mental breakdown. A MI5 report on 'Claud Cockburn and "The Week"' says that 'T.B.F. Sheard, shown [?] as manager, is no longer employed. He had a particularly sharp bout of what is known as "financial irresponsibility", in the course of which he removed the funds.' MI5 had intercepted a begging letter from Claud to Nancy Cunard, an heiress with radical sympathies, asking her to make up the loss. Confirming Sheard's breakdown, another MI5 officer wrote that Sheard had written to King George V, asking him 'to interest his influential friends' in the newsletter.⁶

The Week was mailed to subscribers, who paid an annual twelve shillings, on a Wednesday so that they would read it before they saw other weekly magazines. 'All the things that always happen on such occasions happened,' wrote Claud about the first publication day. 'None of us had ever used a duplicating machine before and stencils cracked like sails in a gale and the place was bespattered by sticky brown ink. The valuable Pekinese dog belonging to the secretary [Crystal] became disgusted and spitefully chewed up the reserve tubes of ink.'⁷

Nevertheless, given the short time between planning and publishing, The Week did well in providing serious insider news to the politically engaged, mostly about the struggle for supremacy in Europe. Claud assumed the powers that be would pursue their own partisan interests, regardless of whatever they claimed to the contrary. Often accused of cynically expecting the worst of political leaders, he defended his attitude as simply reflecting the Realpolitik motives and interests of individuals, nations, classes, business and media. Standing firmly with the have-nots against the haves, he saw his little newsletter as a pistol firing back at the heavy artillery of the rich and powerful.[8]

Claud set out what he intended to do in a letter to potential subscribers sent on 3 April, which was duly preserved by MI5.[9] Claud wrote that 'everybody is aware of the more or less concealed motives, financial, political, personal, that dominate the news policy of the big press. In addition, the big press, precisely by reason of its bigness, tries to select all its news for all its readers. The wider it spreads the shallower it gets. What it does not suppress, it dilutes.'[10] He stressed that his newsletter would be news driven, in contrast to the existing weekly press in Britain, which consisted primarily of commentary on events. Contributors were to be paid one pound per page and were asked to give as many facts, figures and names as possible: 'It is no use telling us that the situation is terrible; we know that.'[11]

The Week was able to live up to its founder's ambitions because it was correct about the catastrophic direction of events. The unstable post–First World War order, which had remained in place since the Treaty of Versailles, was visibly collapsing as Hitler tightened his grip on power. Claud took it for granted that negotiations about disarmament and economic cooperation were illusions. As 'a premature anti-Nazi', he was certain that another European war was inevitable.[12]

Claud believed that explosive events would lift his fragile craft into the air. 'Don't you understand', he told friends anxious about his lack of resources, 'that a glider doesn't *need* a bloody engine.'[13] He meant that a state of perpetual crisis might provide both news and readership. Some in high office already saw the danger posed by the Nazis, and *The Week* could make their views public knowledge.

An example of this process came in the summer of 1933, when the retiring British ambassador to Germany, Sir Horace Rumbold, wrote a ferocious and far-sighted valedictory dispatch to the Foreign Office in which he denounced Hitler and the Nazis root and branch. He said that Hitler himself was 'not normal' and that the policies pursued by the Nazis would

inevitably lead to war.[14] *The Week* summarised Rumbold's pro-
phetic telegram as saying 'the correct attitude [of the British
government] towards the Nazi government should be the attitude that might be adopted towards a group of gangsters
temporarily in control of a territory'.[15] It described Rumbold's
last dispatch as 'not merely critical but violently hostile to the
Nazi government', contradicting those in the Foreign Office
who believed that 'the Hitler government, in spite of some
regrettable lapses, is a healthy and stabilising factor in Europe'.[16]

The Rumbold telegram 'scoop' is instructive not merely
because of its insights but because it shows how *The Week* could
overturn the government's traditional method of keeping information from the public by limiting knowledge of it to a few
trusted journalists. A letter from the Foreign Office about the
leak to *The Week*, sent to MI5, explains that the Rumbold telegram had been shown 'confidentially to certain reputable
diplomatic correspondents and editors' on the condition that
they did not reveal its full text.[17] The official was annoyed that
The Week had disrupted this cosy arrangement and speculated
about the identity of Claud's informant, with suspicion falling
on one named correspondent.

Claud learned about Foreign Office rage that 'the customary
diplomatic procedure of simultaneously informing and muzzling
newspapermen' had, in this case, been flouted. He denied that
his source was one of the Foreign Office's trusted correspondents, but officials thought this 'might be an attempt to throw
dust in our eyes'. Alternatively, they suspected that the source
might be a young German refugee named Herbert Stahl or 'a
kind of clearing house of official secrets' operating 'somewhere
near Kingsway'.

Civil servants were unaccustomed to being criticised by name
and reacted with splenetic fury when *The Week* did so. When
the newsletter alleged that a senior official, Rex Leeper, head of
the Foreign Office press department, had associated with industrialists selling arms in Eastern Europe, an MI5 official reported,

Mr Norton [from the Foreign Office] rang me up to say that Sir
Robert Vansittart [permanent under secretary at the Foreign

Office] was extremely angry over the reference to Mr Rex Leeper which had appeared in No. 77 of 'The Week', and he wished the paper to be brought to the notice of the D.P.P [director of public prosecutions] with a view to considering whether any form of action – apart from legal – could possibly be taken against Claud Cockburn.[18] [I] showed the copy in question to D.P.P. and he arranged to see Sir Robert himself. D.P.P. actually told me that he considered any legal action on this to be out of the question, and he definitely turned down the possibility of doing anything in the nature of warning Claud Cockburn.[19]

The Foreign Office mandarin had suggested Kingsway as a source of leaked secrets, and there was a reason for this. A major source for *The Week* were American and continental European foreign correspondents stationed in London whose own news outlets, out of disinterest or bias, were not running what the frustrated journalists considered to be important stories. Unable to publish these in their own outlets, the foreign journalists were open to sharing what they knew with *The Week*. Claud said that the exchange of news was conducted for the most part on a barter basis with a group of what he considered to be the best informed and most lively-minded correspondents in London.[20] Two or three times a week, this group met in the London office of Negley Farson, the correspondent of the *Chicago Daily News*, in Bush House on Kingsway, in the Aldwych. It was Farson who had originally proposed to Claud a regular exchange of information. Among those attending these informal meetings were Frederick Kuh of United Press, who had been forced to leave Berlin, where he was UP bureau chief,[21] Paul Scheffer of the *Berliner Tageblatt* newspaper,[22] and Paul Littauer of the Polish News Agency.[23] An advantage for the foreign journalists was that they could quote from a story in *The Week* – thereby avoiding taking full responsibility for it themselves – even though the information originally came from them.

As political turmoil increased, foreign embassies in London and foreign ministries abroad were deeply concerned – and divided – about what might be the latest steps towards a European war. A valuable source might be 'the councillor of an embassy, who was convinced of the wrongheaded policy of the Foreign Office and the Ambassador and wished without exposing himself to put a spoke in their wheels'.[24] He pointed out that historians had found that foreign diplomats in Tudor England were among the best-informed people about what was really going on in the English court, so their secret reports to their home governments were filled with confidential information available nowhere else. He felt that, likewise in the 1930s, the best informants about British policy towards Hitler and Mussolini were often to be found not in London but in Paris, Brussels, Vienna and Geneva.

Claud also established *The Week* to bring news from Europe to an English audience. It reported often on the intensifying repression in Germany, shared by well-informed anti-Nazis inside the regime. Such informants became fewer in number after the Night of the Long Knives on 30 June 1934, when SS gunmen killed several hundred of those whom Hitler saw as hindering him in achieving absolute control of the German state.

The Week reported on what it called 'the silent pogrom' against the Jews as well as the beatings and murders. Claud reported the end of a Jewish-owned bookshop he had used in Berlin, calling it one of the best bookshops in Germany. 'It was run by Hans Preiss and was located opposite the State University Library, and supplied students and scholars with the latest works of science, economics and philosophy; but Preiss was "of Jewish origin",' he wrote. 'Universities and libraries one after another cancelled their orders, students dared not be seen entering "a Jew shop". Business came to a full stop so in order to survive, Preiss was forced to emigrate.'[25] The story, for once, had a more or less happy ending, with Preiss opening a new shop close to the British Museum in London.

Communists were also in flight. Willi Münzenberg, 'marked A1 on the Nazi blacklist' as 'a leading Red deputy' in the Reichstag, was campaigning in his constituency on the day of the Reichstag fire. Learning of his imminent arrest,

he instantly hired a luxurious Hispano-Suiza [car], dressed up two Communists in livery, one as chauffeur, the other as footman, obtaining a passport of somebody 27 years younger than himself, drove, lolling on cushions, puffing on a big cigar, off to the nearest frontier. As soon as the typical German frontier officials saw this equipage, they saluted obsequiously, hardly glancing at his passport and allowing him to proceed on his journey.

Another Communist deputy, Babette Gross, fled without a passport by train to near the Swiss border. She called 'Marxists' on the Swiss side of the border, who crossed it ostensibly to attend a village fête; when they returned to Switzerland in the evening, they smuggled Gross back with them past unwary frontier guards.[26]

Ordinary Germans, even when not Jewish and politically neutral, found their lives disrupted by Nazi policies. A Dusseldorf married couple were victims of the Nazi wish 'to set the feminist clock back by supressing all manifestations of the emancipation of women as a Marxist perversion of the true spirit of Germany'. On the instruction of local Nazi bosses, the wife was fired because she worked in the same factory as her husband. They prevented her getting a job elsewhere, 'quoting Hitler about the place of the married woman [being in the home]'. The couple consulted a lawyer who suggested that they get a divorce, though he warned that if they went on living together, they might be arrested 'for living in un-German sin'.[27]

Claud believed, as did many, that only the German army had the power to overthrow the Nazis, probably acting in concert with right-wing politicians like the vice-chancellor Franz von Papen. He had helped Hitler into office in the mistaken belief that the conservative establishment could control him. Though von Papen and senior generals were ambivalent about a showdown with Hitler, their staffs contained dissidents who, if they could not stage a putsch against the Nazis, could pass on information about them to sympathetic journalists like Claud.

Among his informants was Herbert von Bose, the director of von Papen's press bureau and at one time his chief of staff. Claud does not identify him by name but gives enough details to leave little doubt who he is talking about when he says that 'this man,

who at times acted as Von Papen's chef de cabinet, was an energetically devout Catholic and an astute anti-Nazi.'[28] For a year
and a half after he became German chancellor, 'it was still necessary for Hitler to treat Von Papen with caution and a kind of
respect, so that it was impossible to conceal from the Von Papen
bureau more than 30 per cent of what the Nazis were really up
to.' Claud says he took every precaution to keep his link with
von Bose a secret, asking him not to write anything down but
to talk instead to a visiting foreign journalist, whom nobody
suspected of having a connection with *The Week*. The journalist
then passed on his information by word of mouth when he was
next in London.[29]

Claud was hopeful that the German army might act against
the Nazis sooner or later. In an analysis of the German political
scene on 23 August 1933, presumably drawing on von Bose's
information, Claud writes at length about

> the increasingly important role of the Reichswehr, saying that
> before the advent of Hitler to power, the rank-and-file of the
> regular army were divided between right and left, though 'the
> younger officers up to the rank of captain were predominantly
> Nazi, and the higher ranks were chiefly anti-Hitlerites of the
> Right, more or less sympathetic with Stahlhelm and Von
> Schleicher.

He discusses the chances of the army intervening against Hitler,
saying that 'the Reichswehr officers, even many of those formerly favourable to Hitler, are now alarmed by the possibility
of their present status and future prospects being damaged by
the growth of importance of the Storm Troopers.'[30] They saw the
million-strong paramilitary Brownshirts as a socialist-inclined
rabble, while 'our present information leaves no doubt that Von
Papen himself – naif aristocrat built on Wodehouse lines – is
now bitterly antagonistic' to the regime.

The Week emphasised the up-to-date nature of its information as the Nazis consolidated their grip on government and
society. When they moved to abolish the old German states in
January 1934, the 17 January issue detailed the changes

envisaged but said that the regime was undecided whether or not to issue the decree on the anniversary of the creation of the Nazi Party on 19 January or on 30 January, the first anniversary of Hitler becoming chancellor.[31]

Regarding the Nazification of German culture, *The Week* described the minister of propaganda, Dr Goebbels, dragooning literati into joining a state organisation called Reichsverband Deutscher Schiftsteller in a bid to counterbalance 'the vacuum on the literary field which resulted when all the bearers of great names, Thomas and Heinrich Mann, Arnold and Stephen Zweig, Wassemann, Ludwig, Feuchtwanger and others were burned vicariously on the bonfires, and preferred to go into exile'.[32]

In the event, Hitler struck first against the Brownshirts and the anti-Nazi conservatives in the Night of the Long Knives. Claud wrote a lead story ten days before the purge saying at the top of its front page that 'all news now reaching us from Germany confirms our previous information about the advanced stage now reached in preparations for a decisive attempt to establish a military dictatorship'.[33] Among those killed by SS squads were the former chancellor von Schleicher, whose newsletter had been an unwitting inspiration for *The Week*. Von Papen was also arrested. Among those who died was von Bose, though *The Week* suggest that he was not on the original SS death list, saying that 'it is clear from accounts reaching us that that the murder of von Bose, Papen's chef de cabinet, which occurred at 12.45 on Saturday afternoon, was the result of one wing of the repressive forces – namely the SS – getting out of hand. Six of them walked into his office and shot him as he sat at his desk.'[34]

At first *The Week* expressed optimism that the disbanded but still armed Storm Troopers might cause trouble for Hitler, but it soon revised this position, saying that military experts in Britain and France believed that the effectiveness of the Reichswehr had been increased by the purge of its paramilitary rivals. It was scornful of press reports that the inter-Nazi divisions exposed by the killings meant that 'the German threat to European peace' had diminished, when in fact it had increased.[35]

11

Frank Pitcairn of the *Daily Worker*

Claud writes for the *Daily Worker* under the name of Frank Pitcairn [wiki commons]

'I have arranged for two casual agents to take up the investigation of "The Week" from different angles,' wrote an MI5 officer in a memo on 23 October 1933. Their reports give a worm's-eye picture of Claud and *The Week* office in its early days, though the agents expressed some bafflement about him and his newsletter. Posing as freelance journalists and potential contributors, they visited the office at 34 Victoria Street at different times.

The first agent reported that he did not meet Claud but spoke to 'to two women typists working in the office one about 30, dark haired (A); the other fair-haired and a little younger (B)'. They explained to him that Claud was out and only visited the office for short periods. The agent was put out by these irregular office hours and noted censoriously in his report that 'it seems remarkable that the editor of this paper should only visit his editorial office for half an hour a day'. A second agent did meet Claud at the office and overheard intriguing scraps of information, including one end of a telephone conversation in which Claud was trying to find out more about a banker in Cologne, at whose house 'Hitler and Papen had a meeting on January 5 1933, and added that he knew what had happened at the meeting'.

The agent boasted in his report about his success in getting Claud to talk, though this was scarcely an achievement since he was compulsively sociable. 'He swallowed my story and asked for an article which I accordingly prepared today,' wrote one of the agents. 'He is either very crafty or very gullible, for he invited me to have a boozing evening with him tomorrow, which I unfortunately cannot afford in present circumstances to do, and therefore invented an appointment.'[1]

Five days later, the first agent had tea with Claud, saying that 'he told me that war was imminent, so much so that "if I polish my S.B [Sam Browne military] belt for Armistice Day I shan't need to polish it again for mobilisation." He thinks the Far East the likeliest spot. If Japan gets involved with anybody they will try to cut off her supplies of oil, 80 per cent of which comes from Borneo.'[2]

Claud twice asked the agent 'who put me on to him', suggesting that he was suspicious of the supposed freelancer.[3] But he probably would not have cared very much if he had known that the man was reporting back to MI5 since he took it for granted that journalism annoying to the authorities led to surveillance by the security services, as was automatically the case in Central Europe. He felt that more dangerous to the public than the inevitable telephone tapping and spying on journalists like himself was 'the pretence that the high-minded British government wouldn't dream of doing anything so terribly un-British'.[4]

This was his relaxed view twenty years later when he came to write his memoirs, yet at the time he expressed outrage at government surveillance and was less dismissive of the threat of arrest. On one occasion, he sent a special note to subscribers saying that his dossier had been requested from the Home Office by an unnamed but furious government department. 'Combing anxiously through this mass of useless information which is so laboriously collected', officials had been annoyed to find nothing more criminal than Claud's arrest for taking part in a 'free speech' meeting protesting against a police ban on such gatherings where unemployed men gathered outside labour exchanges. Well informed about the contents of his file, or able at least to make a good guess about what was inside, Claud said it was 'filled for the most part with elaborate details of what is jokingly referred to as one's "private" life'.

He expressed annoyance that an apolitical young woman, who was a close friend, had been placed on the suspect list along with elderly ladies and gentlemen, 'actually her uncles and aunts, but hence forth suspected of heaven knows what international conspiracy'. He said the department found the dossier 'fruity rather than fruitful' and claimed that department officials had made unstated threats, presumably of arrest and prosecution, against himself.[5]

MI5 was primarily interested in Claud's contacts and sources of information, though its senior officers expressed doubts about ever identifying them. Responding to an inquiry from the Committee of Imperial Defence, the long-time chief of MI5, Sir Vernon Kell, wrote discouragingly, 'I rather doubt whether any special enquiry would be productive of results, as I imagine that the surface [sic] of possible leakage must be considerable.'[6] Another concern of the security services was about where Claud stood politically. Clearly he was on the radical left, but they wondered: How far to the left? And was he connected to any left-wing organisations? They had difficulty taking on board that The Week was, by design, very much a one-man operation.

Past journalistic colleagues were interviewed, including his old boss Norman Ebbutt, still the Times correspondent in Berlin, though he was by now at odds with his newspaper over its sympathetic coverage of the Nazis. A report from a Special Branch superintendent is gossipy in tone and contains some mistakes but is probably a fair summary of journalistic opinion about Claud in the Times and elsewhere in Fleet Street. The police officer said he had been told Claud was so highly regarded by the *Times* that he could return to its staff any day he wished, if he kept his work to the desired policy of this newspaper. According to the officer, among 'his former colleagues on the "Times" he is regarded as a clever fool rather than a dangerous knave'.[7]

Not all police reports were so complimentary, one describing him as 'a heavy drinker, and [he] is said to be dishonest and unscrupulous as a journalist. He is a daring commentator, and has also been described to me as a professional mischief maker, who delights in causing mischief' and publishing what other newspapers 'did not care to publish'. Also suspicious were his contacts with foreign embassies and foreign journalists, leading the superintendent to remark that 'Cockburn is said to have become quite Communist in outlook'.[8]

Six months later, Claud's political allegiance became clearer when he accepted a commission from the Communist newspaper the *Daily Worker* to report on the Gresford Colliery mine disaster near Wrexham, in northeast Wales. Early in the morning of 22 September 1934, an explosion and fire deep underground had killed 266 miners in one of Britain's worst mine disasters. Accusations followed of management neglect of safety measures, which had led to a lethal build-up of inflammable gases. An official inquiry into the disaster was unable to identify its cause, a failure that was inevitable – though critics said intentional – since the mine shafts had been sealed with suspicious speed after only eleven bodies had been recovered.

As early news of the calamity and the high death toll reached London, Claud received a telephone call from Harry Pollitt, general secretary of the Communist Party of Great Britain, who asked 'if I could take the next train in twenty minutes or half an hour, and report a mine disaster at Gresford in north Wales'. Pollitt had a feeling that there was a lot more in it than met the eye. He also explained that he was a regular reader of *The Week* and felt that a piece by Claud would add 'reader appeal' to the *Daily Worker*.[9] Claud's account of the disaster, datelined 'Wrexham, Sunday' and appearing in the *Daily Worker* on Monday 24 September, is graphic and polemical:

Ventilation was so bad in that mine that for months a lot of them worked naked except for their clogs. Every so often they had to take their clogs off to empty the sweat out of them. That is what workers in the Wrexham district say about the condition of the Dennis Deep of the Gresford Colliery before the terrible explosion on Saturday morning in which scores of workers lost their lives. That is one of a damning series of hard facts behind the smokescreen enveloping the greatest mining disaster in Britain since the war.

Here is another: On Wednesday afternoon of last week, little more than two days before the catastrophe, the workers in a section of the Gresford mine near the section where the explosion actually occurred, had to be pulled out of the mine in a hurry on account of the dangerous quantity of gas in the mine. Today at least 100 workers are entombed in the blazing mine, where they sweated half-naked and in known danger, for an average maximum wage for highly skilled men of less than £2 per week. The barrier behind which they are imprisoned is still blocking rescuers nearly half a mile from the coalface, where the trapped men were working when the explosion came.

'The very stones are burning,' a rescue worker told me in the early hours of this morning. The force of the explosion was so terrific that all along the main way leading from [the] pit bottom to the fall blocking the road, the big structural girders are lying bent and twisted like pieces of wire. Three of the first workers who volunteered to go to the help of their colleagues were themselves killed – 'gassed' as the official announcement admitted.[10]

The piece goes on to accuse the mine company of using electrical machinery likely to ignite the heavy concentrations of explosive gas: 'wires carrying 500 volts are protected only by thin rubber tubing', which could easily be cut or damaged by rock falls. So unsafe was the pit considered by local miners in Wrexham that, prior to the economic depression, they refused to work there, so the colliery owners had to recruit men 'from Yorkshire and South Wales'. But as unemployment grew and under pressure from the Means Test, Wrexham miners were left with no option. Loss of life had been so great because many miners were pulling a double shift at the time of the blast so that they could attend a local football match later in the day.

Pollitt was not alone in admiring Claud's journalism; he had also become the first London correspondent of *Time* magazine and of *Fortune*, the American big business magazine. Receiving no regular salary from *The Week* aside from the uncertain flow of twelve-shilling postal orders, these jobs provided useful additional income. Not long after his Gresford report, Pollitt asked Claud how much he earned and was told that it was probably in excess of thirty pounds a week. 'Well, how'd you like to work for about £4 a week and half the time you won't get even that?' Pollitt said. 'How'd you like to work for the *Daily Worker*?'[11] Claud instantly agreed, writing under the nom de plume Frank Pitcairn, made up of his second Christian name and the surname of his maternal grandmother.

Claud says in his autobiography that he would probably have found this offer irresistible at any time, but that at this moment he was feeling particularly disillusioned with the British Labour Party: 'The Labour people seemed to me to be about where I had come into Germany years and years before.'[12] He is referring to the sympathy of the Labour Party for Germany as a victim of the Treaty of Versailles, its pacifist approach to foreign affairs, and its lack of activism in opposing fascism, capitalism and state oppression at home and abroad.

He found no such ambivalence among the Communists, writing, 'I felt that they were a lot nearer being a creative force in British politics than any other force that I could see. Also, they were a force that were small, poor and adventurous.'[13] Given that he had just witnessed the near collapse of capitalism in the US and the Nazis take power in Berlin, he said that he was only surprised that more people did not join the Communist Party as a movement to achieve revolutionary change from a calamitous status quo. In speaking of the Communists as 'creative' and 'adventurous', Claud meant a willingness to engage in concrete action, such as helping to organise hunger marches or setting up civil rights organisations to resist any extension of state powers.[14]

He took part in two hunger marches, causing much alarm among his volunteer co-workers on *The Week*. Averse though he was to physical exercise, he bought a pair of army boots, took a train from London to Aberdeen, and joined a contingent of unemployed workers who were walking to Glasgow via Dundee and the Fife coalfields. He was encouraged when the bedraggled little band was cheered along the way by factory workers, farm labourers and professionals, saying that for 'the first time I really believed there is another nation here'.[15] Poverty was everywhere, and he wrote to Hope, telling her that the Means Test had further reduced the dire living standard of the working class: 'I know of a girl earning an average of 30 shillings per week who is forced to contribute out of this to the support of three brothers and two other sisters.' He was encouraged, however, by signs of popular resistance, describing a strike in Lancashire, which he said was 'seething with revolutionary feeling'.[16]

His expectations of a revolutionary upsurge may have turned out to be exaggerated, but at the time the government took the threat seriously and made elaborate plans to supress protests. On 1 November 1932, the Metropolitan Police had mobilised as many as 70,000 men, including thousands of 'special constables', to confront hunger marchers arriving in London from deprived areas after three weeks on the road. When the marchers tried to deliver a petition to Parliament with a million signatures protesting against a 10 per cent cut in unemployment benefits and a new Means Test, the petition was confiscated by the police and the leader of the march, Wal Hannington, was arrested and denied bail.[17]

Violent repression by the authorities proved counterproductive, shocking, among others, a former journalist, stage manager, publisher and bookshop owner named Ronald Kidd. Reacting to what he had seen of police brutality and the alleged use of agent provocateurs, he set about establishing a society whose initial purpose was to monitor police behaviour and campaign more generally for civil rights and against state repression. His practical activism attracted Claud, who, whatever his reservations about Britain, was cheered by the thought that 'there are more organisations saying "Stop it, you brutes!" per square mile in the British Isles than anywhere else in the world'.[18]

Three days before another hunger march was due to arrive in London on 25 November 1933, Kidd called a meeting attended by some twenty people, of whom Claud was one, in the crypt of St Martin-in-the-Fields church on Trafalgar Square. 'Before we had to clear out to make room for another society, we had a society ourselves,' Claud wrote.[19] It was to be called the National Council for Civil Liberties (NCCL), which had the immediate purpose of stationing well-known public figures, for the most part from literary London, to observe police actions during the upcoming demonstration. The intention was that the presence of well-known people, like the novelists A. P. Herbert and E. M. Forster, might provide credible witnesses in the event of the police again using excessive force against the demonstrators.[20] Kidd, whom Claud described as looking like the canon of a forward-looking diocese, volunteered to be the unpaid secretary of the new society, whose first headquarters was in 'a hovel-like dwelling' where he lived, close to Shaftesbury Avenue.

Kidd had done a lot of preparatory work in the recruitment of distinguished monitors, but on the morning of the demonstration, Claud says that 'Kidd became nervous that some of our big guns would fail to turn up – the day being one of the chilliest of London's Sunday afternoons.'[21] Members of the executive committee of the new society were dispatched to the homes of the cultural celebrities all over London to make sure of their attendance. Claud went to the apartment of H. G. Wells and, though the great science-fiction writer was recovering from an illness, he loyally abandoned his lunch and followed Claud to Hyde Park where they could see mounted police in the distance and the hunger marchers' temporary platform closer to hand. The plan was for the high-profile monitors to patrol the space in between so as to deter or observe any attacks by the police on the demonstrators like the one two years earlier. Claud described what happened next:

Suddenly Mr Wells dug his umbrella into the mud and said, 'I refuse to go any farther. I detect', he said, turning to me, 'your plan. At any moment now, as a result of some prearranged signal on your part, the situation will get out of hand, the police will charge, a dozen prominent authors and legislators will be borne to the ground and you will have the incident you desire.'

Just at that moment it seemed to me like quite an idea and I was sorry I had not thought of it earlier.

In actuality, the demonstration passed off peacefully, an outcome many attributed to the presence of the NCCL, making it nationally well known, though Claud pointed out that nobody really knew 'what might not have happened if we had not been on the spot'.[22]

Cautious though the government was in its response to the hunger march, the authorities remained edgy about the threat of popular unrest. In its issue published the day before the meeting in St Martin-in-the-Fields, *The Week* noted that an indication of police concern was that they had taken the trouble 'to remove the tens of thousands of little notices of the march pasted up on the walls and elsewhere in Greater London'.[23]

The newsletter added that the police were particularly worried by the sympathy for the marchers and their cause shown by the public and, most worryingly of all from the government's point of view, by some policemen. During the earlier march, the violence of the 'special constables' had generated outrage; in the future, such would be deployed only in traffic duty, while the regular police dealt with the march.[24] The government took very seriously the prospect that protestors would suborn policemen or soldiers into disobeying their orders. It therefore introduced the Incitement to Disaffection Bill, better known as the Sedition Bill, which mandated heavy penalties for anybody seeking to sway the loyalty of the security forces away from the government.

The NCCL campaigned vigorously against the bill, leading to Claud spending a night in jail later the same year. He had gone as a committee member to the society to observe a public meeting opposing the Sedition Bill outside a labour exchange in Battersea. Though the meeting was taking place in an alleyway, the police sought to close it down on grounds that it was too close to a labour exchange. Giving evidence in a police court the next day, an inspector Bailey said that when the police demanded the removal of the speaker's rostrum, 'Cockburn demanded to know why they could not hold a meeting there and refused to leave'. With Claud was Graham McLennan from the National Unemployed Workers' Movement, who shouted: 'This is an outrage! This is Fascism! We demand free speech!'[25] He and Claud were duly arrested.

Both men were represented by Dingle Foot MP, while a Special Branch officer took notes and wrote a lengthy report on the trial.[26] The prosecutor sounded rattled by the high-profile proceedings, saying that 'the case was simple, and nothing he said would convert it into a State trial, though he was alarmed to see the books Mr Foot had got in court'. The magistrate said the case gave rise to 'questions of grave constitutional importance', adding grudgingly, 'I suppose that you want me to inflict a small fine so you can pursue it further [in the courts].'[27]

As Claud was already carrying out multiple acts of opposition before he joined the Communist Party, why did he sign up? Friends told him that once it was known he was a party member, he would alienate many who might otherwise have supported him. He retorted that those urging him towards moderation never did anything active themselves, while committed radicals, the 'Reds', usually provided the organisational backbone for protests against injustice, authoritarianism and fascism.

12

Project Revolutionary Baby

Hope Hale with daughter Claudia [Hope Hale]

On 11 February 1933, Claudia Cockburn, daughter of Claud and Hope Hale, was born in Presbyterian Hospital in New York. They called her conception and birth 'Project Revolutionary Baby', a name which turned out to be even more appropriate than they could have imagined. 'When I was in Presbyterian Hospital both Hitler and Roosevelt came to power,' wrote Hope. 'I read the news between my earnest sessions with Trotsky's *History of the Russian Revolution*.'[1] Politics and love intertwined, deeply affecting the future of mother and child.

In the following months Hope was increasingly anxious, though she reminded herself that it had been her idea to have a baby with a husband who was leaving the country, probably never to return. Self-confident and professionally successful, Hope was initially sure she could look after Claudia on her own while continuing to edit a magazine. Her letters, diaries and memoirs show her to be emotionally intelligent and articulate about her relationship with Claud. But there is also a strain of naivety and wishful thinking, some of it born of inexperience in dealing with babies, not realising how all-consuming the task would prove to be. She felt Claud's absence more and more keenly, writing that 'neither Claud nor I have foreseen [the] pain, this time of not sharing that first experience of her [Claudia]'.[3]

Personal and political priorities pulled in opposite directions. A friend warned her that marriage was never a 'technicality', as Hope had just told him, and urged her to join Claud at once in Europe. 'I tell him that I had resolved never to let the baby hamper his work,' she wrote. But in early 1933 the backers of her magazine pocketed the profits and closed it down. She and Claudia moved to stay with her sister Mimi, who was living in the countryside in Virginia, just outside Washington.

'Project Revolutionary Baby' was certainly the fruit of revolutionary romanticism, combined with a semi-conscious desire on Hope's part to maintain her relationship with Claud. From early in her pregnancy, she looked hopefully for any signs of him becoming a genuine husband. In the weeks before he sailed for Europe from New York, she would later recall 'those mornings in the sunny Lafayette Hotel café when he helped me get down a few spoonfuls of cream of wheat'. Nor was the wishful thinking all on her side, since he told her that he was wondering if their 'parting need be for very long. Why shouldn't I, in fact, come over soon and work with him for the revolution?'[3]

At times it seemed just possible that this might happen, with Hope taking up a job as a *Time* magazine stringer (part-time correspondent) in London. In the event, he took the job himself, having presumably failed to persuade the management to appoint his wife instead of himself.[4] After Claudia was born, he could be effusively affectionate, writing, 'I am amazed to feel such strong emotions about somebody I have never seen.' But by July, as his letters first dwindled and then stopped, Hope became increasingly unhappy about the limbo in which she found herself:

> Claudia's beauty is a constant hurt, with her father missing each phase. The mailman keeps dashing the daily hope, leaving louder silence. I tell myself that *The Week* is communication. I imagine the frenzy and pressure of getting those stunning stories, some from sources close to Hitler. I work, sell a few pieces but by August [1933] the vacuum is asking for an implosion.[5]

In the event, the vacuum was filled by an economist called Hermann Brunck, who, like many other left-wing intellectuals, had come to Washington to work for one of the New Deal agencies, in his case the National Recovery Administration. An American of German extraction, he had experienced European troubles as his family had by chance been on holiday in Bavaria in July 1914, a piece of bad luck which led to his father and himself ending up in the German army during the war. As a Marxist and far-left sympathiser, he turned out to be a reader of *The Week* and was doubtful if the New Deal reforms would really work. In conversation with Hope, he likened 'Roosevelt to a blind sculptor'.[6]

She soon got a job herself with the New Deal, working for the Consumers' Council. She and Brunck became lovers, and by December 1933 she and Claudia were living in an apartment he had found for them at Kalorama on Rock Creek, near Washington Zoo. Despite more or less living with Hermann as her partner, Hope still had mixed emotions about Claud as her official husband and the father of her baby. She still subconsciously resented Claud's departure:

> In this mood of doubt and indecision, I had a bad dream. Claud and I are lying in my big bed with Claudia between us, just as I pictured us in my scenarios. Resting on his elbow Claud is looking down at her. But what is he doing? Quite consciously, still smiling, he is letting ashes from his cigarette fall into the baby's

eyes. I hated and resisted the dream, Claud was always so considerate to everyone around him.[7]

She havered a long time about travelling to London to meet Claud, whom she had not seen for twenty months. She was finally decided to go by Bertold 'Berti' Wiesner, the Austrian Jewish biologist and member of the Eugenie Schwarzwald circle, who had been a political mentor to Claud in Berlin in the late 1920s. Wiesner had suddenly called Hope from New York, where he was attending a conference, and said he must see her to talk about Claud. When they met, he said that she must go to London to prevent Claud going off the rails personally and politically. Hope found it a peculiar story, but Wiesner was insistent, countering all her arguments until she fell back on simple pride – Claud had not invited her to join him. Wiesner's response to this was peculiarly political: 'This is no time to think of such small things,' he said, speaking of Claud's unique talents – political shrewdness 'combined with the ability to disarm and neutralise possible enemies of the movement.'[8]

When Hope mentioned Hermann, Wiesner suggested that they take the train to Washington and ask him about the proposed trip. 'He and Hermann were at once congenial,' wrote Hope. 'And I was overruled. For his own reasons Hermann wanted me to see Claud, to know where we [all] stood.'[9] Hope needed to know the status of her marriage in order to choose between Hermann and Claud.

In May 1934 Hope sailed with Claudia to London on board a modest ship called the USS *American Farmer*. Her first meeting with Claud in almost two years went far better than she could have hoped for. The ship was due to dock at Tilbury, twenty-three miles downriver from London, on 21 May 1934, and up to the last moment Hope was uncertain that anybody would meet her. But an hour before landing, Hope and Claudia were waiting on deck when 'a stir at the starboard rail caught my glance. And, as I watched, astonished, a head appeared – Claud's. He had hired a motorboat to come out to us in midstream. And then, the least athletic of men, he had climbed up the side of the ship on a rope ladder.'[10]

For over a year, Hope had been wondering what Claud's first meeting with his daughter might be like, but Claudia immediately took his hands. 'Claud had turned to me, too, and suddenly, after all those night time fears, I saw him exactly as I had known him – unsinister, warmly eager, familiar and dear. And with the extra shared delight in Claudia.' Claud had taken a room for them in a hotel in Bayswater, and in the afternoon the reunited family went to feed the swans in Kensington Gardens.

Later in the evening, after Claudia had gone to sleep in their room, Hope and Claud went to the bar of the hotel, and it was here that the brief idyll ended. 'During the first half hour, as we drank our Scotch,' Hope recalled, 'it seemed like old times. I realized only gradually that we were both trying to make conversation, trying rather hard.'[11] Claud talked exclusively of politics, emphasising the prospects for revolutionary action in Britain. As they chatted in the small hotel bar, Hope noted:

> We were trying to talk through the same preoccupation – the night ahead. A sort of final silence fell at last, and he asked if I was tired. At that moment I could have said yes; I felt my exhaustion suddenly. But how could I rest in this situation? He had dismissed women who delayed and teased. And we were married, after all. We had parted at the height of our passion, and had met again with the joy of sharing our child for the first time. So, when he asked, 'shall I come up with you?' I nodded.

But the time spent apart was too long. Hope was no longer the dashing, reckless girlfriend, but a mother living with another man. Claud was himself at the beginning of a serious relationship, which was to last five years, and he was more than usually preoccupied with politics. 'In the room where we lay hearing Claudia's breathing,' wrote Hope, 'the test came that we did not pass. In loving simulation, we each gave what we thought the other expected. It was only after further whiskies in a different bar could we find words to admit, reluctantly, that something was missing, some essential had gone.'[12]

They realised that the pretence that everything was as it had been when they first met was an illusion. Hope wrote that after such a long separation, 'you can't pick up a relationship where you left off: We were not the lovers we had been.'

The only surprise is that their relationship had survived as well as it had after two years apart, during which they had both been open about their other lovers. Hope was more or less living with Hermann in Washington, and Claud had been equally frank in his letters about sleeping with other women. Soon after Hope arrived in London, she was to meet one of them, Jean Ross, a twenty-two-year-old actress and scriptwriter who had recently returned from Berlin.

Hope first describes Jean in the garden of a small house in Chelsea that Claud had taken for Hope and Claudia. 'This afternoon a beautiful girl came into the garden,' Hope wrote to Hermann. 'She represents in Claud's life what you do in mine.'[13] She described her as 'brown-eyed, dark-haired, level-browed with a classic oval face'. Explaining to Hermann why she did not feel any jealousy towards Jean, Hope told him that this 'may be due to my throughness with Claud erotically . . . or that I can be unjealous of anybody I really know for a good person'. It was a sign of the times that 'good' refers to political rather than moral virtue, Hope emphasising that she was predisposed to approve of Jean because she was a political radical. As a result, Hope neither objected then to Jean as Claud's latest girlfriend, nor was this fact, in Hope's words, to 'check my friendship with Jean, which lasted all her life'.[14] With so much in common romantically and politically, Jean was more open with Hope about her past and present life than she was with anybody else.

Hope must have been correct in saying that her emotional attachment to Claud had waned; otherwise, even by her permissive standards, Jean's 'frank and forthright' account of her affair with Claud would have shocked her, since she was, after all, still his wife. Jean was equally uninhibited about her experiences in Germany. 'Her proper upper-class accent describing those shocking Berlin vices made her sound curiously innocent,' wrote Hope.[15] Less innocent was her intrigue at the beginning of her relationship with Claud. 'I had to hold Claud off for at least a month,' Jean told Hope, 'because you see I had told Eric that I was pregnant, and I had to wait to see if he would marry me.'

The prospective husband referred to was Eric Maschwitz, a composer of popular songs, his most famous – 'These Foolish Things Remind Me of You' – most likely to have been inspired by Jean.[16]

In point of fact, she was not pregnant, and her ploy to marry Maschwitz failed. But while there was still a chance that it might work, Jean said she postponed sleeping with Claud, telling him that the stars and planets needed to be in a favourable orientation. Hope says Claud told her this 'with an indulgent smile, because Jean's reason beguiled him'. She also asked Jean about it. 'Well, I could not tell him the truth, could I?' Jean replied, as if any reasonable person should have been able to see that. 'If I had, Claud would have been off and running.'

Hope admits to mixed feelings, as a feminist, about these revelations, saying, 'I couldn't help being amused to see male arrogance brought down so easily, but at the same time I was shocked at her female wiles. Didn't Claud deserve fair warning? Yet how could I betray another woman's confidences?'[17]

One evening twenty years later in Northampton, Massachusetts, Hope showed W. H. Auden an old snapshot of herself, Claudia, Claud and Jean Ross sitting in the garden of the house in Chelsea that Claud had rented for them. Auden placed his large forefinger next to a small face in the photograph. 'That's her,' he said. 'That's Miss Sally Bowles.'[18]

Hope writes:

In the picture, a pure featured young woman sits pensively watching a baby ... The young woman is Jean Ross, recently returned from a wild period in Berlin ... Perhaps at that moment Christopher Isherwood is beginning to shape his memories of her into one of his Berlin Stories, 'Miss Sally Bowles', to be published in 1937 ... From the composed, patrician face in the photograph it is difficult to imagine Jean drifting from bed to bed in the decadent circles in Berlin between the wars. But that same evening, after she has gone, I wrote in a letter [to Hermann] about 'the beautiful girl' in our garden: 'she is supposed to have slept with over 200 men in Berlin alone, and she is only 22' ...

Jean had come back to London when Hitler took power.[19] Introduced by a current lover to Claud she had reached for him almost from habit. And by manoeuvres she described to me with the candour of Sally Bowles, she had succeeded. I had arrived to find my husband captivated. Yet I also write that I like and admire her, that she is 'a great young woman'.[20]

Isherwood himself wrote in his later years that he could no longer distinguish between the real Jean Ross, with whom he had shared a flat in Berlin, and the fictional Sally Bowles as she appeared in his novella and as she was played by a succession of actresses on stage and screen. 'I wish I could remember', he wrote, 'what impression Jean Ross – the real-life original of Sally Bowles in *Goodbye to Berlin* – made on Christopher [Isherwood] when they first met. But I can't. Art has transfigured life and other people's art has transfigured Christopher's.'[21]

This will happen when any life is fictionalised, but the vividness of Isherwood's writing style in the original novella created an ineradicable image of Jean that obscured the reality, colouring even the recollections of those who were her closest friends.[22] There was already a distance between real-life Jean and fictional Sally in *Goodbye to Berlin*, which grew wider as successive readaptations, such as the play *I Am a Camera* in 1951 and the film version in 1955. In the trailer for the film, Sally is introduced as 'brash, brazen, outrageous Sally Bowles whom I first met in one of those third-rate nightclubs in wild and wanton Berlin in the early Thirties'. Asked by the narrator why she paints her nails green, she simply replies with a bubbly, seductive laugh: 'to attract men'.[23]

This version of Sally was further readapted for the musical *Cabaret* in 1966 and the vastly popular film with the same name in 1972, with Liza Minelli in the lead and with the choreography by Bob Fosse. In the musical Sally is hoping to become 'a famous film star, if booze and sex don't get me first'.[24] Sally has become a spectacularly talented singer and dancer, which Jean was not according to Isherwood.[25]

Jean never saw *Cabaret* and died a year after it appeared in 1973.[26] At first, as the fame of Sally Bowles grew and she was known to be the original model, she was angered by what she saw as a distorted picture of herself as an attractive but vacuous good-time girl, too self-absorbed to notice the terrible tragedy unfolding around her as Hitler prepare to take power and Storm Troopers beat Jews to death in the street. In reality, Jean had returned to England a few months before Hitler became chancellor, deeply conscious of impending horrors and determined to do what she could to avert them.

As for being unaware or uncaring about anti-Semitic violence in Germany, Jean's sister Billee reports that she arrived back in London with a German Jewish girlfriend called Hippy, and that they managed to find lodgings on the top floor of a very elegant house in Cheyne Walk on the Chelsea Embankment. While Isherwood shows Sally speaking rudimentary German, in fact, after eighteen months in Berlin, Jean had learned German well enough to earn a living in London by translating German film scripts into English.

Isherwood may have dumbed down Sally in terms of intelligence and political awareness, but otherwise his portrait of her was pretty close. When he and his editor John Lehman feared being sued for libel by Jean, Isherwood successfully pleaded with her to give her permission for publication. Nonetheless, she objected in particular to the description of her abortion, which Isherwood had witnessed and then attributes to Sally. When Isherwood pleaded poverty unless his book was published, Jean reluctantly gave way. She later regretted doing so, as what she felt were the greatest distortions in the book – her empty-headedness and ignorance of the Nazi threat – became more and more exaggerated in successive portrayals as she achieved a sort of unwanted immortality.

She would explain in private why she thought that Isherwood had misunderstood her, and women in general, saying that Isherwood was gay, as were many his close friends. 'You see', she said, 'I was the only girl Chris had ever really known.'[27] Sarah Cockburn, Jean's daughter with Claud born in 1939, had a less sympathetic view of Isherwood's characterisation of Jean as Sally, saying that, though he presented himself as a member of the artistic avant-garde, he was in practice highly conventional.

She argued that 'convention requires that a woman be either virtuous (in the sexual sense) or a tart. So Sally, who is not virtuous, is a tart.'[28]

The success of *Cabaret* as a film in the early seventies led to renewed media interest in Jean as the woman known to be the model for its main character. Bright young reporters asked her for interviews that always ended in mutual disappointment according to her daughter Sarah: 'The journalists always wanted to talk about sex and my mother always wanted to talk about politics.'

'They say they want to talk about Berlin in the Thirties', Jean would complain. 'But they don't want to know about the unemployment or the poverty or the Nazis marching through the streets – all they want to know is how many men I went to bed with. Really, darling, how can anybody be interested in that?'

'I suppose a lot of them [reporters] have pursued you,' reflected Hope, who would become Jean's lifelong friend. 'What do you do?'

'Shut the door,' Jean shrugged. 'Hang up the phone.'[29]

13

Sally Bowles and the Party

Jean Ross – the model for Isherwood's Sally Bowles [wiki commons]

Jean Ross was born in Alexandria in 1911, the eldest of the four children of Charles Ross, a cotton expert working for the Bank of Egypt. She grew up in great comfort in a house full of servants called Maison Ballassiano. Charles was moderately wealthy but politically liberal: 'My father, all his life,' recalled Jean's youngest sister Billee, 'was first and foremost a champion of the poor, and gave away far more than he kept for himself.'[1] Jean's mother Clara, the daughter of industrialist and landowner Charles Caudwell, was a cultivated woman who had intended to study architecture but instead married and moved to Egypt.[2]

After an idyllic childhood, Jean was sent at the age of eleven to Leatherhead Court, an expensive girls' boarding school in Surrey, which she detested from the start. Academically precocious, she completed her final examinations at the school by the age of sixteen and was desperate to leave but was told that she might have to stay on for another year. Many teenagers rebel against their school over frustrations like this, but Jean chose a spectacularly dramatic means of guaranteeing her departure from Leatherhead Court. The first her family in Egypt knew about it was in July 1927, when Charles Ross received a cryptic telegram from Jean's headmistress, a Miss Ash, which read: 'Regret to request the removal of Jean and Peggy [a younger sister] from Leatherhead Court as soon as possible. Writing. Signed Ash.'[3]

The promised letter, coupled with Jean's own defiant account of her exit, explained what had happened. The full story tells much about Jean's utter determination to get what she wanted, come what may. Her school expulsion also gives an insight into the confusion caused by English upper-middle-class circumlocutions when referring to anything to do with sex:

> It appears that, while washing her hands in the changing room after games, a fellow student, standing beside Jean said 'Jean you do look pale' to which Jean replied, 'well so would you in my condition'.[4] Her neighbour eyed her with surprise but said no more. Two days later Jean was summoned to the headmistress's study. There sat Miss Ash, flanked on either side by a row of tight-lipped school mistresses, silently awaiting the inquisition. Miss Ash asked Jean if the report she had received that 'Jean was in an interesting condition' was true?
>
> Jean was completely taken aback; she was standing beside the fireplace and clasped the corner of the cold marble mantlepiece to steady herself. It seemed that the touch of that hard unyielding stone, in the palm of her hand, travelled up her arm to her pulsating brain and said 'this is your chance, take it.' She hesitated for a moment and then, looking straight at Miss Ash, she answered 'yes'.
>
> Horror was expressed on the faces of Miss Ash, and of her colleagues, and the verdict of expulsion was delivered. The

Matron was sent for; she was asked to take Jean Ross to the
school sanatorium where she stayed until she left school.[5]

Bizarrely, Peggy, though obviously blameless for whatever Jean had
done, was expelled with her.

At first Jean stuck to her story, perhaps fearing that if she
admitted that she was not pregnant she might be sent back to
Leatherhead Court. After her aunt Janet, a conventional lady
who lived at Porlock in Devon, had picked up the two girls, she
asked: 'Jean are you then in the state of the Virgin Mary?' Jean
again said, 'Yes.' Only when they reached Janet's cottage in
Porlock did she admit 'quietly, but unrepentantly', that it was all
untrue, and that the idea of spending another year in Leatherhead 'was so horrendous to her that she had decided to go to
any lengths to avoid it'.[6]

Jean's expulsion from school was in keeping with her taste for
melodrama and yearning for independence. Billee says that Jean
made friends easily at school, but that 'she loathed being insti-
tutionalised, loathed what she felt was the atmosphere of
self-righteousness of the staff and the insensitive greed and self-
satisfaction of England's upper class'. Returning to Alexandria,
which she loved, she swam, played tennis and went to endless
parties, though Billee says she never forgave her father for sending her to Leatherhead Court, 'away from the people and places
she knew and loved'.

In the spring of 1928, she was sent to a finishing school in
Neufchatel in Switzerland to perfect her French, learn German
and go skiing. But she wanted, above all else, to be an actress
and went to the Royal Academy of Dramatic Art (RADA) in
London for a year. She thought the teaching poor in quality,
but she won a prize for acting in a French play, entitling her
to choose her part in an upcoming production. She chose
Phedre, Jean Racine's tragedy about an ageing queen who
develops a passion for her stepson Hippolytus. But one of her
teachers objected that Jean was too immature to play the role,
saying: 'You are only seventeen and have no experience of
life.'[7] She was, in any case, the teacher continued, 'destined
to be a comedienne'.[8] Angered by this criticism, Jean left

RADA and started looking for work in the theatre and cinema.

She got a small part in a film comedy called *Why Sailors Leave Home*, in which a Cockney is put in charge of a sheikh's harem. Jean played the part of a slave girl, at one point saying something in Arabic for added authenticity, though nobody else in the film company or among English audiences understood what she said. Only when the film reached Egypt and was shown in a cinema in Alexandria did Egyptian servants working at Maison Ballassiano, who had gone to see it, report back to her shocked parents the risqué words.[9]

Jean's meagre earnings from acting and modelling were supplemented by an allowance from her father and from a trust fund left by her recently deceased maternal grandfather, Charles Caudwell. The money was just enough for Jean to live independently in London, though she found that jobs were scarce. She heard that she might do better in German where film studios needed English-speaking actors. Only two years out of school, but energetic and adventurous, Jean and a friend, an Egyptian-born Hungarian actress named Marika Rökk, travelled to Berlin, where they arrived in 1930 as the cataclysmic impact of the Great Depression in America was beginning to capsize the fragile Weimar Republic.

The turning point was the general election on 14 September 1930, when the vote for the Nazis soared from 800,000 to 6.5 million.[10] Menacing though the political prospects might be, Bohemian life in Berlin was the most innovative in Europe, while notoriously offering forbidden fruit, both cultural and sexual. More practically for Jean, she was living in a city where 'young artists had the best chance of launching themselves on a literary or dramatic career'.[11]

Work in film and theatre was more difficult to find than Jean and her friend had hoped, but Jean stayed on in Berlin singing in nightclubs and modelling for fashion magazines. She finally did get theatre parts, such as the role of Anitra in Max Reinhardt's production of *Peer Gynt*. By late 1931, she was a dancer in his production of Jacques Offenbach's *The Tales of Hoffman*, the nightmarish fantasy famed as the last great triumph of the

Berlin theatre before the Nazi takeover. Jean's life sounds insecure, but her hand-to-mouth existence was not so different from that of any late teenager seeking excitement, independence and the beginnings of a career.

One advantage which made Jean's move to Berlin less of a leap in the dark than it might appear was that she could speak and read adequate German. Comical evidence of her proficiency is a story Jean later told about sharing lodgings with a morphine-addicted actress called Erika Gluck, who was the girlfriend, and later the wife, of Richard Crossman, a British academic who would become a Labour Party cabinet minister. Erika reputedly knew no English and Crossman no German, difficult though it is to see how they could have achieved such intimacy without at least some rudimentary verbal communication. Jean would translate Crossman's love letters to Erika, the contents of which, she would tell people, made it impossible for her in later years to take him seriously as a political leader.[12]

Jean was younger than the circle of British intellectuals – Christopher Isherwood, Stephen Spender, W. H. Auden – with whom she socialised in Berlin, but she had packed a lot of experiences into her first twenty years[13] – all of which became the carefully recorded raw material for Isherwood's fictional and autobiographical writings. His most significant departure from real life was the need, essential at the time, to conceal the fact that he and many of his English and German friends were gay. His male fictional characters, modelled on people he knew, had to be remodelled as heterosexual. Jean, for example, first met Isherwood and Spender in early 1931 in the apartment of Franz von Ullman, a gay philanderer who appears in the 'Sally Bowles' story as Fritz Wendel, who boasts continually of his affairs with women.

Going by Spender's memory of his and Isherwood's first meeting with Jean, she dominated the conversation by speaking of her many lovers, with a freedom that startled him. She provoked further alarm by taking a diaphragm out of her handbag and waving it in front of the two writers. After she left, Isherwood asked Spender what he thought of her, and Spender replied: 'I think she is utterly repulsive.' More sympathetic, though still patronising, Isherwood replied: 'I think she's really a little girl. Next time I see her I'm going to throw a cushion at her.'[14]

Jean was belittled by Isherwood in her Sally Bowles guise as a charming, zestful libertine who is also attention seeking, self-absorbed, and uninterested in political convulsions in the streets. She spends much of her time pursuing toxic boyfriends, who invariably let her down in one way or another.

But what was the reality of Jean's life in Berlin? Could she have been as unaware of apocalyptic developments in Germany as Isherwood suggested? The point is important because she became for Isherwood – and subsequently for millions of readers, theatre and filmgoers – the symbol of 'the whole idea of militant Bohemia'.[15] The rampant sexuality of the Bohemian quarter of Berlin in its last doomed pre-Nazi days helps explain the enduring appeal of the Sally Bowles character. 'Here the sexual games were as varied, frowsty and complex as in the court of Nero,' Hope Hale wrote after talking to Jean a couple of years later. 'Jean may not have understood all she saw, but she made a brave effort not to be outdone.'[16]

This comment sounds a little crude, and there is another more nuanced way of looking at Jean and her life in Berlin. In a persuasive defence of her mother, her daughter Sarah says that 'the plain, almost documentary quality of Isherwood's style has beguiled a wide audience into believing that the events and characters of *Goodbye to Berlin* are closer to factual reality than is commonly the case with a novel'. She argues that what Isherwood persuades readers to see as 'lifelike' is often not so much true to life as 'to the reader's expectations of life – expectations based not on direct experience but on the conventions of existing literature'.[17]

In Isherwood's portrayal of Sally, he certainly inclined towards a view of her as a sort of younger and updated version of Giuseppe Verdi's courtesan Violetta in *La Traviata*, transferred from upper-class Paris to Bohemian Berlin. The words in Isherwood's story that provoked most outrage on the part of Caudwell come when an apolitical Sally refers to 'an awful old Jew', summoning an image of an empty-headed middle-class English girl thoughtlessly allying herself 'with attitudes that led to Dachau and Auschwitz'. In fact, Caudwell says, 'Such a phrase would have been as alien to my mother's vocabulary as a sentence in Swahili; she had no-more deeply rooted passion than a loathing of racialism, and so, from the outset, of fascism.'[18]

Paradoxically, it is Isherwood himself – forty years after he had first met Jean and shared an apartment with her at Nollendorfstrasse 17 – who provides the most convincing picture of her at that time. Though he said his memory was blurred between the fictional Sally and the real Jean, he kept a detailed diary which he used in his autobiography, *Christopher and His Kind*, where he comes out publicly as gay and seeks to correct the distortions previously forced on him.[19]

'Jean was more essentially British than Sally,' he wrote. 'She grumbled like a true Englishwoman, with her grin-and-bear-it grin. And she was tougher. She never struck Christopher as being sentimental or the least bit sorry for herself. Like Sally, she boasted continually about her lovers. In those days, Christopher felt certain that she was exaggerating. Now I am not so certain.'[20] He explains how in the film *I Am a Camera*, it was left ambivalent as to whether or not Sally was really seducing all those men. Isherwood shows bitterness at how in the musical *Cabaret*, the Isherwood figure, named Brian Roberts, is portrayed as bisexual, sleeping with Sally and by the end of the film wanting to marry her. She turns him down, hinting that his lapse into homosexuality is the reason for her rejection. Isherwood remarks sourly that 'Brian's homosexual tendency is treated as an indecent weakness to be snickered at, like bedwetting.'[21]

Isherwood describes himself and Jean as having an asexual relationship, sometimes even sharing a bed in the crowded flat, but one which he says was more intimate than that between Sally Bowles and her lovers in the novel, plays and films. 'Jean moved into the Nollendorfstrasse flat after she met Christopher early in 1931,' he writes.

> Soon after they were like brother and sister. They amused each other and enjoyed being together, but both of them were selfish and they often quarrelled. Jean never tried to seduce him. But I

remember a rainy, depressing afternoon when she remarked 'what a pity we can't make love, there's nothing else to do', and he agreed that it was and there wasn't.[22]

During this period, Jean had an abortion after she became pregnant by a musician called Gotz von Eick and almost died as a result of the operation, after an incompetent doctor left a swab inside her. Isherwood visited her in the clinic, and the abortion scene is the high point of the novella. It was something that Jean almost certainly did not want her family to know about – after all, abortions were illegal in Britain and frowned upon even by the tolerant – which would explain why she was later reluctant to give Isherwood and his publisher John Lehman permission to put out even a fictionalised account of her abortion.

Jean met Claud briefly in Berlin in the autumn of 1932, shortly before she left the city and soon after he had returned to it after three years in America. They met again in London a year later, but it was a year that was upending the world in which they lived.[23] The Nazis were in power and hunting down Jews, Communists, socialists and gay people, along with everybody who criticised, disliked or differed from them. From early 1933, an unprecedented exodus from Germany was underway. 'The exiles Hitler made were the greatest collection of transplanted intellect, talent and scholarship the world had ever seen,' writes Peter Gay, a historian of Weimar culture.[24] Jean moved sharply to the revolutionary left and joined the Communist Party of Great Britain. This most likely happened, or was in the process of happening, before Jean encountered Claud for a second time.

Hope who, for all her easy acceptance of being displaced by Jean as Claud's partner, may have nursed a subconscious feeling of resentment towards her, attributed Jean's politicisation entirely to Claud's influences. Isherwood likewise noticed a change in Jean about this time, though he did not attribute it specifically to Claud. He wrote that 'her way of expressing herself already showed the influence of her new London friends – left-wingers who were humorous but dedicated; sexually permissive, but politically dogmatic'.[25] More likely, however,

Jean had already been radicalised by witnessing Nazi savagery in Berlin and the mass misery everywhere caused by the Great Depression. By now she spoke fluent German, had many German Jewish friends, and would have known that the decadent, cosmopolitan bohemian culture, the world in which she had been deeply embedded, was a prime target of Nazi rule. Apocalyptic events in Germany are enough to explain her swift conversion, in the course of a few months, from aspirant actress to political activist. This would have made her all the more attractive to Claud, whose long-term relationships tended to be with intelligent, adventurous and politically sophisticated women.[26]

Jean and Claud had other factors in common, such as similar family backgrounds, as both were born far from Britain – he in Beijing, she in Alexandria – with parents who had lived most of their lives in far-flung corners of the British Empire. At sixteen, Claud was travelling backwards and forwards to war-ravaged Hungary and Central Europe, an experience that would shape his political attitudes for the rest of his life. At the same age, Jean was going to and from Alexandria and being expelled from school, and she was more at home in Egypt than England. It was unlikely that either of them would have developed conventional English attitudes towards politics or sex.

Both were eyewitnesses to the near collapse of capitalism – he in America, she in Germany – and saw the fascist triumph in Germany and Italy as a hideous tragedy that threatened to repeat itself in the rest of Europe, not excluding Britain. The urgency of this menace – and the fact that Hitler was no passing phenomenon – may appear obvious in retrospect, but this was not necessarily true at the time, even among those who saw firsthand the Nazi takeover. Isherwood, who stayed on for some months in Berlin after Hitler became chancellor, told himself optimistically that Hitler's appointment was a blessing in disguise as 'he would now reveal himself as an incompetent windbag, he would be forced to resign and the Nazis would be discredited'.[27]

By the time Jean and Claud met each other again in the second half of 1933, he was editing *The Week* and using the Café Royal in Piccadilly as a meeting place with friends and contacts. 'It made – since a bottle of good wine cost three shillings – an almost free place to do business in,' he said.[28] It had to be 'almost free' since at this point 'the circulation of *The Week* was awfully steady at thirty-six' and he had no money. According to one anecdote about his first encounter with Jean, he cashed a cheque on her for five pounds but rang her up the following day to warn her that it would bounce if she took it to a bank.[29]

During these frantic years, politics took precedence over sex and romance for many politically engaged people, propelled into frantic ant-fascist activity by cataclysmic events. Politics shaped Claud's and Jean's personal relationship, which was initially rather spasmodic. Jean's fifteen-year-old sister Billee observed the beginning of their affair: 'I think Jean at first was rather reluctant, she was very tied up with her work. She knew Witney Strait [a famous racing driver] at that time and enjoyed his fast driving, and also she knew Nigel Playfair [a theatre director] and enjoyed his entourage, but I think it was Claud's belief in communism that finally tipped the scales in his favour.' MI5 recorded her phoning Claud at *The Week* in November 1933 to talk about a film synopsis she was reading.[30]

By 1934 the Nazis had shown that they were not going to self-destruct through incompetence, as people like Isherwood had hoped. Furthermore, there were ominous signs that fascism was spreading from continental Europe to the British Isles. *The Week* may have overstated the threat, but after what had happened in Germany and Italy – and was about to happen in Spain – this was understandable. Claud took seriously the powerful Blueshirts movement in Ireland led by General O'Duffy and, closer to hand, the menace posed by the British Union of Fascists (BUF) led by Sir Oswald Mosley.

One day Claud returned home bruised and battered from a BUF mass rally of 10,000 people at Olympia in West London, addressed by Mosley, which took place on 7 June 1934. Communists, socialists, liberals and other anti-fascists had disrupted it with organised heckling and had been set upon and beaten up by BUF Blackshirts.[31] 'Seeing Claud with those bruises must have had a powerful effect on Jean,' wrote Hope. 'And perhaps the Nazi Brownshirts in Berlin, had, after all, taught her about the menace of fascism.'[32] But this muffled rebuke was misleading, as Jean had helped to organise the disruptions, according to her sister Billee, whom Jean had recruited as a timid and unwilling assistant. By now Jean had moved from Cheyne Walk to Gunter Grove, where she was staying with Olive Mangeot, another friend of Isherwood and a Communist Party member. Billee found the two women folding up leaflets and tying them in bundles, which Jean asked Billee to take to a house on the New King's Road, warning her to tell any policeman who asked about the leaflets that they had been given to her by an unknown woman. 'I felt it was all rather sinister, but I did not dare decline,' recalled Bill, deciding in her own mind, however, that, if a policeman came anywhere near her, she would drop the leaflets and run away.

Later in the afternoon, a car picked up Jean, Olive and Billee and took them to an empty shop in the suburb of Shepherd's Bush, where a group of men and several women were waiting in a back room before sallying out to fight the Blackshirts. 'It soon became clear to me that I had temporarily joined the Communist Party,' wrote Billee. She felt apprehensively that if she did not keep out of the way, she might soon be caught up in the violence. Confirming her fears, the backdoor of the shop was suddenly flung open and a man burst in, bleeding profusely from a cut on his left cheek, his jacket torn, and his shirt covered in blood. 'Those bloody fascists,' he said. 'There are men out there swinging stockings filled with broken glass.' Billee listened nervously to the sounds of mayhem and wished she was back at her school in Kent.[33]

By now Jean had largely given up acting and was translating film scripts from German into English, a skill that was in demand because several German and Austrian directors were in exile in London.[34] Jean later became film critic of the *Daily Worker* under the name of Peter Porcupine, a nom de plume originally used by the English radical William Cobbett. In Berlin, she had often gone to the cinema with Isherwood, Spender and Auden, and remained part of their circle in London.[35]

It was because of her connection with the Germanic film world that Jean was able to do Isherwood one more giant favour.[36] In October 1933, he was back in London and short of money and a job. One morning Jean phoned him up to say that she had persuaded the Austrian Jewish film director Berthold Viertel, who had previously never heard of Isherwood, to consider him as a replacement for a scriptwriter who had suddenly dropped out of a film project. Isherwood did not at first take this possible job offer seriously, because he says Jean was always thinking of money-making schemes. But she persisted and bought a copy of his novel *The Memorial*, which she gave to Viertel. After reading a passage, the director said that he found it 'genial', which sounded like faint praise, but it turned out that he was using the word in the German sense of 'gifted with genius'. The job with Viertel was the beginning of Isherwood's long and successful career as a Hollywood scriptwriter.[37]

Jean's relationship with Claud may have started as a casual affair on both sides, but she was soon helping him to run *The Week*. He was living with her at Gunter Grove, and she was to go with him to Spain at the beginning of the Spanish Civil War in 1936, where she became a war correspondent for the *Daily Express*. But her later journalistic career was so far from the 'Sally Bowles' stereotype wished on her by Isherwood and subsequent plays and films that her front-line war reporting was soon forgotten. When Claud was fighting as a soldier on another front, she ghostwrote his copy for the *Daily Worker* and for *The Week*.

By the time of the anti-fascist riot at Olympia, Hope had decided that her marriage to Claud was truly over, and she yearned for Hermann back in Washington. The parting was amicable on all sides, with Claud taking Hope, who was to sail from Southampton, to see his mother, who was living on the Isle of Wight. Hope was to stay in touch with her in the coming years, sending her photographs of her granddaughter Claudia as she grew up.[38]

Claud did not see Hope again for several decades, but the ending of their marriage was to have a final, curious twist which affected him. Hope had said that she saw her marriage to Claud in 1932 as a technical formality, and she had a similarly light-hearted attitude to their divorce. Looking to marry Hermann as soon as possible, she 'sent a hundred dollars to a lawyer in Juarez, Mexico. Soon, it would be time to send the other hundred, and receive the document which, however dubious legally, would let us start a true and solid marriage.'[39]

As for Claud, she did not believe when she left Britain that his relationship with Jean would last or that he was likely to get married again any time soon. But he must have realised at some point that what was a 'dubious' divorce in the United States would certainly not be recognised as legal in Britain. Hope, too, must have come to realise this in time because in the spring of 1938, she says in a friendly letter intercepted by MI5 that Claud should come to America: she said they might be able 'to work out a much quicker way to get a divorce, as there are short cuts in the U.S.'[40] He did not take up her offer, which might explain why, though he and Jean were to be partners for six years, they never got married, though they clearly wanted to give the impression that they were. Jean was to change her name by deed poll to Jean Cockburn on 3 March 1939, shortly before the birth of their daughter Sarah.

The same concern about the legality of Hope's Mexican divorce explains why Claud's third wife, Patricia Arbuthnot, with whom he would live for more than forty years, also changed her name to Patricia Cockburn by deed poll soon after they started living together. They finally married on 20 March 1978 in Westminster, three years before he died in 1981.[41]

14

'If a Mistake Can Be Made, They'll Make It'

Claud as a revolutionary agitator [author]

'If you go on like this', said Mr John Wheeler-Bennett, then head of the Royal Institute of International Affairs at Chatham House, 'you will soon, I should think, be either quite famous or in jail.'

'Lots of people', I said, 'have been both.'

'That', he said, turning upon me his luminous smile and beaming as though an awkward question had been satisfactorily resolved, 'is so.'[1]

Claud's account of the conversation has a detectable note of pride on his part in the success of his 'pirate craft', *The Week*, in exerting an influence out of all proportion to its size. It had been launched at just the right moment, when detailed insider stories about the threat posed by fascist regimes and movements were being substantiated daily by real-life events. Many who had previously hoped the fascist threat was overstated were changing their minds. 'I admire passionately the people who are standing up now and telling the truth,' wrote Christopher Isherwood in a letter on 7 July 1934. 'Especially I find myself warming to [Claud] Cockburn – I get *The Week* regularly. Misinformed or not, he does slash out at these crooks and murderers and he's so inexhaustibly cocky and funny like a street-boy throwing stones at pompous windows.'[2]

Gratified though he was that his newsletter was attracting attention, Claud wanted to be more than a gadfly doing its mischievous best at a moment in history when capitalism was in a crisis and fascism was sweeping across Europe. In such an apocalyptic era, he thought there was nothing surprising in his decision to become a Communist since he was already opposed to capitalism, imperialism and fascism before he joined the party, and he was to hold the same opinions after he left.

His reasons for joining were in part ideological, but also utilitarian: he believed the Communists to be the one serious political movement with the commitment and organisation capable of fighting with any hope of success for the same political goals as himself. In conflicts in Germany, Britain and Spain, he was convinced that only the Communists were really doing anything positive, whether it was organising hunger marchers in Fife or turning brave but untrained militiamen into regular soldiers in the Spanish Civil War.

Despite recognising the need for organisation, he had an inherent suspicion of organised groups rooted in a conviction that they functioned, and in most cases malfunctioned, in the same way. When he had started working for *The Daily Worker*, everybody had confidently told him it would be entirely different from his old employers at the *Times*. He found that such advice – like many pieces of unquestioned conventional wisdom – was mistaken.

'True', he wrote, 'the plain-clothes detectives of the Special Branch of the C.I.D. bulging in the saloon bar just across the street, struck a note unusual in Printing House Square.'[3] Otherwise, he found that the two offices had much in common, especially in the atmosphere of mounting panic as the final print deadline for the paper approached and editorial writers pondered their copy. Both papers had ostensibly rigorous but, in practice, dysfunctional means of safeguarding their journalists from bothersome intruders:

> At *The Times,* I had always been given to understand, [they were] protecting the editorial staff against the onset of people with plans to reorganise the Church of England, people who wanted it to publish a five-column letter demanding state subsidies for otter hunting and people who were going to beat up the racing correspondent because of the ruinously misleading thing he had foreshadowed about the third race at Newmarket.
>
> At the *Daily Worker,* the job of the man on the door was rather to keep out people with plans to reorganise the Communist Party, people who wanted to get a five-column letter published demanding state subsidies for Esperanto and people who were going to beat up the racing correspondent because of the ruinously misleading thing he foreshadowed about the fourth race at Wolverhampton.[4]

Claud was fascinated to discover that a key member of the *Daily Worker* staff appeared to be a Burmese gentleman who sat ensconced in the paper's library at a table covered in books, brochures and papers. Claud supposed that he must be at work on a lengthy series of articles about the situation in Burma, but he turned out to be the greyhound-racing correspondent.

Some readers were disgusted by the devotion of a section of the paper to greyhound tips and results instead of focusing on revolutionary agitation and wrote in to say that the Tolpuddle Martyrs, farmworkers severely punished after forming a trade union in 1834, were rolling in their graves. But other readers were 'delighted, for, however shaky he may have been on Burma, as a dog tipster he was the tops'.[5]

Forced to go to press early because the paper was banned by press proprietors from the newspaper trains, the *Daily Worker* was sold earlier than others on the streets of London. Ingeniously, the paper had turned this early availability to its advantage by printing the greyhound race results before anybody else and thereby increasing circulation by 25 per cent in the capital.[6]

Using 'Frank Pitcairn' as a nom de plume – only in 1937 did the paper admit that his real name was Claud – he felt that the *Daily Worker* gave him a small platform from which he could reach out to a radical working-class audience, in contrast to *The Week*, which targeted a small but influential elite.[7]

The *Daily Worker* was not the only publication trying to employ Claud at this time. As *The Week* gained notoriety with a number of notable scoops, other publications began to seek him out. Particular though Claud was about whom he worked for on a permanent basis, he had the normal instincts of a freelance journalist, a notoriously ill-paid branch of the profession, who must think twice before turning down any commission. Money was tight: the circulation of *The Week* might be rising quickly, but it sold for only twelve shillings per annual subscription, while at the *Daily Worker*, the party had ruled that nobody should be paid more than the wages of a semi-skilled worker.[8]

Aware of his employability though he was, Claud was surprised in late 1933 to be called by Ralph Ingersoll, the newly appointed editor of *Fortune*, the American business magazine, asking to meet him urgently in the foyer of the Savoy Hotel, on the Strand. *Fortune* was part of the magazine empire of the right-wing media magnate Henry Luce, who also owned *Time*, *Life* and *Sports Illustrated*.[9] Claud was even more astonished when Ingersoll told him that he was in London to hire the first British and European correspondent, and that the short list had been reduced to two names: Claud and Randolph Churchill, the only son of Winston Churchill.

Claud liked Ingersoll, whom he describes as charmingly impetuous, but he found the potential job offer so unlikely that he asked if Ingersoll might have mistaken him for somebody else. According to him, Ingersoll asked why I thought he could have made such a mistake? I referred to my pretty well-publicised political views: a man, to put it delicately, of the Left. He shrugged and waved a grand hand in a gesture seeming to indicate astonishment and some resentment that anyone should suppose *Fortune* to be affected by any such consideration. *Fortune*, he said, simply wanted the best man available for the job.[10]

He then went off to interview Randolph Churchill, who was almost as far to the right as Claud was to the left.

So convinced was Claud that Churchill would get the job that he went to Paris, only to receive on his arrival at his hotel urgent messages from Ingersoll asking him to return to London. At a second meeting at the Savoy, it emerged that 'Randolph was out, myself in', thanks to Brendan Bracken, a close associate of Winston Churchill and the owner of the *Financial News*, who had made a disastrous, though well-meant, bid to help Randolph get the job. Ingersoll was offended by Bracken's intervention, which he found heavy handed and patronising, and promptly crossed Randolph's name off his short list. Bracken, Claud reflected later, was an able man, but not one who inspired trust. When Bracken became Churchill's minister of information during the Second World War, Claud said 'he was a man of such all-pervading duplicity that his natural hair must come to resemble a wig'.[11]

Claud accepted the well-paid job, sending a telegram to Ingersoll on 1 November 1933 reading: 'thank you. all set ready to start immediately.'[12] But he found working for the magazine a disconcerting and even eerie experience because nothing he wrote ever appeared in print.[13] He was beginning to wonder how long his employment might last when he got a telegram from Ingersoll in New York informing him that a special correspondent called Hilton Railey was coming to London to research and write up a project about the armament manufacturers, whom many in Britain and the US saw as the 'merchants of death', responsible in large part for the First World War. *Fortune* had already published a highly praised long article called 'Arms and the Men' in 1934, and its editors were eager to follow it up.[14] Claud privately believed that arms manufacturers might find the prospect of imminent war in their business interests but not its actuality, which they disliked for being dangerously unpredictable in duration and outcome: 'It can end, as in Russia in 1917, in ruinous revolution. Or, short of that, the patriotic war-battered tax-payers may go berserk and sequester the bulk of the profits.'[15]

Claud had a lifelong liking for adventurers and Americans, and Captain Hilton Railey, the *Fortune* special correspondent, was the quintessence of both. He had worked for US military intelligence in Poland and had recruited Amelia Earhart to make her solo flight across the Atlantic.[16] He had a scheme to gain access to the wreck of the *Lusitania* to show that it had been carrying weapons, contrary to the British claim that a German U-boat had torpedoed a wholly civilian target, killing 1,195 people, including 123 Americans and making the entry of the US into the war against Germany more likely. He also carried out unofficial, confidential missions for President Roosevelt relating to the League of Nations.

Now in London, Railey outlined to Claud his plans to penetrate and expose the secrets of the great European armaments companies: Krupp, Vickers, the Comité des Forges, Škoda: 'I warmed to this enthusiastic man of goodwill immediately and reflected that if he seemed just a little bit crazy, that was all to the good, since a man would need to be at least half crazy to attempt seriously to carry out our assignment.' The captain planned to carry out his initial investigations in Britain and then move on to Germany.[17]

Claud was eager to get back to Germany to find out what life was like under Nazi rule. But he knew that this would be lethally risky for him using his own name and passport. He thought, however, that he stood a good chance of getting in and out of Germany safely using a forged British passport if he presented himself as the correspondent of a famous American business magazine accompanying a well-connected American-passport holder working for the same magazine and with connections to the White House.

The gambit worked well when the two men landed at Frankfurt Airport, German security men being more suspicious of the flamboyant captain than they were of Claud, with his dubious passport. His troubles did not end there, however, because he dared not submit his passport to close scrutiny by the authorities in Germany: 'I could stay neither with friends for fear of compromising them nor in hotels because passports had to be surrendered for police examination.' The only way around this was for him to spend the night in railway sleeping-cars, where there was no such inspection, which involved crisscrossing the country between cities he had no reason to visit. He split off from Rainer for some days, travelling nightly by train between Hamburg and Essen and learning as much as he could from dissidents, subversives on the run, disappointed liberals, disenchanted Nazis, 'and not least from blabber-mouthed enthusiasts for the regime'.[18]

Reconnecting with Rainer in Berlin, they were able to stay in a hotel which the American embassy used as a guest house to put up visitors who were not required to register their passports. But another risk had arisen in the shape of Rainer's heavy drinking – which must have been spectacular as even Claud noted it as excessive – during which the captain loudly denounced the Nazi regime. 'We talked much of the sufferings of the Jews, liberal democrats, social democrats, and Communists under Hitler's barbaric rule,' said Claud.

On the night before their departure from Berlin, Rainer became overconfident. In a fit of nostalgia, Claud took him to a little bar-restaurant where he used to meet his friends in pre-Hitler times. By now its clientele included Brownshirts and men in business suits with Swastika badges pinned to their lapels. As Rainer and Claud dined and drank copiously, Claud rashly volunteered, 'Many of the friends I used to meet here were now dead, in concentration camps, or in exile.'[19] Moved by their fate, the by-now very drunk Rainer began to rant against the Nazi regime at high volume and was starting to attract the hostile attention of the Brownshirts.

Claud and the barman manhandled Rainer out of the bar and into a taxi. Later, as their train crossed the frontier out of Germany, the captain made up for his dangerous outburst by diverting official attention from Claud 'by snarling and shouting

in English and broken German, waving important-looking letters and claiming diplomatic privilege'.[20] Claud parted company
from Rainer, who pursued his investigations, but, as had happened to Claud in the past, the *Fortune* editors had gone cold
on the project and the story never appeared.

In a lengthy article in the *Atlantic* magazine in July 1974,
Claud wrote about how he had been hired by Ingersoll and visited Nazi Germany with Captain Rainer. But he was discreet
about the identity of 'the international organisation for the relief
of Nazi victims', which somehow had the ability to produce a
forged passport at short notice, even if it was not a very good
one. The organisation was, in fact, a committee of the Communist International (or Comintern), founded by the Bolsheviks
in 1919 to spread Communism and world revolution, called
the World Committee for the Relief of the Victims of German
Fascism, established in Paris soon after Hitler took power.[21]

Sometime in 1934, Claud received an urgent message from
the committee asking him to come to Paris, where they were
based. When he visited their office, they explained that they
needed to rescue two small children of a prominent Communist
sympathiser who were living in Germany, though their father
had fled the country. It was feared that the Nazis might use the
children, who were staying with a politically neutral aunt near
Hamburg, for purposes of political blackmail. What was needed
was somebody with an impeccable British passport to go to
Germany to extract them. Claud said that since he was certainly
on the Nazi blacklist, he was the last person who should under-
take the rescue mission and that they should get somebody else.
'I might get 100 yards into Germany, but I certainly shouldn't
get out and about again,' he told them.

The members of the committee pondered this and came up
with a solution: We'll forge you a passport.' Taken aback by
this, Claud said that he thought the whole idea was that who-
ever went to Germany should have an unimpeachable British
passport and be in a position to call up the British consul in the
event of trouble. 'Give us the name of someone with that sort
of passport who'll be willing and able to do the job,' said the
members of the committee. When Claud confessed that he

could not, they went ahead with their plan to supply him with a fake passport.

Claud was always derisive about fictional tales of the sinister but seamlessly efficient Comintern, saying that 'whatever happens there is going to be a bloody muddle. When dealing with that lot, you must always remember that if a mistake can be made, they'll make it.'[22]

In this case, his forebodings turned out to be all too correct. He thought the passport photograph looked more like that of a Nordic boxer, with no feature resembling his own. The aunt looking after the endangered children had supposedly been alerted to his arrival, but she turned out to know nothing about him, and he had to spend an hour persuading her that he was who he said he was and not a crackpot or a Nazi provocateur. 'In her place, I wouldn't have been convinced at all,' he said afterwards.

A further problem was that the aunt was unconvinced that the children were truly at risk from the Gestapo, whom she dismissed as infantile idiots, and that all Claud needed to do was take them to the nearby Danish border, flash his British passport, and all would be well. Claud found that the Paris committee had failed to provide essential travel documents for the children, which had to be hurriedly obtained from the relevant government department in Hamburg. Fortunately, the great commercial city had never been sympathetic to the Nazis, and the necessary papers were obtained within twenty-four hours.

The aunt, persuaded at last that the children were at risk, arranged somewhere safe for Claud to stay overnight and for a man living between Hamburg and the Danish border to pose as the children's uncle and take them, under assumed names, across the frontier into Denmark. Claud thought the plan ramshackle, but it worked, and he pointed out later that 'paradoxically, and on the whole encouragingly, that all the most dangerous practical part of the job was done by people who considered themselves neutral and non-political, but could understand a human need when they finally saw it'.[23]

↬

In all likelihood, one reason the committee in Paris was so incompetent in helping Claud in his rescue mission in Hamburg was that it had been set up for a different purpose. Its aim was to expose and publicise Nazi crimes, but it was never designed to carry out clandestine operations inside Germany. As the cutting edge of anti-Nazi propaganda, however, it was admirably speedy and effective in exposing the new German regime's record of persecution and murder, at a time when much of the British and American media were predicting that Hitler would water down his fanaticism once settled in power. Underlying this optimism was a sense of relief within the established order that Hitler, Mussolini and, in a few years' time, General Franco would provide a barrier against the rising tide of social disorder and revolution in the midst of the Great Depression.

Claud was a connoisseur of the techniques of propaganda, a word which had no negative connotations for him because he believed that an information war was an inviolable part of political conflict. He approved of the propaganda counter-offensive launched by Willi Münzenberg, the German Communist media specialist, through the committee in Paris in the weeks after the Reichstag fire on 27 February 1933, which destroyed the German parliament and for which Marinus van der Lubbe, a Dutch Communist, was arrested. Though the circumstances of the fire were murky, Hitler suspended civil liberties and grasped the golden opportunity offered by the fire to establish his absolute dictatorship by blaming the arson on the Communists, claiming that they were poised to stage an uprising. Acting with a speed and determination equal to that of the Nazis, Münzenberg organised a group of journalists and writers, for the most part Communists, many of them Jews, to produce an alternative scenario, making a credible case against the Nazis, supported by copious and detailed evidence, that they had staged the fire themselves. It was much in their political interests to do so, but to turn suspicion into something nearer to a certainty required producing a convincing alternative narrative before the Nazi version of events jelled in the public mind.

On 15 May 1933, the Paris committee did just that, publishing the *Brown Book of the Reichstag Fire and Hitler Terror*, which gave a headline-grabbing explanation for the fire. Put together at a frantic pace by talented writers and propagandists, of whom the most important was Otto Katz – also known as Andre Simone, among other aliases – a Czechoslovak Communist widely seen as the chief engineer of 'the Münzenberg machine'. The book, which sold in vast numbers globally, demonised the Nazis as a force of exceptional evil, who might well have fabricated the fire. Much easier to prove was the Nazi record of atrocities and violent anti-Semitism, all of which were described in vivid detail in separate chapters in the second half of the *Brown Book*.[24] The book caught the nightmarish tone of developments in Germany by quoting a popular Nazi song: 'When Jewish blood spurts from under the knife / Things will be twice as good as before.'[25]

Claud believed that a committed and disciplined organisation was essential to oppose the Nazis and to fight for revolutionary political and social change. But he also had an ingrained suspicion of all organisations as tending towards incompetence and authoritarianism. He had far-greater faith in action by individuals who might be ideological supporters of the revolutionary cause but were also practical, professionally skilful, utterly determined and, above all else, effective. Münzenberg, whom he had met in Berlin in the winter before Hitler took power, was one of these people. Claud described him as a media expert of genius who 'made a vital impact on the politics of Europe'. He quoted those who said that Münzenberg was the most dynamic force in the German Communist Party. 'He had snatched the journalism of the extreme Left', Claud wrote, 'from the hands of the pedants, insisted that a modern revolutionary newspaper could be as "popular" in today's terms as an old-time revolutionary broadsheet and that the technical tricks, skills and "appeal" of the stunting, pandering, sensation-mongering of the capitalist press were not to be despised but imitated.'[26]

Münzenberg's picture magazine *AIZ* became the largest circulation weekly in Central Europe, while his office on the Wilhelmstrasse was filled with what became known as 'Popular Front' organisations in which 'the Communists provided the inspiration and driving force, [and] did at moments of crisis rally many sorts and conditions of non-Communists and anti-Communists who wanted to get moving and found no other bus going their way'.[27]

Claud already knew two of Münzenberg's team, one of whom, the Czechoslovak journalist Egon Erwin Kisch, had once worked with Claud's Viennese girlfriend Berta Pölz at the end of the First World War. Like Berta and Claud, he became a member of the Schwartzwald circle in Berlin. He was by then already known as a brilliant journalist, having edited the German-language magazine *Bohemia* in Prague before the Great War, his greatest scoop being his revelation that the Austro-Hungarian authorities were desperately trying to cover up the fact that their late chief of military intelligence, Colonel Alfed Redl, had also been a top Russian spy.

Having served as a reluctant soldier in the First World War, Kisch had joined with Berta in establishing a revolutionary movement in Vienna – the Federation of Revolutionary Socialists 'International' (FRSI) – which was part of the general upsurge in Central and Eastern Europe. A year later, the FRSI was absorbed into the newly established Communist Party of Austria, which Berta and Kisch found too tame. Kisch remained an active Communist for the rest of his life, moving to Berlin, where he became an associate of Münzenberg and produced, among many other anti-Nazi writings, a scathing investigation debunking Hitler's account of his military career as a corporal during the war.

Arrested in the Nazi roundup after the Reichstag fire, Kisch, whom Claud said was a born survivor, was lucky to be deported to Czechoslovakia in May 1933 as a Czech citizen. Highly conscious that his chances of long-term survival were low, Kisch once said to Claud that he was fortunate 'being a Central European Jew of the twentieth century to have lived a long time without being tortured even once'.[28]

Regarding Kisch as a 'revered genius', Claud credited him with snatching journalism in Central Europe away from the writers of ponderous 'think pieces', and towards hard news reportage in the tradition of British and American journalism. Claud described how his 'bustling, thickset figure, vehicle for gipsy-sharp eyes and his inquiring nose – he looked rather as a Scottish terrier would look if it were Jewish – first hustled him into the back streets of Prague . . . [at a time when] the term reporter was not noble in Europe'.[29]

Not only was he a famed reporter, who became part of the Münzenberg team in Paris, but he was an anti-fascist political agitator of great energy and determination. Denied an entry visa to Australia in 1934, he jumped from the deck of his ship onto the dock at Sydney, breaking his leg in the process. The government's bid to exclude him entirely backfired, turning the previously little known Kisch into a celebrity whom the Australian Supreme Court finally allowed into the country.

Claud liked and admired Kisch, with whom he travelled in France and Spain, but it was that other Czech Jewish Communist, Otto Katz, also a member of the Münzenberg machine, whom Claud believed was the best embodiment of the spirit of the 1930s. Claud later wrote:

> Though he died abruptly at the end of a rope, pronouncing me responsible for his misfortune [when Katz was hanged by the Communists in Prague in 1952], historians ought not to forget Otto Katz. No portrait gallery – rogues' gallery, some would say – of the period would be quite complete without the putty-coloured visage of that most talented of propagandist and intriguer . . . Pretty soon every schoolboy will think that he knows all about that time, certified as having been full of starry-eyed do-gooders with pink illusions which, when darkness came at noon, blew up in their faces and turned them a neutral grey or else deep blue. Not so much, probably, will be heard of the late Katz – a man nevertheless reeking of eighty-five per cent *Zeitgeist*, and producing some pervasive practical effects upon events. Manuals of journalism should have a bit about him too.[30]

Claud found Katz to be effective, alarming and amusing in equal quantities. He first encountered him at the World Congress Against War held in Amsterdam on 27–29 August 1932, soon after Claud had stepped off the boat from America. Organised by Münzenberg with the assistance of Katz, the majority of the 2,000 delegates were committed anti-fascists, but not Communists. It was an early example of 'the Popular Front' in action long before it became the party line. At the end of the conference, Claud found himself in a hotel bedroom late at night helping translate the final communiqué of the meeting from German into English. The experience was stressful as the translators all agreed that the final product had 'to be as jolly popular in style as the *Daily Mirror* and as rigidly exact as the Athanasian Creed'.[31]

Among his fellow translators were the British left-wing intellectuals John Strachey and Gerald Hamilton, a much-distrusted political chameleon who was to be the model for Mr Norris in Christopher Isherwood's Berlin novel *Mr Norris Changes Trains*. Others included a Hungarian woman who, because she knew German better than the others, wrongly believed that this must also be true of her English.

Into the crowded hotel room, there periodically popped a man whom Claud had never met, acting as a sort of master of ceremonies and general morale raiser for the exhausted translation team. Claud describes him as a light-footed man with a large head and 'abnormally broad shoulders, hunched in a way to suggest that his burdens were indeed heavy, but he could bear them, and yours, too, if you cared to confide them to him'. When Claud asked the others who the man was, they replied, 'You don't know who Otto Katz is? Oh!'

In the morning, after a sleepless night, Claud was invited by Katz to drink brandy with him on the hotel terrace where they discussed the outcome of the congress. Claud expressed enthusiasm for its work, mentioning that he had until recently been a foreign correspondent for the *Times* in New York. Soon after they parted, Katz issued a press release in which 'the distinguished former foreign director of the *Times*'s fully endorsed the conference's aims and made some sharp criticisms of the British government.

Claud was both horrified and amused by the brazenness with which Katz had exaggerated his former importance on the *Times*. 'But it's preposterous to describe me like that,' he protested, demanding a correction. 'People will think that Wickham Steed [a former editor of the *Times*] has turned Red in the night.' Katz dismissed his objections airily, retorting that 'as a sincere supporter of our cause and an experienced journalist, you appreciate that any retraction could be damaging to the excellent effect already obtained. *The Times* will doubtless issue any denials necessary. It will help stimulate discussion.'[32]

Wary though Claud was of Katz's manipulations, he did not believe that they were much different from what British propagandists did in the Second World War. Katz was also assiduous in seeking to create a common front between people of very different political stripes in order to oppose fascism. This produced bizarre and unlikely alliances. Claud was told by the Roman Catholic Prince Löwenstein that during a visit to the United States with Katz, he had seen him 'genuflect three times and kiss the ring of a cardinal to whom he then presented a Marxist professor just out of jail in Rio de Janeiro'.[33]

Claud tried to assist Katz in his travels, which Western governments tried to impede with visa bans. The Special Branch reported in May 1934 that Katz had been appointed Paris correspondent of the Labour-supporting *Clarion* newspaper 'in order the more easily to gain access to this country'. They believed that Claud, who briefly worked for the *Clarion* at this time, had got him the job.[34]

Claud felt at home with these Central European Communists, often German or Jewish or both, who were committed to fighting Nazism relentlessly and knew how to do so effectively. Few of them survived very long, since they were not only high up on Nazi death lists, but – and this applied also to Claud – suspected by orthodox Communists in Moscow of departing from the party line and acting as independent operators.

Münzenberg lost his job and became increasingly anti-Stalinist before being found hanged in a forest in southeast France in 1940 by the Gestapo or by the Soviet security service, the NKVD. Kisch and Katz escaped to Mexico during the fall of France the same year, both returning to Communist Czechoslovakia in the late 1940s, where Kisch died of natural causes. Had he not done so, Claud believed that he might have joined Katz on the gallows in Prague in 1952, where he died after confessing during his show trial to being recruited by Claud Cockburn as a British spy.

15

Reporter in Spain

Claud with Fred Copeman, British battalion commander of the International Brigades during the Spanish Civil War in 1937. Photographer Gerda Taro was killed soon after [wiki commons]

On 17 July 1936 the Spanish armed forces launched a putsch to overthrow the democratically elected government in Madrid. The plotters were surprised when their coup only half succeeded and they faced stiff resistance from those opposing the old order of army, church, big landowners, industrialists and bankers. Frightened by the victory of the left, united in the Popular Front, in the general election on 16 February, the military leaders launched a counter-revolution of great ferocity and violence – though no revolution had as yet occurred.

Within days, the anti-government uprising turned into a civil war in which outside powers were quick to take part and would play a decisive role. The Nationalists, as the coup supporters came to be called, were strongly backed by Hitler and Mussolini, and, in the first mass airlift in history, German and Italian military aircraft flew General Francisco Franco's Army of Africa from Spanish Morocco to mainland Spain. Seeing the war as 'a battle of the forces of order and true religion against a Jewish-Bolshevik-Masonic conspiracy', the well-equipped Nationalist columns slaughtered those they identified as favouring the Republican government.[1]

The defenders of the Republic, though less united than the right, brought together the poor along with the progressive secular middle class. The cause was at its strongest in the big cities, above all in Madrid and Barcelona, and in the separatist regions of Catalonia, Galicia and the Basque Country. The Republicans also had their massacres, but they were less widespread and systematic than those carried out by the Nationalists. The odds were always against the Republic since it was fighting not only against the professional Spanish Army – with its veteran Moroccan and Legionnaire units – but, after the first few months, against 80,000 Italian troops and 20,000 Germans, including the elite Luftwaffe force that was soon to achieve infamy by bombing the Basque town of Guernica.

The International Brigades, drawn from pro-Republican volunteers all over the world, were to become famous, but they did not counterbalance the powerful Italian and German contingents. The Soviet Union supplied arms and military advisers, wishing to prevent another fascist victory, but did not want to alienate France and Britain as potential allies by appearing to spread Red revolution. Britain and France declared an embargo on the export of arms to Spain in the name of 'non-intervention', though in practice this only applied to the Republican side, as Germany and Italy poured in weapons through pro-Franco Portugal. Listing the forces arrayed against the Republic – the trained Moorish troops, intervention by Mussolini and Hitler, the arms blockade by Britain and France – Claud concluded after the war that 'the real wonder of it was not that the

Republicans were defeated, but that they held out for as long as they did'.[2]

On the day of the putsch, Claud was already in Spain on what he said was a holiday, resting up and sunbathing on a beach in the village of Salou, near Tarragona, sixty miles south of Barcelona.[3] Friends were sceptical that a man who seldom took holidays should have coincidentally visited Spain, where he had been only once before, on the same week as the military tried to seize power. He himself was always adamant that his presence in Spain was fortuitous, having intended to go on holiday in the South of France but taking the wrong train in Paris. In his book *Reporter in Spain*, published only three months later in October 1936, he refers to 'we' staying in an otherwise deserted hotel in Salou, so the likelihood is that he was accompanied by Jean Ross, who was certainly with him in Madrid some weeks later.[4] A waiter at the hotel explained to Claud that the absence of guests was because they feared an impending crisis, something of which Claud must have been well aware in general terms since a little over a month earlier, on 4 June, he had published a short item in *The Week*, which turned out to be a scoop, under the headline 'Spain':

Intensive underground activity suggests that the long-delayed attempt at a Fascist putsch by the higher ranks of the army officers is not likely to be delayed much longer. The reorganization of the army which will, in fact, amount to a certain democratization of the army is due this month. The disorderly elements of the Right are believed determined to try to get in their blow before the reorganization can be carried out.[5]

Claud took the train to Barcelona, where the military uprising was being crushed, largely because of the determined armed resistance of the working-class districts, often led by the National Confederation of Labour (CNT), the powerful anarchist trade union federation. The failure of the coup here and in Madrid gave the Republicans breathing space and a fighting chance, even if the odds were still heavily against them. Claud's train was delayed and finally stopped by fighting on the line ahead.

'The train went no further', wrote Claud, 'and I walked across Barcelona in the beautiful freshness and light of the early southern morning, with the noise of rifle and machine gun fire growing louder and louder, as I came towards the centre of the city.'[6]

He saw people crowding around radios to find out the latest news and medical students tending those wounded in street battles. After the fighting ended with the total victory of Republicans, Claud interviewed the ill-armed but triumphant militiamen manning the barricades, who, despite their victory, suspected treachery on every side – and often with good reason. He contacted the Republican authorities, obtaining press credentials and the use of a car as a correspondent writing under the name of Frank Pitcairn for the *Daily Worker*.

As a Red journalist, working for a paper fully supportive of the Republic, he presumably received special treatment. But this had its drawbacks since his militiaman driver promptly crashed the car, afterwards admitting that his sole previous experience consisted of driving a delivery van in Barcelona. He had volunteered his services, wrote Claud, because he felt that it 'would be a swell time driving a member of the Military Committee and a foreign journalist up to the front'. As a replacement car and driver were being secured, the Military Committee member accompanying Claud remarked that the car crash was symbolic of the difficulty the Republicans would have in trying 'to create a war machine right from the beginning'.[7]

Driving towards the front on his own, Claud tried to catch up with the first counterattack launched by the Republicans, which had left Barcelona on 23 July with the purpose of recapturing Saragossa, the capital of Aragon, from the Nationalists. The counter-offensive consisted of three columns, the largest led by the Catalan anarchist leader Buenaventura Durruti, a revolutionary hero revered in Catalonia as a Robin Hood figure who had personally led the final assault on the last rebel barracks in Barcelona.[8] At dawn, Claud came in sight of the two-mile-long column stationary on the grassy Aragon plateau as the militiamen, who were not all anarchists but included socialists, trade unionists and Communists, ate their breakfast of sardines and bread beside the road. Their vehicles were of every sort – trucks, buses, taxicabs, private cars and even confiscated Rolls-Royces – many with red-and-white striped mattresses strapped to their roofs as bedding and to provide minimal protection against shrapnel. The weapons of the militiamen ranged from army rifles to pistols and sporting guns, but, while 'they had considerable experience of street fighting in Barcelona [they had] almost none of any kind of warfare'.

Claud's car was stuck at the rear of the column, which was strung out along the narrow road. At this vulnerable moment, two Caproni aircraft provided by Mussolini but, in Claud's estimation, probably crewed by Spaniards appeared over the column. Flying low, the aircraft started dropping small anti-personnel bombs which had the destructive power of a large grenade:

> Hardly anyone present had ever been bombed before and many who had fought like tigers at Barcelona were now overcome by a horrible sense of helplessness. The road, which had been the road of victory leading to Saragossa, turned into a trap. The story that it really was a trap, that treachery had been at work again, spread like poison gas. I saw a group of tough fellows crouching in a shallow ditch repeating over and over again 'We are betrayed. They have brought us here to kill us.'[9]

Some of the militiamen, feeling less intimidated, jumped onto the roofs of their trucks and vans, firing their pistols at the bombers. Other drivers panicked and tried to turn their vehicle around on the road and instead overturned them. In the midst of this turmoil, some of the fighters were defiantly shouting 'On to Saragossa,' though this had become impractical as the road was blocked.

Claud abandoned his car and ran forward on foot. 'Trotting as fast as possible through the chaos of vehicles, wounded men and men firing their pistols impotently into the air, I made my way to the column's head where, in a small farmhouse which was also a low-grade inn, I found Durruti's headquarters.'[10]

Unfortunately for him, Claud had already run a little way past Durruti's headquarters, down the road leading towards Saragossa. His small mistake threatened lethal consequences: 'In a flash every one could see that I was a spy – a man in foreign clothes running off towards the enemy to report on the effects of the bombing. There were shouts, which I didn't understand, and then shots, which I did.' Walking back towards the farmhouse with his hands in the air, he thought that the misunderstanding would soon be cleared up. To his horror, he found that the militiamen had other plans for him. 'I realised that what was really going to happen was that I was going to be shot immediately – as surely as if I had jumped out of one of the Capronis.'

He shouted and swore at the militiamen, who only spoke Catalan and were pushing him up against the wall of the farmhouse in preparation for his execution. As the volunteer firing squad assembled, the noise attracted the attention of one of Durruti's guards, to whom Claud spoke in Castilian Spanish explaining that he was there to see Durruti. The guard gestured to the militiamen to let Claud go, and he entered the farmhouse, where he again thought that his troubles would shortly be over.

But Durruti, a rebel who had been engaged in armed struggle against the authorities for decades, was as quick as his men to suspect hidden enemies. Sitting at a table in the kitchen of the farmhouse, he glanced dismissively at Claud's credentials showing him to be the correspondent of a Communist newspaper. Though this placed Claud nominally on the same side of the barricades as Durruti, it did not make him a comrade in arms, as the anarchist leader angrily pointed out. 'In a low voice, vibrant with hatred, [he] denounced the Communists and all their works. So far as the undisputed anarchist boss of Catalonia was concerned, I might almost have been a fascist.'

Realising that Durruti was sitting in judgement on him, Claud yelled at him, writing later that acute fear always provoked him to rage. He told Durruti that the column outside was part of the Popular Front, and it even had a Communist contingent. Grudgingly, Durruti ceased to treat Claud as an enemy agent but insisted that there must be 'no writing about the Frente Popular [Popular Front] as the liberators of Saragossa. It will be Anarchists who will liberate Saragossa. Understood?'

Claud persisted in praising the Popular Front until Durruti asked him about political attitudes in Britain towards the Civil

War. Claud spoke optimistically of public sympathy for the Republic, but Durruti said he did not believe it. 'Words,' he said. 'Nonsense. Nothing will come of all that.'

On parting, Durruti told Claud that he had been lucky: 'You understand, you might very easily be dead. We don't have time to waste and are quick on the draw. We have to be.' Scribbling a few lines in Catalan on a piece of paper, he handed it to Claud who had it translated the same day, 'To whom it may concern,' it read. 'Comrade Cobun [sic] has a violent temper and an offensive tongue, which may lead him into trouble. He is also ignorant of a great deal. Notwithstanding, it is desirable that all possible consideration should be shown to him.'[11]

This was not the only occasion that Claud came near to be being executed by his own side. Paul Callan, working for the 'Londoner's Diary' on the *Evening Standard* in the 1960s, says that he went to interview Claud on his latest book. He took with him a photographer called Vic Drees who was a man of few words, but Claud kept staring at him. Finally, he said: 'Haven't we met somewhere before?' Drees glanced briefly at him and replied: 'Yeah. It was in that bleeding cell near Barcelona during the Spanish war. They were going to shoot us in the morning, but you talked them out of it.' Claud Cockburn looked thoughtful and just said: 'Oh yes, I'd quite forgotten.'[12]

Durruti's column pressed on towards Saragossa, but it was unsupported by the two other columns and narrowly failed to seize the city.[13] After fighting for a couple of months in Aragon, Durruti took his anarchists south to Madrid, where they arrived on 14 November and played a key part in stopping an attack by Moroccan troops on the university area. Durruti did not survive long and was shot dead, probably by accident, by one of his own men whose weapon caught in a car door. For morale-boosting reasons, the anarchists claimed that he was killed by a Nationalist sniper, while the Communists put out the story that he died at the hands of anarchists who objected to his strict discipline and to his cooperation with the Communists.[14]

Claud arrived in Madrid in August before the first full-blooded Nationalist assault on the city in November, which came close to succeeding. Claud knew that all wars were fought in 'a savage muddle' and the muddle was even worse in civil wars. The first weeks of the war in Spain left him in no doubt about the ferocity of the conflict as Franco's forces, behaving much as they had done in quelling native resistance in Morocco, spread terror by mass executions, torture and rape in the cities, towns and villages. He stayed at the Florida Hotel, the base for many foreign correspondents, and drove forty-five miles north into the Sierra Guadarrama to view from about six or seven hundred yards distance what he took at first to be men in the Republican front line, but which turned out to be the advance patrols of the enemy. A few days later, driving to the crumbling government positions west of the capital, he was reassured to see a senior Republican officer calmly driving towards the front, but it later emerged that the officer had only been doing so in order to switch sides.

Claud wrote about the fighting in early August, as the Nationalists tried and failed to seize Madrid by a coup de main. In the lull that followed, he drove south in a yellow Hispano-Suiza limousine across the heart of Spain to see the equally shaky front there. 'He is now at the Southern Front of the fighting in Spain, with the Government troops centring on Cordoba,' reads an MI5 report on his movements dated 26 August.[15]

He praises the excellent Spanish highways that enabled the car to travel fast across the plain of La Mancha, where Don Quixote had once fought with windmills, to Alicante and Villafranca in Andalusia. Peasants and townspeople armed with shotguns and sporting rifles were everywhere, vainly trying to stop the Nationalist columns.[16] Another MI5 report notes that by 31 August, he was back in Madrid, where he joined the Fifth Regiment, which was to be the nucleus of a disciplined and better-trained militia force being raised at frantic speed by the Republicans to offset their crippling shortage of regular troops. More specifically, it was being organised by the Spanish Communist Party along the lines of the Red Army during the Bolshevik Revolution in Russia. Discipline requirements included a ban on militia units debating their officers' orders before obeying them.

Claud was obviously of more use to the Republican cause as a skilled professional journalist than as an amateur soldier who might be killed at any moment. But, aside from romantic revolutionary zeal, he felt that he – and the same applied to other foreign intellectuals who fought in Spain – could write more graphically and authoritatively if they had actually fought with a rifle in their hand. As for the *Daily Worker*, he suggested that Jean Ross, who must have been with him in Madrid, should temporarily take over writing articles in his name.[17]

The Fifth Regiment of Militia, as it was officially known, was headquartered in a former school of the Salesian religious order in Cuatro Caminos, a working-class district in northern Madrid. Its name is deceptive as the regiment was not a single military unit but hopefully the beginnings of a new model army divided into 'steel companies', one of which Claud joined and found to be only a step above a rag-tag militia when it came to training and equipment. 'It was considered in those days a long training if you had more than twelve hours of it,' Claud wrote. 'In one of the first battles on the Sierra, men who were to handle the extremely complicated Spanish hand grenade, which [would] go off in your hand and blow you to pieces unless you handled them just right, had to undergo their whole course of instruction in an armoured train going up to the front. The journey lasted just forty minutes.'[18]

By the time Claud joined the regiment, recruits were doing a little better, receiving eight days training before being rushed to the front and thrown into battle. He himself had some basic military knowledge thanks to the Officers' Training Corps at Berkhamsted. The Steel Company recruits took an oath not to retreat without orders and to shoot any other member of their unit who did. When Claud wrote about the shortage of rifles, his mind went back to what he had witnessed aged eleven or twelve in the First World War:

When I was a child, I saw Northumberland miners who had joined Kitchener's First Army, drilling with broomsticks in the fields at Berkhamsted. In Francisco Rodriguez Street, I saw men tearing planks from a neighbouring ruin with their bare hands, and trying to break them into something approximately of equal length and weight to a rifle, so as to have something to train with.[19]

In mid-September, Claud's platoon was posted to a mountain position overlooking the town of Guadarrama, near Somosierra, a low range of mountains north of Madrid. It took them two hours of driving and seven hours of marching, making long detours to avoid heavy artillery fire and spotter planes, to reach their position. At first sight, this appeared to be easily defended, situated on a hill on the flank of a mountain with a clear field of fire on three sides, though with a grove of pine trees on the fourth. The soldiers they were relieving had built a stone wall around the little encampment as well as a score of dugouts, 'half hut and half burrow' covered in pine branches where a militia-man could lie down comfortably out of the wind and safe from rifle fire. Soon after they arrived, they heard rumours that the enemy had received German Junker bombers with heavier bombs and with German crews. Men wounded in air attacks trickled through their position, where Claud was on guard duty with an old 1914 Oviedo rifle. A sergeant gave him a piece of wood, half an inch thick and six inches long, telling him to clench it between his teeth to avoid shell shock in the event of their position being bombarded.

Some hours later, the bombing did begin, though not yet directly on Claud's platoon. But he witnessed its results when he saw three wounded men making their way up the hill towards him. Two of them had dirty bandages bound around their wounds and were carrying a third man, whom Claud had known in the barracks back in Madrid: 'I saw that the bottom half of his face had been literally blown off, and that as his body sagged between the bearers, blood oozed horribly from the small of his back.'[20] Bleeding, dazed and stone deaf from the bombardment, the men staggered into the little camp, but by then the most seriously wounded man was dead.

The seventy-two soldiers in two platoons who had arrived with Claud, along with some paramilitary Assault Guards and survivors from units already overrun by the enemy, were expecting the Nationalists to follow up the bombardment with a ground attack. But it never came, and the exhausted Republican fighters crawled into their shelters to sleep, only to be reawakened by their sergeants telling them that their commanding officer had ordered a counterattack to disrupt any enemy offensive the following day. The Republican attack on positions high on a hill two miles away was to take place immediately, under cover of darkness, to avoid German bombing.[21]

A few days later, Claud wrote a detailed account of the assault as his memory was still fresh. 'In silence', he wrote, 'broken only by the constant noise of men falling down among the thorns and rough boulders of the tiny mountain track we moved out of camp, down one side of the ravine between us and the enemy [on the] mountain, and began the long climb towards the summit, where the Fascists lay entrenched.'[22] After climbing up the far side of the ravine, they came to the edge of an open space 150 yards across, sloping gently upwards towards the enemy positions.

Given that the dug-in Nationalist troops possessed machine guns and grenades, while the Republican militiamen had neither, the attackers had little chance of success and every likelihood of suffering heavy casualties. The militiamen and Assault Guards opened fire and were answered by a ragged volley, followed by half a dozen grenades pitched down the hill. Claud wrote: 'One of the Guardias [Assault Guards] lying a little in front of me to the right, got a grenade full in the back and was blown into bloody fragments of flesh and blue cloth.'[23]

Courageously, the militiamen made a rush up the hillside towards the fort held by the Moorish machine gunners. Claud wrote:

The men charged, holding their rifles high above their heads and giving the clenched fist salute with the other. It emerged that they had taken the highly stylized and symbolic posters designed by the Madrid intellectuals, showing a soldier of the Republic in this posture, as illustrations of correct military practice. When they saw me dodging about, bent half-double and taking whatever cover there was, they thought the posture unworthy, despicable. A lot of them were killed or wounded before they were converted to the idea that, as instructional diagrams, there was something wrong with those posters.[24]

The Nationalists moved their machine guns to better positions, from which they could shoot anybody on the slope below them who raised their head above the boulders behind which they were sheltering. Fortunately, the machine gunners were firing high, enabling the surviving Republicans to fall back to where the hill dipped sharply and gave some cover. 'At this point', wrote Claud, 'the belt of my trousers broke.' Along with others in his platoon, he had been issued with an ill-fitting army uniform, whose wide cavalry trousers were not designed for a tall, thin man. As he ran down the hill, jumping from boulder to boulder, his improvised cummerbund broke and his over-sized trousers dropped to his knees, leading him to fall over and lie on the ground 'so paralysed by fear that I did not move'. The Assault Guards he had been with had disappeared, so he was alone, but fortunately for him the pursuing Moors had not followed the retreating militiamen very far before returning to their position at the top of the hill.[25]

Despite the debacle, there were still some Assault Guards, who had received more training than the others, who wanted to continue to fight. They decided to snipe from separate positions and Claud, after distributing fifteen rounds of ammunition he had taken from one of the dead, decided to do the same.

'We scattered,' he wrote a few days later. 'At the end of twenty minutes. I had found no good sniping point, had fired two shots at a small body of men clustered near the corner of the enemy position, and was completely lost.'[26]

This happened shortly before midnight, and Claud spent the rest of the night crawling about the mountainside with enemy snipers firing from above, hitting trees uncomfortably close to him. Most alarming of all, the rattle of gunfire further down the hill below told him that there were now enemy forward outposts between him and the Republican front line: 'At dawn, I was still a long way behind the fascist positions, having accidentally taken a track to the left rather than the right. It was not until a couple of hours after sunrise that I finally crept up the bed of a tiny mountain stream and came out in our lines, a mile or so below our positions.' He immediately went up the hill again to his old encampment, where, he recalls, 'I was received with quite a celebration, everybody having assumed that I had been dead for hours.'[27]

The fighting continued, with the Republican militiamen launching brave but unsuccessful attacks on dug-in enemy positions. He says that the enemy machine gunners were still firing high, otherwise, 'by all the law of common sense we should have been shot off the bare face of the earth'. When they finally did retreat, they carried their wounded, aside from one whom they shot as he was 'too badly wounded to have a chance of living all the way down the hill and we knew what the fascists would do to him if they caught him still alive'. He explains that the purpose of these near-suicidal charges was to rattle and confuse the enemy, hopefully making them hesitate before launching their own ground assault backed by artillery and air strikes.

As the battle ended, Claud was summoned back to London in order to take part in a campaign to influence public opinion, particularly in the Labour Party and Trades Union Congress, against the 'non-intervention' that was starving the Republicans of arms. He had been unwilling to leave the front, where he had been promoted to corporal, and was horrified to find on reaching London that he was billed as a star speaker at a giant meeting in Shoreditch Town Hall on 27 September. This was a bad idea, he wrote later, 'because I am one of the worst public speakers who ever bored and exasperated an audience'.

He was thankful when he was called to Communist Party headquarters by Harry Pollitt and ordered to write a book. Called *Reporter in Spain*, by Frank Pitcairn, it was published in October 1936. It is a polemical but gripping read, showing few signs of the breakneck speed with which it was produced and gains in atmosphere and freshness from being written within a few weeks of the events it describes. Given that the purpose of the book was to garner support for the Republic, its tone is upbeat, but Claud leaves no doubt that he is writing about a defeat in this small battle, albeit a heroic one.

In later years, he gave a more caustic account of the doomed assault in which he took part, blaming the commander of the Republican forces, a former captain in the Spanish Foreign

Legion, who had ordered it. Shortly before he died in 1981, Claud told an interviewer:

> Imagine trying to move about four hundred totally untrained peasants through a ravine in the middle of the night in silence. What had actually happened, we discovered later, was that shortly [after] giving this order, he [the Legionnaire captain] had in fact deserted to the other side, and the night attack was proof that he was a genuine Francoite. He'd get us all killed.[28]

16

The Sinking of the *Llandovery Castle*

The Battle for Madrid [wiki commons]

On 25 February 1937, Claud was on board a British ship, the 10,000-ton *Llandovery Castle*, travelling from Gibraltar to Marseilles, two miles off the Spanish coast just south of the frontier with France, when it struck a mine laid by the Italian navy. The mine ripped a hole fifteen feet by fifteen feet in the port side of the ship, which came close to sinking.[1] Claud wrote that the explosion 'blew the heavy forward hatches high into the air, [and] sent a column of water over the deck, wrecked two cabins completely, tearing the fittings from the wall. And filled the whole ship with the acrid smell of burning cordite.'²

Fortunately for the crew and the one hundred passengers, the hole blown in the side of the ship flooded the forward hold containing a cargo of cement and cork that slowed the inrush of water. 'If the mine had struck a matter of a few yards further forward it would quite certainly have killed a score of the crew who were then in their quarters,' wrote Claud. Even so, the damage was severe, and the *Llandovery Castle* was soon down by the bows with lifeboats swung out and the crew and passengers standing by in their life jackets. A second mine was spotted in the water but passed by harmlessly.³

Steaming slowly so as not to increase pressure on a weakened bulkhead, the *Llandovery Castle* made for Port-Vendres, close by on the French side of the border. She limped into the little port, where a contemporary photograph shows her off a beach with her bows low in the shallow water. Claud was by this time on the bridge acting as an interpreter between the British ship's officers and the French port authorities. Later, he went ashore to explain why the crew and passengers needed to be rescued immediately. 'It was at first hoped that possibly, with a British destroyer standing by, she might still progress to Marseilles in the morning,' he wrote. 'Within a few hours this hope and the bulkhead collapsed together.'

As the wind rose and the sea grew choppy, the crew fired distress rockets and within an hour all on board had been brought ashore. Claud dispatched a telegram to London, reading in capital letters 'MINE IMPEDES PROGRESS RING PORT-VENDRES 33 (THIRTY THREE) AT TWELVE THIRTY.'⁴

A British naval officer in Gibraltar had warned Claud that Italian trawlers were dropping mines between the Balearic Islands, which had become an Italian-Nationalist naval base, and the coast of Republican-controlled Spain. From the bridge of the *Llandovery Castle*, officers had seen two mines in the water and what they thought might be the periscope of a submarine. They may have been right since, from the first months of the civil war, Italy had been conducting a covert naval campaign against Republican-held ports on Spain's Mediterranean coast. Later in the war, the success of Italian-Nationalist attacks on ships carrying Soviet arms and fuel supplies from the Soviet Union to Spain was to be one of the deciding factors in the Republican defeat. The *Llandovery Castle* was unlucky to be an early casualty of the Italian blockade.

Claud had returned to Spain the previous year, in November 1936. Back in Madrid after the publication of *Reporter in Spain* in October, Claud arrived as the Nationalist forces were preparing for their all-out assault on the capital. 'When I returned to Spain', he wrote, 'the atmosphere was a great deal more harsh, the aspect of the whole war more grim than it had seemed in the summer but – although Franco was literally at the gates of Madrid – hardly anyone, I believe, ever imagined we could be defeated.'[5]

The International Brigades fuelled this optimism, as did the first deliveries of Soviet arms and ammunition. The formation of the International Brigades stared on 12 October and by November, the XI International Brigade was fighting and suffering heavy losses in street battles as Franco's veteran Moorish troops advanced into the centre of Madrid. 'Those of us who were here', Claud wrote in a diary he briefly kept at this time, 'will never be able to convey, and nobody who is not here will ever be able fully to imagine, the emotions and significance of this moment. Last night, at University City, for the first time in Europe and in the history of Europe, Frenchmen, Germans, Italians, Hungarians, Poles, Bulgarians and Rumanians, went into action together. The [foreign] contingents were small, rushed up prematurely from Albacete, to prevent a total breakthrough.'[6]

Claud himself joined the International Brigade only later in 1937, dealing primarily with propaganda and political intelligence.[7] As the siege of Madrid tightened, he reported on the ground fighting and air attacks in the city and countryside.[8] On one day in December, he had been driving back from the front line north-west of Madrid when his car had engine trouble, forcing him to stop in a small village called Majadahonda. As the driver 'tinkered' with the engine, Claud saw a squadron of twenty Italian bombers approach, sending villagers running out of their houses into the fields. 'I saw a girl of fifteen to twenty years run by', he wrote, 'her hands spread out on her breasts, her head flung back and her eyes staring madly at nothing. She stumbled wildly forward with little harsh sobs across the ploughed land, running crazily nowhere in particular.'[9] Overall, however, the tone of his dispatches is defiant and upbeat, though he makes clear that the Republic would lose unless they could turn brave militiamen into 'efficient infantry'.[10]

After a brief return to London, he was back to Spain in February, travelling south to Málaga, on the Mediterranean coast just east of Gibraltar. He and the Republican commanders did not realise until it was too late that this isolated Republican enclave was about to be assaulted by a powerful newly landed Italian expeditionary force equipped with light tanks and supported by Italian air power. Between December 1936 and April 1937, Mussolini sent some 80,000 Italian regular troops, mostly recruited from the Italian fascist militia, to Spain.[11] Italian conscripts were surprised to find themselves in Spain rather than Abyssinia, where Mussolini had also intervened militarily.

The *Daily Worker* proudly announced that Pitcairn was the first foreign correspondent to get into Málaga, though Claud said, more modestly, that he believed five other foreign journalists had visited Málaga since the war started six months earlier. One of these was Arthur Koestler, another Communist associate of Münzenberg and one of the authors of the anti-Nazi *Brown Book*. When Málaga fell faster than anybody expected to the Italians, Koestler was captured and only narrowly escaped execution. Claud said that he had warned Koestler at the last minute to get out of the city, but that Koestler felt he had been unfairly criticised for retreating too precipitately earlier in the war and did not want to be accused of faint-heartedness a second time.[12] In reality, there had never been much chance of 12,000 poorly led and -trained militiamen, a third of them without rifles and divided between anarchists and Communists, could have held Málaga against the Italian motorised columns which attacked on 3 February, though they might have resisted purely Spanish forces.

Claud had initially expressed edgy optimism that the city could be held: 'Six hours before I got into Malaga, I thought that Malaga would fall. Now I doubt it.'[13] He describes the church bells ringing out two or three times a day as a warning that another Italian bombing raid was about to start. People fled their flimsy houses, which had no cellars, to seek safety in the caves and rocks.[14]

When the defences of the city collapsed on 8 February, Claud was surprised and a little embarrassed, writing that his mistaken overconfidence had sprung from his visits to all the Republican front-line positions, interviews with Republican commanders and with enemy deserters. He wrote that 'in the General Staff Headquarters in Malaga [just before the start of the attack] we discussed reports from the Paris press of the landing of Italian troops and German troops, and particularly the landing of 100 Italian planes', but they had discounted the Paris reports as exaggerated.[15] Republican military intelligence must have been appalling if it failed to know about the landing of an entire Italian army.

Observing the exodus from Málaga along the narrow coastal road, Claud describes peasant carts drawn by oxen and horses, piled high with women, children and their belongings, being machine-gunned from the air as they tried to escape. Their terrified flight was understandable since as soon as the Italians turned over control of the city to the Nationalists, they promptly executed some 4,000 Republican supporters and militiamen.[16] 'The nationalist revenge in Malaga was perhaps the most horrific of the war', writes Antony Beevor in his *Battle for Spain: The Spanish Civil War 1936–1939*, 'judging by the British consul's report of 20,000 executions between 1937 and 1944.'[17]

By then Claud was in Valencia, having narrowly escaped the final debacle, and a few weeks later was in Gibraltar. A message from MI5 in London to a local security officer sent on 25 February warned of Claud's presence in Gibraltar, speaking of his high abilities making him 'a formidable factor', and said that he might soon be joined by Jean Ross, currently believed to be in Paris, who 'was with Cockburn in Madrid during the early stages of the Spanish war'.[18] By the time the message was sent, Claud had already left Gibraltar on board the *Llandovery Castle*, whose voyage was about to be abruptly 'impeded' by an Italian mine.

On coming ashore at Port-Vendres, Claud called the Spanish News Agency (EFE) in Paris, a publicity arm of the Republican government whose French office was headed by his friend Otto Katz. Another reason for his call may have been that Jean also worked for the agency. Katz insisted that he come straight to Paris.

'What I want now', he told Claud when he arrived 'is a tip-top, smashing, eye-witness account of the great anti-Franco-revolt, which occurred yesterday at Tetuan [in Spanish Morocco], the news of it having been hitherto suppressed by censorship.'[19] Claud replied that he had never been in Tetuan and knew of no such revolt there. 'Not the point,' replied an impatient Katz. 'Nor have I heard of any such thing.'

He explained that field guns essential for the Republican military were being held up on the French–Spanish frontier under the non-intervention policy. But, supposing French prime minister Leon Blum's Popular Front government was to learn about a mutiny in Spanish Morocco, the very place where Franco had launched his putsch, then Blum might be less certain of a Francoist victory and let the guns through. Claud liked cunning stratagems of this sort, often not so different from a politically inspired practical joke, which might damage the enemy. He thought there was just a chance that Katz's ploy 'would work and for me, who had briefly fought in Spain, and had watched so many battles as a non-combatant, the idea of actually helping to roll those guns toward the front was exhilarating'.[20]

He and Katz relished concocting evidence of their imaginary anti-fascist revolt. 'We spent many hours on the story,' wrote Claud.

We had the *Guide Bleu* and a couple of other guide books which might be seriously out of date, and Otto had been to one of the big libraries and copied a few facts from books not available in bookstores. From one of them, he had slashed, with a razor blade, a street map of Tetuan. Unfortunately, there was nowhere any clear indication of contours, so there was always the danger that we would have the alleged rebels – Moorish and European soldiers joining in democratic indignation against miserable conditions and hopeless war – firing at the Fascist forces along some street which had a great hump in the middle of it.

It was a long and detailed story of battle, with the outcome still uncertain. It was important, Otto pointed out, not to claim too much of a victory. We must admit some setbacks. Lieutenant So-and-Sos attempt to capture Such-and-Such strong point had ended in failure and the death of the gallant lieutenant. Many names were given but I insisted that we should display some frank uncertainty – thought to be under the command of Captain Moreno, who was among the leaders of the revolt in 1936 and [is] now believed to have turned in disgust against Franco. It is not, however, clear that this is the same Captain Moreno.[21]

Claud claimed with some professional pride that the article that finally emerged was one of the soundest, most factual pieces of war correspondence ever published. He believed, moreover, that it had a significant impact in swaying the Blum government towards telling French frontier guards to briefly close both eyes and allow the artillery pieces to reach the Republican forces.

Twenty years later, Claud was to tell the story of the fake uprising among Franco's veterans at Tetuan and was astonished when many people expressed shock that a professional journalist should not only have fabricated the mutiny but openly admitted to doing so. Given that he was working full-time for the Republican government at the time, he thought this criticism was absurd. He quoted Richard Crossman as saying that he was 'disgusted' by the story of the fake mutiny and the exuberance with which Claud claimed credit for it. He thought it amusing that Crossman could write that 'black propaganda may be necessary in war, but most of us who practiced it detested what we were doing'.[22]

Nevertheless, Claud's open admission that he and Katz had made up the tale of the Tetuan mutiny did him reputational damage down the years. Phillip Knightley expressed shock in *The First Casualty*, his book on war correspondents published in 1975, over Claud's unconcealed identification of himself as a polemical Republican supporter, saying that this 'rendered Cockburn unfit to report the Spanish Civil War'. Knightley was especially outraged that Claud was 'unrepentant' about exaggerating the Republic's chances of victory.[23]

In fact, Claud was convinced that all wars were information wars and that this is inevitable since people who are trying hard to kill each other will not hesitate to tell lies about each other. He thought that such partisanship was impossible to avoid and that what was important was for the public to know about such undeclared bias. Knightley gives a telling example of the latter, writing about how an internationally significant scoop by Herbert Matthews, the *New York Times* correspondent in Madrid, had been suppressed by his newspaper because it was contrary to their political prejudices.

Most journalists are uncomfortably aware of the mutability of events which may appear to be inevitably moving in a single direction one day, only to reverse course the next. Generally, they play down this changeability in order not to undermine the credibility of their reporting, but Claud rather gloried in the sheer unpredictability of human affairs. An article he sent from Spain to *The Week* at this time was prefaced by the following message: 'Seek to use this fine assessment of the situation before some *schweinerei* committed by God or Hitler or some others I can see in the café across the street proves it utterly mistaken.'[24]

Ironically, one group of people convinced that Claud was now working for the Republican regime was the British government in London. When he submitted his passport to the Foreign Office in 1937 to get an essential stamp that he would need to cross the French frontier into Spain, he was turned down. His passport was returned to him but invalidated for Spain, something which provoked a public row with the Foreign Office over his right to report in Spain.

In its campaign to get the validation, the *Daily Worker* announced for the first time that 'Frank Pitcairn'[25] was the pen name of Claud Cockburn.[26] Questioned in the House of Commons about this on 28 March, the foreign secretary, Anthony Eden, said that 'so far as he could ascertain Mr Cockburn had been engaged in press and propaganda work on behalf of the Spanish government'. [27]

Despairing of getting official sanction, Claud had already left Britain, travelled by way of Newhaven and Dieppe to Paris, and then on to the French Pyrenees.[28] Unable to cross the frontier legally, he learned that there were two alternative, unofficial routes available. One was long but fairly safe, going over the mountains, while a shorter, riskier route went across flat land closely observed by bored and trigger-happy French frontier guards. After considering the options, Claud felt that he would do almost anything rather than 'climb even a small mountain, let alone a bit of the Pyrenees', so he took the riskier route back into Spain.[29]

As Claud was crawling across the Franco-Spanish frontier, another British journalist and author was fighting in the Republican front line before the Nationalist-held city of Saragossa, in Aragon. This was George Orwell, who had arrived in Spain in December and joined the militia of a dissident Communist party, the Workers' Party of Marxist Unification (Partido Obrero Unificacion Marxista) (POUM), which had distant links to Leon Trotsky, then in exile in Mexico. The leader of POUM, Andreu Nin, had once been Trotsky's secretary.

Orwell's membership of the group was in large part accidental, since his sole purpose in going to Spain was 'to fight fascism'. He wrote later, 'I was not only uninterested in the politics of the situation but unaware of it.'[30] He had first tried to go to Spain under the auspices of the Communist Party of Great Britain but had been turned down by its general secretary, Harry Pollitt. He had instead used his contacts with the Independent Labour Party, which had put him on to POUM. He trained in a former cavalry barracks in Barcelona, not dissimilar to Claud's in Madrid. Orwell describes the other recruits as 'mostly boys of sixteen or seventeen from the back streets of Barcelona, full of revolutionary enthusiasm but completely ignorant of the meaning of war . . . if a man disliked an order he would step out of the ranks and argue fiercely with the officer'. After a few days training in Barcelona, Orwell had gone with his POUM militia unit to spend three and a half months in freezing temperatures in the hilltop trenches before Nationalist-held Saragossa. His location was not far from the spot where Claud had nearly been executed as a spy by anarchists of the Durruti Column the previous July.

Claud and Orwell have certain obvious points in common – as well as some deep differences.[31] Both were the sons of civil servants in the British Empire, Orwell born in Bengal in 1903. They had each turned sharply to the revolutionary left, impelled by the Great Depression and the rise of fascist regimes in Italy, Germany and Spain. Their political experiences varied widely, Orwell's radical political views developing gradually after a brief career as a police officer in Burma, then as a radical journalist and author writing mostly about Britain. Claud, by way of contrast, had been heavily influenced by the ferocious politics of Central Europe, and above all of Germany, during the final years of the Weimar Republic and the Nazi seizure of power.

Orwell said he was surprised on his arrival by the hatreds dividing the Republican side. Claud, in contrast, already had plenty of experience of this infighting, saying that 'to be ideologically at variance [had] . . . not very much difference from being on the other side altogether'.[32]

These differences covered a great range of issues, the most important of which was how to win the war against greatly superior forces. The Popular Front government in Madrid – made up of moderate socialists, bourgeois Republican parties and Communists – was in alliance but also at odds with the anarchists of the National Confederation of Labour (CNT) and the Trotskyists in POUM, whose strength lay in Catalonia. The government wanted to avoid divisive revolutionary changes while fighting the war and to create a regular army capable of resisting Franco. All this was complicated by the fact that the Republic could not survive without arms supplies from the Soviet Union, where the great purges were getting underway in a paroxysm of state violence and paranoia.

And, if this were not enough, the Republic was all too clearly losing the war. Claud had witnessed the fall of Málaga in the south in February, and now the Nationalists were advancing through the north. On 26 April the German Luftwaffe, operating as the Condor Legion, had obliterated the town of Guernica, killing some 1,645 of its inhabitants.

Furthermore, a confrontation between central government and semi-independent Catalonia was inevitable. Orwell, briefly back from the front on 3 May, was surprised when the government's paramilitary Assault Guards tried to seize the telephone exchange controlled by the anarchists since the start of the civil war. Heavy street fighting erupted between government forces on one side and the anarchists and POUM on the other, in a conflict which became known as 'the May Days', ending on 8–9 May with a government victory. Claud, who was in Valencia, wrote a piece in the *Daily Worker* published on 11 May saying that this was a decisive moment in the war since 'the Germans and Italians are at the gates of Bilbao [the Basque city that fell on 19 June]'.

He continues that foreign agents working behind the lines in Catalonia were disrupting the Republican war effort, accusing the POUM of acting as their proxy. More of a diatribe than a reasoned article, it demonises POUM as being filled with Trotskyist saboteurs.[33] On 17 May he wrote another piece claiming that POUM was heavily equipped with 'arms they had been stealing for months past, and had hidden, and there were arms such as tanks, which they stole from the barracks just at the beginning of the rising. It is clear that scores of machine guns and thousands of rifles are still in their hands.'[34]

Orwell was particularly incensed by the accusation that POUM was well armed and went to considerable lengths to show that they possessed only 'some dozens of machine guns and several thousand rifles'.[35] Asked about this accusation many years later, Claud was unapologetic, saying that he might have been 'misinformed about the quantity of tanks, arms and so on that they had', but that he had believed what he had written at the time. He thought that Orwell's account of the 'May Days' in Barcelona was as polemical as his own, though from the opposite side in what was 'a civil war within the civil war'.

As for the ferocious onslaught on POUM by the Soviet security service, the NKVD, he is more sympathetic to Orwell, saying that there were genuine reasons for people to become disillusioned with the Republican cause, and with the Communists in particular, because of 'the preoccupation of some Communists with the rooting out of heresy; there is no question that in '37, at the time of the Stalinist purge, this did become an evil preoccupation, and I can imagine that anybody who saw that at close quarters would indeed feel horrified'.

At the same time, he said that most of the Russians advisers in Spain were not involved in the purges.[36] 'This was not the case at all,' he said. 'Although they were certainly saying that we must not push our opposition to the Stalinist fanatics to the point that everything collapsed and we lost the war.'[37]

Orwell had every reason to feel enraged by the persecution of the POUM militiamen alongside whom he had been fighting. After returning to the front line in Aragon, he was shot through the throat by a sniper and evacuated to a hospital in Tarragona. When he re-emerged in June, he found that POUM had been declared illegal; shortly thereafter, he and his wife were on the run for the French frontier. The leader of POUM, Andre Nin, was kidnapped, tortured and, after refusing to confess to being a Nazi agent, murdered by Russian agents. Claud thought that the Republic had to have a unified central government and a professional army if it was going to have any chance of winning. He attacked in print anybody who opposed this. But the probability is that whatever the Republican government did, it was bound to go down to defeat, given the overwhelming superiority of the forces ranged against it.

Claud did not take the spat with Orwell very seriously in the context of a war which the fascists won and half a million Spaniards were killed. Orwell ultimately came to much the same conclusion, saying that 'in essence it was class war. If it had been won, the cause of the common people everywhere would have been strengthened. It was lost, and the dividend-drawers all over the world rubbed their hands. That was the real issue; all else was froth.'[38]

17

Scoops and Abdications

Claud plots with John Strachey during the abdication crisis as a policeman spies on them [author]

As Claud was writing about the battle for Madrid in the early winter of 1936, friends in London standing in for him at *The Week* were divided on how to handle an entirely different type of story. Should they focus solely on the titanic struggle between fascism and democracy being fought out in Spain, or should they carry more stories about the love affair between Edward VIII and Mrs Wallace Simpson?

The latter appeared frivolous and diversionary while the fate of Europe was being decided on Spanish battlefields. But at the same time, the king's determination to marry a divorced American woman, in the face of objections from Prime Minister Stanley Baldwin and his cabinet, was a real constitutional crisis. It was also one in which the British press was exercising the sort of self-censorship which *The Week* commonly derided and had promised to ignore. It was peculiarly well placed to do so because the impending divorce of Mrs Simpson and her likely marriage to the king were being written about copiously in American news outlets in October and November 1936, though the British only broke their silence on 2 December.

Astonishingly, the British distributors of *Time* and other American magazines had instructed their employees to cut out with scissors any articles referring to the liaison between Mrs Simpson and the king. It was an ideal story, therefore, for *The Week* as its small voice would inevitably reverberate in this vacuum of information. Moreover, its earliest and best-informed contacts were American foreign correspondents in London who were reporting daily on the royal scandal. Frustrated by their editor's and proprietor's prohibition on covering the story, British journalists were likewise likely to pass on what they knew to the newsletter.

The first cryptic reference to the king's troubles came in the issue dated 14 October, reporting on a plan for 'a social bombshell to explode under the king . . . The ideal method would be for a reference to be made from the pulpit to the very different standards of conduct set to his subjects by the late King [George V].'[1] This report was at the bottom of the final page and claims that those behind the plan were hoping that the Archbishop of Canterbury, Cosmo Lang,[2] might deliver the sermon.

In the event, it was a different clergyman, Alfred Blunt, Bishop of Bradford, who spoke out on 1 December. But, as had been forecast, his vague reference to the king's need for divine assistance was sufficient for the British newspapers to end their embargo on the story. The first to use the bishop's words as a hook to highlight the royal affair was the *Yorkshire Post*, owned by the family of the wife of the foreign secretary, Sir Anthony Eden – a coincidence suggesting a government hand in pushing the king towards abdication.

Possibly *The Week*'s scoop was a lucky chance, but more likely it was proof of Claud's contention that rumours were politically important and should be published.

Readers may have been perplexed by this odd little piece of royal gossip in an issue otherwise dominated by revelations about the illegal export of arms to the Spanish Nationalists and the political troubles in Ireland. But the significance of the item was made clear a fortnight later, on 28 October, when a longer article appeared with the headline 'The King and Mrs Simpson'. It said that 'yesterday at the Ipswich Assizes, Mrs Ernest Simpson was granted a decree nisi', explaining that the American press was giving the news greater coverage than any story since the kidnapping of the Lindbergh baby.

Distancing itself a little from its own report, the newsletter asserted that 'the reason for this stupendous and vulgar bally-hoo' was the view, then openly expressed in the American press, that the king was about to marry Mrs Simpson. It offered some uncertainty about this belief, assuming that readers would disregard these doubts. 'The evidence that the King is planning a political and constitutional innovation of this magnitude is extremely slender,' it warned. 'It has been known for some time that Mrs Simpson has been a member of the inner circle of the King's friends and this apparently is the sole fact upon which the American press has proceeded.'[3]

The article cannot have been written by Claud, as he was in Madrid, showing that the newsletter was by now well enough established to publish scoops even when he was away. Revelations on the brewing abdication crisis boosted *The Week*'s credibility and circulation. A memo in Claud's MI5 file notes that 'the circulation of this bulletin has greatly increased in the last few weeks', attributing this to the 28 October article 'dealing with the relationship between His Majesty the King and Mrs E. Simpson'.[4] The same memo from the Special Branch says that Claud visited the office on 23 November, indicating that it was under police observation, and mentions his return from Spain the previous week. It adds that while he was away, the newsletter had been run by Geoffrey Bing, a radical barrister on the executive of the National Council for Civil Liberties. Claud stayed in London until after the king's abdication on 10 December, writing at length about the final stages of the crisis.

Other left-wingers thought it strange that Claud should give so much attention to Edward VIII's problems, which they dismissed as an intense but trivial struggle within the establishment that only served to divert public attention from the terrible menace posed to Europe by the unstoppable spread of Nazism and fascism. For all Claud's revolutionary radicalism, he showed a clear preference for Edward in his confrontation with the government, explaining that he supported anybody, even a reactionary monarch, who was opposed to Baldwin and his ministers in a year when they had failed to resist Hitler's occupation of the Rhineland and Mussolini's invasion of Abyssinia. Moreover, the British government was now helping stifle the Spanish Republic by a grossly unfair non-intervention policy. Claud rejected the suggestion that he was suffering from an unexpected bout of royalism, but he evidently felt an instinctive sympathy for anybody battling the powers that be.

Claud would also have guessed that the weaker party in any unequal struggle may decide to even up the odds by leaking damaging information about their enemies to journalists like himself. *The Week* had a distant connection to the circle around the king through John Strachey, a politically active intellectual on the far left whom Claud had first encountered at the anti-fascist peace conference in Amsterdam in 1932. Strachey had diffidently approached Claud to ask him for a short, potted autobiography in the spring of 1936. Mystified by the request, Claud repeatedly asked Strachey what it was for, and Strachey finally disclosed to him that it was intended for the king.

It turned out that a friend of Strachey's was an intimate of Lord Louis Mountbatten, somebody whom Claud approved of as an isolated anti-Nazi among right-wing courtiers. He was also a reader of *The Week* and had conceived the idea that if the king could be persuaded to read the newsletter, then he might take a radically different view of European affairs than that presented to him by Baldwin and the cabinet.

Understandably, Edward asked why he should take seriously an obscure scandal sheet edited by somebody he had never heard of. It was to answer this query that Claud had been asked to produce a brief account of his background, which he now swiftly produced, showing himself to be 'one of the Right People with ancestors, and an Oxford accent, and a former connection with the *Times*. I reached for my halo and rapidly presented Mr Strachey with a glowing testimonial to myself in four hundred words.'[5]

Viewing the episode with some jocularity, Claud continued to meet Strachey, in absolute secrecy, in various London parks. When Claud returned from Madrid in the second half of November, Strachey approached him again to say that Edward VIII's supporters had concluded that because of the 'suffocating [press] silence, the trend was running strongly against the King'. Mountbatten had made a plot, of which the king as yet knew nothing, to leak sensational information damaging to Baldwin and his government to *The Week*. Though the nature of this super-secret bombshell was not revealed, Strachey wanted to know: Would Claud, 'in principle', be prepared to publish it?

'I was rather far from being a passionate champion of the monarchy', Claud later recalled, 'but the atmosphere of pompous discretion was almost unbreathable and anyway it looked as though whatever happened we should have a lot of fun. Also, one got the impression that Lord Mountbatten was a bonny fighter who ought to be encouraged. I accepted of course.'

Claud also took elaborate precautions to ensure that copies of a special edition of *The Week*, which would contain the information that might rock the government, was to be distributed by hand to circumvent any attempt to suppress them. Learning one evening that the explosive material would be in his hands within hours, he mobilised typists, assistants and delivery boys, but by one o'clock in the morning, the dispatch rider delivering the documents had still not appeared. Then Claud heard the distant sound of a motorcycle:

I rushed down five flights of stairs and got to the street door at the same time as the dispatch rider, who had shot past and had to turn. He handed me a small unaddressed envelope, and I knew from the size of it that it was going to be no good. I called to him to wait – there might be an answer. He said no, he had been told there would be no answer. Inside the envelope there was a single sheet of plain paper with this typewritten line. It read: 'the situation has developed too fast.'[6]

After the abdication which took place on 10 December, Claud expressed some disappointment in *The Week* that the king had not been up for a fight, lacking personal determination and political skills. He had been 'comprehensively outmanoeuvred and outgeneralled', failing to expose dirty work by his opponents that might 'have blown up those trying to force him out'. As it was, the 'vital factor in the situation was the inability or unwillingness of the Duke [of Windsor, as the former king was now known] to hit back'.[7]

Shortly after the abdication, Claud returned to Spain, where Franco's forces, powerfully supported by Italian infantry and German air strikes, were to advance inexorably throughout 1937. Málaga fell on 8 February, Guernica was destroyed by the Condor Legion on 26 April, Bilbao was captured on 19 June and Gijón and Asturias on 21 October. Government offensives – such as that at Brunete, fifteen miles west of Madrid in July – tended to be initially successful and then falter under the weight of Nationalist counterattacks. Many people were being killed and had often been with Claud a few days before they died.

When in London at the end of 1936, Claud learned of the death of Hans Beimler, a Bavarian Communist who was one of the few prisoners to have escaped from Dachau concentration camp and had been killed while fighting in the International Brigades in Madrid. 'Eighteen days ago', wrote Claud, 'we were sitting in a frontline position on the Casa del Campo front, outside the city, and he eased himself up to pull a map or something out of his pocket, and a bullet missed his head by a millimetre.'[8]

British intellectuals who had gone to fight in Spain were also dying. Among these was Ralph Fox, a historian, novelist and journalist who was killed in Madrid on 28 December 1936. 'He was a highly politically educated man, very life-loving, very realistic,' said Claud.

> But he insisted on going to the front with the British Battalion [of the International Brigades] as a political commissar. He almost pushed himself into battle – I saw him at the base at Albacete, where he was dodging the orders of the high political chiefs who naturally thought it monstrous that a man like this – an internationally known, influential Communist writer, should be let to get himself into a position where he could be killed like an infantryman, which he was three weeks later. But Ralph's certainty was that unless he personally and physically fought he would cease to function as a writer.[9]

Not all of Claud's friends who died were combatants. Among them was Gerda Taro, a twenty-six-year-old German Jew who was probably the first female war photographer. Born Gerda Pohorylle in Stuttgart, though her family came originally from Galicia, she had been brought up in Leipzig, where she was highly educated, speaking German, French and English. She was not at first politically minded, but this changed when she and her family became victims of Nazi anti-Semitism, her father's business ruined and their house confiscated. Her two brothers joined the anti-Nazi resistance; she was jailed for three weeks for distributing anti-Nazi leaflets and was only released because she had a Polish passport. Forced to leave Germany, she moved to Paris, where she had a job in a photographic agency. But in a city bulging with anti-Nazi refugees, her prospects of making a living as a photographer were low, until she teamed up with two other Jewish exiles, André Friedman and David Seymour (the first from Hungary, the second, also known as 'Chin', from Poland). They thought of an ingenious stratagem to sell their photographs, which was to do so under the collective nom de plume of Robert Capa.

Capa was an entirely fictional American photographer who was supposedly visiting Paris. His pictures – in reality all photographs taken by three highly talented immigrants from Central Europe – sold for three times more than the amount they could have charged under their own names, if they could sell them at all. On the outbreak of the war in Spain, they travelled to Madrid, where they were intrepid in photographing all aspects of the war – military, political and social.

To this day, their black-and-white pictures powerfully convey the flavour of the conflict, showing Republican militiamen as they inch through buildings shattered by bombs and artillery fire that look like the ruins of Stalingrad. Soldiers advance half crouched against incoming fire, while another picture shows them as they stagger back carrying their wounded on their shoulders. One iconic photograph shows a Republican militiaman in Andalusia at the moment he is hit by a bullet.[10]

In one of the photographs taken by Taro, Claud is shown looking scrawny and older than his thirty-three years, wearing a white shirt, round glasses and with dark unruly hair and a domed balding forehead. Beside him stands Fred Copeman, a former sailor in the Royal Navy who briefly commanded the British battalion in the International Brigade. Behind the two men is scrubland at Brunete in July 1937, where Taro was to be killed in battle a few days later.

Though no photographs have survived of Taro and Claud together, they covered the Brunete offensive by government forces, which aimed to relieve Nationalist pressure on Madrid and persuade the outside world that Franco's victory was not assured. In their response, the Nationalists launched a devastating counterattack backed by German air strikes. Claud and Taro arrived at the front on 22 July, where they were strafed by German aircraft. Claud said that he and Taro came 'around to the calculation that we had, this time, very little chance of getting out alive. She then stood up and began to take photographs of the planes, saying "in case we do get out of this, we'll have something to show the Non-Intervention Committee".'[11]

In the event, they were not hit, Taro later saying to Claud that 'when you think of all the fine people we both know who have been killed even in this one offensive, you get the feeling that it is somehow unfair to be alive'.

They went back to the Alianz, a cheap place to stay for foreign journalists in Madrid, and she was planning to travel to Paris on 26 July to meet up with Friedman. Claud is said to have moved into the hotel to be near her. At the last moment, she decided on one more visit to the front, which by this stage was caving in under the weight of the Nationalist assaults. She went with a friend called Ted Allan, a young Canadian attached to a medical unit, but conditions had got so dangerous that their driver abandoned them short of Brunete and they walked the last part of the journey.

Once there, they went to see the Republican commander, but he ordered them and other journalists to leave immediately because Franco's forces were about to attack. Ignoring his advice, they stayed, but the Republican troops started to panic and retreat pell mell back down the road to Madrid. Taro jumped on to the running board of a car carrying wounded soldiers, but an out-of-control Republican tank accidentally side-swiped the vehicle, mortally wounding Taro, whose stomach was ripped open. A photograph shows her on a stretcher with blood streaming from her mouth. She died in a hospital at El Escorial, her last words being, according to an American nurse: 'Are my cameras smashed? They're new. Are they there all right?'[12]

Many of the greatest writers and intellectuals of the age travelled to Madrid in the months after the start of the civil war. 'Everybody who wanted to be in on the decisive thing of the century', wrote Claud, 'the thing that was going to prove that Democracy was going to stand up to the enemy there and then or else that Democracy – it was the phrase that people used at the time and they believed in it – was going to take a terrible beating, and after that there would be a bigger and worse war.'[13]

Among those who came was Ernest Hemingway, perhaps the best-known American writer of the time, who was considered something of an expert on modern warfare because of his experiences on the Italian front during the First World War. In September 1937, he was staying in the Florida Hotel, in a part of Madrid under fire from Nationalist artillery on Monte Garabitas. This moved him to give a briefing on the military situation that Claud attended.[14] Shells were exploding nearby but were not actually striking the hotel. In his room, Hemingway laid out a map on a table and was explaining to an audience of politicians, generals and correspondents that, for some ballistic reason, the shellfire could not hit the Florida. 'He could talk in a military way and make it all sound very convincing,' wrote Claud.

> Everyone present was convinced and happy. Then a shell whooshed through the room above Mr Hemingway's – the first actually to hit the Florida – and the ceiling fell down on the breakfast table. To any lesser [person] than Mr Hemingway, the occurrence would have been humiliating. While we were all getting the plaster out of our hair, Mr Hemingway looked slowly round at us, one after the other. 'How do you like it now, gentlemen?' he said, and by some astonishing trick of manner conveyed the impression that this episode had actually, in some obscure way, confirmed rather than upsetting his theory – that his theory had been right when he expounded it – and this only demonstrated that the time had come to move on to a new one.[15]

Claud advised the Republican government on how to deal with visiting intellectuals. He found that many wanted somehow to get close to the Spanish people or take part in the fighting for reasons with which he sympathised but thought impractical. 'Quite a lot of literary people of the 30s had an exaggerated idea of physical action,' he reflected years later. 'They discovered in Spain that every Tom, Dick and Harry who knew the innards of a bren-gun was better at it than them; then came disillusionment which could easily lap over into a feeling that the whole thing was no good.' An instance of this was a visit by W. H. Auden to Valencia in late January 1937, a few weeks before the fall of Málaga. Claud said that through some awful mischance it was taken for granted that he knew the aims and objections of any Anglo-American who sought a visa for Spain. When Auden came out, Claud laid on a car for him. The Republican authorities hoped that Auden would be whisked up to Madrid, write poems saying 'hurrah for the Republic', and then go home.

But not at all: the bloody man went off and got a donkey, a mule really, and announced that he was going to walk through Spain with the creature from Valencia to the Front. He got six miles from Valencia before the mule kicked him or something and only then did he return and get in the car to do his proper job.[16]

The story about Auden and the mule has been often quoted to Auden's discredit, portraying him as a stereotypical fellow traveller unable to cope with the beastliness of war or the wiles of Republican and Communist propagandists. Auden was to write long afterwards that nobody he knew who had gone to Spain 'came back with his illusions intact'.[17] But his brief journey did produce a magnificent poem, 'Spain 1937', with its rallying cry: 'I am your choice, your decision: yes, I am Spain.'[18]

Despite occasional irritation or amusement at the misadventures of visiting foreign intellectuals, Claud thought that those who belittled Auden and others for wishing to see the war were themselves making a mistake. He believed, on the contrary, that it was the government and supporters of the Republican cause who were being simple-minded in imagining that writers and poets could produce great works to order, and that 'the alternative to their getting killed was that they would pour out marvellous books. But it would be more likely that the writer would mentally drop dead.'[19]

The visits of VIPs and celebrities boosted morale in the shrinking government-held enclave, but they also promoted a false sense that public sympathy abroad might do the Republic much good. Claud believed that talking up the chances of his own side coming out a winner was right, but he was depressed by those who believed too much of their own propaganda. In these fraught circumstances, he increasingly preferred the company of the Russians in the Palace Hotel as they 'were the only people who could live without this illusion [that outside powers were going to rescue the Republic] but still not become defeatist'.

Claud's best Russian friend in Madrid was Mikhail Koltsov, and they remained close until Koltsov was arrested in Moscow in December 1938 and executed a little over a year later. A veteran Bolshevik since the revolution, he had founded the satirical

magazine *Krokodil* and was one of the among the best-known
journalists in the Soviet Union. At the time Claud met him, he
was foreign editor of *Pravda* and, more importantly, was the
confidant, mouthpiece and emissary of Stalin in Spain. Claud's
admiration for him was unstinting:

> He was a stocky little Jew – from Odessa, I think,[20] with a huge
> head and one of the most expressive faces of any man I have ever
> met. What his face primarily expressed was a kind of enthusias-
> tic gleeful amusement – and a kind of hope that you and everyone
> else would, however depressing the circumstances, would do
> your best to make thing more amusing still. He had a savagely
> satirical tongue and an attitude of entire ruthlessness towards
> people he thought incompetent or even just pompous.
>
> People who did not know him well – and particularly non-
> Russians – thought his conversation, his sharply pointed Jewish
> jokes, his derisive comments on all sorts of Sacred Cows unbear-
> ably cynical. And others, who had known them both, said that
> he reminded them of Karl Radek – an ominous comparison
> [Radek had been jailed in a show trial in Moscow in early 1937].
>
> To myself it never occurred that somebody who had such an
> enthusiasm for life – for the humour of life, for all manifesta-
> tions of vigorous life, from a tank battle to Elizabethan literature
> to a good circus – could possibly be described as properly 'cyni-
> cal'. Realistic is perhaps the word – but that is not quite correct
> either because it implies or might imply a dry practicality which
> was quite lacking from his nature. At any rate, so far as his
> personal life or fate were concerned he unquestionably and posi-
> tively enjoyed the sense of danger – and sometimes by his
> political indiscretions, for instance, or his still more wildly indis-
> creet love affairs – deliberately created dangers that need not
> have existed.[21]

As the Spanish war ground towards its gruesome conclusion,
Claud says he found himself looking forward more and more to
his meetings, journeys and conversations with Koltsov. Above
all, he admired his refusal to believe that, though the enemy
might have won a battle, he had not yet won the war: 'He was

a man who could see the defeat for what it really was, could assume that half the big slogans were empty and a lot of the big heroes stuffed shirts or charlatans and yet not let that bother him at all or sap his energy and enthusiasm.'[22]

18

The Cliveden Set

Lady Astor and Lord Astor at the centre of the Cliveden Set [wiki commons]

Claud did not spend all of his time in Spain but travelled widely elsewhere in Europe, explaining that he was able to do so because 'periods of terror and periods of tedium are, alternately, so large a part in modern war'.[1] He moved rapidly between London, Paris, Madrid and Valencia, making occasional forays to Geneva, Brussels and Prague. He never speaks of holidays, aside from the one he took in Spain in July 1936 which coincided so conveniently – and in the eyes of some observers suspiciously – with Franco's military coup. Datelines on his published stories give a guide to where he was and what he was doing, while MI5 noted his arrivals and departures, making copies of his telegrams and letters, which supply further details.

Claud comes across during this period as a person wholly absorbed in politics and polemic journalism, to the exclusion of everything else. His relationship with Jean Ross was political as well as romantic since she was helping on *The Week* and reporting from the front line in Spain. He paid little attention to his own comfort, food and accommodation, or even his frequent lack of money. Many of his telegrams to Jean and the *Daily Worker* were requests for small sums – generally under ten pounds – to be wired to him as soon as possible. 'Can You Possibly Wire Four Pounds Hotel Perigord Paris', reads a typical message to Jean in 1934.[2]

By the beginning of the war in Spain, he had been forced to give up his well-paid job with *Fortune* magazine due to lack of time. *The Week* flourished, and by 1938 he was telling a MI5 informant 'in confidence' that it had between 4,500 and 5,000 subscribers and was making between £1,000 and £1,200 a year.[3] Yet individual subscriptions were absurdly low at only twelve shillings a year, so it was never going to generate much income.

Claud could survive on limited food or a comfortable place to sleep, but he could not willingly do without alcohol and cigarettes, considering it perfectly natural that he should spend his last pennies on them. He had drunk heavily as an undergraduate at Oxford, as did his contemporaries like Evelyn Waugh, Graham Greene and members of the Hypocrites Club and, like them, he continued to do so for the rest of his life. Plain-clothes police, following him from pub to pub in London, concluded that 'it may be said that Cockburn is a heavy drinker of whisky'.[4] In November 1935, a more disapproving police memo writer said that he was 'going down-hill' morally and physically and 'is dirty and unshaven'.[5] Jean's younger sister Clare, known in the family as 'Billee', wrote a closely observed description of at this time: 'He started the day fresh and clean, usually wearing a light shirt, but by evening he usually appeared slightly shop soiled and shabby, due most likely to his constant proximity to cigarettes and newsprint.[6]

His general health appears to have suffered little from his unhealthy lifestyle since a medical check-up in 1943 showed him to be fit and eligible for military service. Despite spending much time in Spain in the front line, he suffered no injuries aside from two ribs broken when jumping from a car during the Battle of Brunete.[7]

Many of the telegrams in Claud's MI5 file were sent to or from Jean, with whom he was permanently living by late 1934 at 8 Brunswick Square in central London.[8] When not with him in Spain, she helped him in running *The Week*, on occasion ghosting his copy, but also working on her own as a war correspondent for the *Daily Express*. By early 1937, according to an MI5 official, 'Cockburn's ablest assistant in his work on "The Week" is Jean Ross. She was with Cockburn in Madrid during the early stages of the Spanish Civil War and has since been largely responsible for publication of "The Week".'[9]

On 17 June 1936 Claud wrote an article in which he described for the first time a political and social network at the centre of which was the vastly wealthy Astor family, who were the owners of both the *Times* and the *Observer*. In addition to the Astors, the core members of this powerful grouping, which eighteen months later he was to pillory as 'the Cliveden Set', were Dawson, Lothian (Philip Kerr) and Lionel Curtis, all former members of 'Lord Milner's kindergarten', the nickname for the bright young men who had been brought to South Africa by the governor, Lord Alfred Milner, to reconstitute British imperial rule and supervise reconstruction after the Boer War.

As with many who were to be associated with Cliveden, members of the Set had multiple other connections, such as Eton, Oxford, Parliament, government service and business. But the Set did bring together a wide circle of politicians, civil servants, aristocrats, editors and the very wealthy who gathered at Cliveden, the Astors' palatial country house overlooking the Thames in Buckinghamshire.

The network was not a cabal, coterie or a conspiracy, since its members saw no need to plot in secret. A measure of Cliveden's power was that it was semi-open about its activities, the most important of these being bringing about a peace agreement between Britain and Germany. By making substantial territorial concessions to Hitler in Eastern and Central Europe, the future of the British Empire, detached from the fate of continental Europe, would be secured.

In an article entitled 'The Best Peoples' Front', Claud outlined the nature of what was only later to be called the Cliveden Set in a narrative that was to vary little in the coming months. The hook for Claud's piece was an editorial that had just appeared in that newspaper. He wrote that 'half the statesman in Europe pored anxiously this week over the increasingly peculiar editorials of "the Times", culminating on Tuesday in the plea for secret negotiations between Hitler and the London government'.[10] He gave a somewhat mocking but well-informed account of links between the *Times*, Dawson and the Astor family, and explained why they were such a powerful combination.

> The Times is a great newspaper. It treats its staff so well that it is full of men that for years have been proclaiming every six months that they are going to get out before it is too late and are still there working for it. Its editor, Mr Geoffrey Dawson, has never, so far as we know, expressed any such desire. An able and charming man, he is the unfortunate victim of a form of society – or rather of a sector of British society – which impresses deeply upon the consciousness and subconsciousness of its youthful [members] a feeling amounting almost to awe in the presence of inherited wealth, inherited security.

The portrait of Dawson, who had edited the paper since the Astors bought it after the death of Lord Northcliffe in 1922, is waspish, noting that his original family name was 'Geoffrey Robinson' but that he had changed it to inherit a family estate from an aunt. The new owners, the Astors, one of the wealthiest families in the US and Britain, exercised a control over the paper that 'was considerably more subtle than the open dictatorship of the deceased Northcliffe'. Claud emphasised that this power flowed not from a single individual but from the family as a whole, 'which in the 1930s shares – and disputes – with the Cecils, an extraordinary position of concentrated political power'.

Best known in the Astor family was Lady Nancy Astor MP, one of the three Langhorne sisters from Virginia, who had married

Waldorf Astor, later Lord Astor, in 1906. For a time, she exerted –
thanks to the establishment figures with whom she associated – a
powerful influence over British politics. Claud said in *The Week*
that she had 'a vigorous – if not very profound – personality',
and attributed her prominence to a sort of historic accident

> when the personal whims, prejudices and well or ill-conceived
> notions of a single individual, play a role of absurdly dispropor-
> tionate importance . . . Lady Astor for instance is obsessed with
> a vivid personal dislike of the French, a sort of antipathy which
> some people have tried to explain by attributing it to the hostil-
> ity between the extremities of Anglo-American Puritanism and
> traditional French Catholicism . . . She has maintained, too, a
> basic belief that Bolshevism is an affair of bombs and knives
> between the teeth – possibly not too clearly distinguished in her
> nimble mind from anarchism.

Superficial though these prejudices were, her hostility towards
France and the Soviet Union mattered much in the late 1930s,
since these countries might be Britain's potential allies in the
event of another war with Germany.

> With this sort of idea [about France and the Soviet Union] latent
> in their minds – and not counter-acted by any more thorough
> understanding of the situation and its terrible dangers – the
> Astors have been the easy and obvious target for German prop-
> aganda and German diplomatic activity during the past two
> months. There is no doubt that at the beginning of the Nazi
> regime they shared – and the Time certainly reflected – the general
> disgust at its methods.[11]

The Astors' dislike of the French and fear of the 'red menace' –
two hostile forces that Berlin claimed were virtually fused
together – had the result that the family 'has today become one
of the most important supports of German influence'. No
wonder the *Times* was urging upon 'a recalcitrant Foreign Office
that failing to begin secret, bilateral conversations with Berlin,
if Berlin wants them, is "mere pedantry"'.

Ownership of the *Times* elevated the Astors to a level of power exceeding that of other press lords. Claud pointed out that when an article appeared in the *Daily Mail* calling for Britain to line up with Germany and Italy against Bolshevism, people paid minimal attention. But when the *Times* and the Astors called for something similar, their views had a real political impact on events. 'For one must recall the awe with which many politicians still regard *The Times* and also from the point of view of numbers of [those who hope] to be called "rising young politicians" invitations to Cliveden are more important than the fact that the end of all these lovely editorials, dinners and garden parties will be war.'[12]

The Week seldom directly abused those it disliked, though it might mock or excoriate their activities. But Lady Astor was an easy target and, by all accounts, was even nastier than *The Week* made out. Among her many prejudices, she was viscerally anti-Semitic. Returning to Britain from New York in 1937, she complained to reporters about 'the appalling anti-German propaganda here'. She warned that 'if the Jews are behind it, they've gone too far. And it will react on them.' When an MP came up to her in a corridor of the House of Commons to say that he disagreed with something she had said, she replied: 'Only a Jew like you would *dare* be rude to me.' Privately she attributed criticism of her politics to 'Jewish Communist propaganda'.

Her poor judgement and outrageous opinions made Lady Astor easy to demonise, but her flamboyant failings divert attention from why Cliveden house parties were such a magnet for the powerful and well connected. Claud usually coupled Cliveden with Printing House Square, a common synonym for the *Times*, as a combination which gave the Astors political leverage far superior to other political salons. To use a modern analogy, in the 1930s, the Astors possessed greater power than Rupert Murdoch half a century later because of the prestige and authority of the *Times*, and because this was an era when newspapers in general were at the peak of their influence in the early days of radio and prior to television.

Much subsequent controversy about whether or not Claud was correct in targeting the Cliveden Set for their vast and malign influence over British foreign policy stems largely from the fact that a 'set' is by definition a loose association of people who may derive much of their power from being in the cabinet, Parliament, Conservative Party or upper ranks of the civil service. But Cliveden provided an essential focus for them and for all those holding pro-appeasement opinions. Though its political attitudes were not entirely uniform or static, Cliveden counted for more and more in the late 1930s, as decision makers closely linked to it came to dominate the government. Most important, Neville Chamberlain replaced Stanley Baldwin as prime minister in May 1937 and Lord Halifax, previously viceroy of India and already in the cabinet, replaced Sir Anthony Eden as foreign secretary in February 1938.

Having identified the Astors and Dawson on the *Times* as representing an extraordinary 'concentration of power', Claud became preoccupied with the Spanish Civil War over the next year and a half. When he resumed writing about Cliveden in *The Week* on 17 November 1937, the occasion was a visit by Lord Halifax to Germany, during which he was to meet with Hitler. What gave his visit such significance was that it was a sign that Chamberlain and the appeasers were taking over control of British policy towards Germany and shifting it significantly towards making concessions to Hitler. This redirection of policy was by and large opposed by Eden, who was already being marginalised, and especially by Sir Robert Vansittart, the permanent under-secretary at the Foreign Office, who was shortly to be sidelined by Chamberlain.

The first scoop about a proposed Anglo-German agreement to be discussed by Halifax and Hitler was to appear in the *Evening Standard* on 9 November in a piece by Vladimir Poliakoff, a former diplomatic correspondent of the *Times*, who had almost certainly got his information from Vansittart's faction within the Foreign Office. Claud was a friend of Poliakoff and received details of the Hitler–Halifax conversation from him, but Claud had other highly informed sources, such as the French foreign ministry, whose vital interests were affected by the prospect of an Anglo-German agreement.

The Week's article on 17 November, published the same day that Halifax arrived in Berlin, confirmed the *Evening Standard* piece but corrected it on one crucial point. It said that the deal's terms were being proposed by London, not by Berlin, and that under the proposed bargain, 'Germany would offer a ten year "Colonial truce" to Britain in exchange for a free hand to attack countries in Eastern Europe'.[13] He said, furthermore, that 'the plan as a concrete proposal was first got into usable diplomatic shape at a party at the Astors' place at Cliveden on the weekend of October 23rd and 24th'.

He referred readers back to the issue of *The Week* published on the eve of the Spanish Civil War that had described 'pro-nazi intrigues at Cliveden and Printing House Square'. He claimed that 'the queer Anglo-American gathering at Cliveden' has decided what colonial concessions should be made to Germany in pursuit of an agreement with Britain. He thought it scarcely believable that 'the little knot of expatriated Americans and "super-nationalist" minded Englishmen' did not see that the British Empire could not be saved in this manner. He expressed mock surprise that they did not understand that giving Germany a 'free-hand' in Eastern Europe was seen as desirable, if not essential, in Berlin as a way of 'securing the backdoor of Germany in preparing for the great Tag (day) when the German armed forces will move through the front door against Western Europe'.[14] Claud's belief that the German attack would be directed west rather than east was borne out in May 1940.

In a follow-up article, *The Week* said that Eden had at one point resigned in protest at the Halifax visit, but this was 'like so many of Mr Eden's nervous gestures "a political event without consequences"', and he soon withdrew it.

The first two articles by Claud on Britain's bid for an accommodation with the Nazis attracted absolutely no attention, making, he complained, 'about as much impact as a crumpet falling on a carpet'.[15] But the third article, on 22 December, placed the Cliveden Set centre stage of the pro-appeasement machinations, while adding that the 'Set' did not yet have the full support of Chamberlain in its struggle with the Foreign Office over policy towards Germany, though this setback was likely to be temporary. 'It is regarded as certain that sooner or later these vast influences emanating from Britain's "other

Foreign Office" at Cliveden will be brought very powerfully to bear on the prime minister.'[16]

Much to Claud's surprise, this third article, which differed little from its predecessors, 'went off like a rocket'. He attributed this to his use of the phrase 'Cliveden Set' as a headline. Within weeks, however, the Cliveden Set was being written about and denounced in newspapers across the world.[17] David Low, the *Evening Standard*'s cartoonist, drew a series of cartoons called 'the Shiver Sisters', one showing Lady Astor, Dawson and Lothian under a banner reading 'Any Sort of Peace at Any Sort of Price' and another portraying them as ballet dancers dancing to a tune as Goebbels conducts.

The sudden pariah status of Cliveden was not confined to the progressive end of British and American politics. On a trip to the US, Eden reported in a letter to Stanley Baldwin that 'Nancy and her Cliveden set has done much damage, and 90 per cent of the US is firmly persuaded that you and I are the only Tories who are not fascists in disguise'.

In London, Claud directed foreign journalists who had turned up in the cramped office on Great Victoria Street to talk about plots hatched at Cliveden to go instead to St James's Square, where the Astors had a splendid townhouse that was by now beset by paparazzi. A year later Lothian wrote from America to Lady Astor: 'The Cliveden Set yarn is going strong everywhere here. It symbolizes the impression spread by the left and acceptable to the average American that aristocrats and financiers are selling out democracy in Spain and Czechoslovakia because they want to preserve their own property and privileges. Chamberlain is their tool.'[18]

Lady Astor similarly had no doubts about the cause of her political eclipse – and, on being introduced to Claud by John Strachey in the House of Commons, pursed her lips as if to spit in his face.[19]

Claud was understandably pleased that his story about the Cliveden Set was having a sustained impact, though he thought that its influence, as a sort of all-embracing conspiracy, was becoming exaggerated. The press likes to portray the world in black-and-white terms, and Cliveden had now been selected as the villain of the piece. What Claud had written in *The Week* was more nuanced than this, but he saw that there was nothing he could do 'to curb the monster I had let loose'. In any case, he considered the story to be essentially true and remarked that, supposing he were to persuade 'the BBC to permit me to announce personally to the listening millions that the story had no foundation, that I had invented it, no one would pay the slightest attention. People would come to the conclusion that I had been nobbled by the Cliveden Set.'[20]

Almost a century later, how well does Claud's story of the Cliveden Set stand up? Pretty well, on the whole, keeping in mind that supporters and critics of the story both take for granted an exaggerated version of what Claud had actually written in *The Week*, transmuting it into an all-purpose conspiracy theory. They picture a plan hatched secretly at Cliveden to appease Hitler, with the plotters acting in ways not dissimilar from those of Guy Fawkes and the Gunpowder Plot conspirators.

'No plot was concocted at Cliveden that weekend,' writes Norman Rose, the author of *The Cliveden Set: Portrait of an Exclusive Fraternity*, speaking of what happened there on 23 and 24 October. But he adds, 'There was no need to [plot],' explaining that what emerged at Cliveden was rather a coincidence of opinion between Lothian, Dawson, the Astors and their friends who were already of one mind about appeasing Germany. After their appeasement project had crashed in flames, they denied any sympathy for Hitler and the Nazis, but this was not really true.

Lord Halifax, for instance, wrote to Baldwin before seeing Hitler in 1937: 'I cannot myself doubt that these fellows are genuine haters of Communism, etc! And I daresay that if we were in their position we might feel the same.'[21] The inner core of the Set had no doubts about their influence as movers and shakers at the top of British government. Lionel Curtis, who was one of them, wrote to Lothian in 1938 that 'your long and persistent efforts were largely responsible for the replacement of Vansittart-Eden by Halifax. Though Chamberlain and Halifax may have diverged from your line (Lothian wanted rearmament as well as appeasement) you will exercise the most powerful influence on their policy outside the cabinet.'

This view was endorsed by Jan Masaryk, the well-connected Czechoslovak minister in London, who reported back to Prague that Lothian was 'the most dangerous because the most intelligent friend of Germany'.[22] Others, including Claud, put greater emphasis on the role of Dawson as editor of the *Times*. According to one study of his influence, he 'played the role of unofficial propaganda minister' for Baldwin and Chamberlain. 'Without Dawson's work, always behind the scenes, appeasement would never have gained the popular influence it achieved.'[23]

Though astonished by the speed with which the 'Cliveden Set' had abruptly become a symbol for that part of the British establishment who wanted a deal with the Nazis, Claud understood how 'the phrase went marching on because it first had dramatized, and then summarised, a whole vague body of suspicions and fears'.[24]

Moreover, he believed that there was much to be fearful and suspicions about. He expressed a little not very convincing sympathy for those who felt that they had been unfairly smeared as pro-Nazi conspirators because of a chance visit to Cliveden. 'I was certainly taken aback by some of the wild improbabilities which some correspondents were writing about the Cliveden Set,' he wrote. 'It looked as though quite a lot of people were getting involved, were being branded as subtly scheming political intriguers, who would not have known a plot if you had handed it to them on a skewer, and quite possibly had gone to Cliveden simply for a good dinner.'

On the other hand, he felt that it required a high degree of naivety not to know the political implications of visiting Cliveden, even if the pay-off was a particularly good dinner among political celebrities. He quoted a favourite Chinese proverb: 'Do not tie up your shoes in a melon field, or adjust your hat under a plum tree if wish to avoid suspicion.'[25]

The reputation and political influence of the Astor family never recovered from Claud's attack on them. By 1938–9, undergraduates at Oxford were singing a song about the Cliveden Set, the first verse of which goes:

In Bucks there is a country house, country house,
Where dwells Lord Astor and his spouse, and his spouse,
And Chamberlain and Halifax,
To manufacture Fascist pacts, Fascist pacts![26]

19

Press Censorship, British Style

Claud working as a journalist [author]

'A satisfactory thing about Herr von Ribbentrop was that you did not have to waste time wondering if there was some latent streak of goodness in him,' wrote Claud about the German ambassador to Britain between 1936 and 1938, who went on to become the Nazi foreign minister and was ultimately hanged at Nuremberg. During his years in London, Ribbentrop came to believe that Claud and *The Week* were at the centre of anti-Nazi intrigue and propaganda.

Proud though he was of the notoriety and impact of his newsletter, Claud was realistic about its influence, which he rated as considerably less than the conspiratorially minded German envoy. He believed, however, that the fact that Ribbentrop

> could be such a fool as to think so – helped to give me a measure of the Third Reich which could employ such an Ambassador. One is not much alarmed about people who are reasonably intelligent. What was terrifying about this man was that he was a damn fool – and could only have been employed by a regime of, basically, damn fools who could blow up half the world out of sheer stupidity.[1]

Yet, contemptuous though Claud might be about the ambassador's paranoia, Ribbentrop's belief in the high influence of a small publication like *The Week* was not entirely absurd. If the Nazis had one area of real expertise, it was in propaganda, and they took media coverage at home and abroad very seriously. They were acutely sensitive to foreign press criticism, as Hitler made very clear to Lord Halifax when he saw him on 19 November 1937, and Goebbels reiterated the same point at a separate meeting two days later. Hitler said that 'a first condition of the calming of international relations was therefore the cooperation of all peoples to make an end of journalistic free-booting'.[2]

Goebbels told Halifax 'that the influence of the Press was under- rather than over-rated. Its power to mould public opinion was greater than was realised.' He went on to ask if 'something could not be done to stop in the British Press personal criticism of Hitler. Nothing caused more bitter resentment than that.'[3] Even the most objective and non-judgemental reportage was unacceptable to the Nazis, as Goebbels had demonstrated a few months earlier in August by expelling Norman Ebbutt, citing 'the spiteful taint given to him in his reports'. Halifax responded to this unsubtle pressure by issuing a statement to the remaining British correspondents in Berlin on 21 November, in which he stressed 'the need for the Press to create the right atmosphere if any real advance were to be made in a better understanding [between Germany and Britain]'.

Back in Britain, the government redoubled its efforts to restrain criticism of the Nazi regime – and in this it was remarkably successful for the rest of the pre-war period. Research into this process by Richard Cockett in his book *Twilight of Truth: Chamberlain, Appeasement and the Manipulation of the Press*, concludes that 'due to the incestuous relationship between Whitehall and the press that had developed during the 1930s, the press in fact could do nothing but help Chamberlain pursue appeasement, as the "free" and "independent" press of Britain is at best merely a partisan political weapon'.[4]

This was very much the line Claud took at this time and later. He was not shocked by it, because he saw the biased nature of the media as being an inevitable fact of political life which had the advantage, from his point of view, of creating a vacuum of information which 'a pirate craft' like *The Week* – engaged in the sort of 'journalistic freebooting' of which Goebbels so disapproved – was designed to fill. Goebbels was correct in cynically supposing that the British government could, in practice, determine what was written about Hitler, contrary to Halifax's protestations about 'the complete independence of the British Press'.[5]

On 31 August the following year, *The Week* itemised the differing phases of self-censorship since the Halifax visit to Berlin in 1937, after which Halifax, by now promoted to foreign secretary, had been 'very much to the fore in urging, and getting, a sort of "autonomous" censorship of the British press, under which it was considered "bad taste" and "not in the interests of international appeasement" to say anything unpleasant to Hitler. Even Mr Low, the cartoonist, was we understand, "approached" on the matter.'[6]

Hitler's annexation of Austria in March 1938 had briefly made the British government less eager to suppress criticism of Germany, but, despite occasional wobbles, news undermining the appeasement policy was played down or omitted. At one moment, Lord Beaverbrook's *Daily Express*, seeking to keep in tune with changeable government policy, variously told its 3 million readers that there would be no war or, less confidently, that such was the newspaper's opinion, a change of course which for *The Week*, was 'full of menace . . . The episode provided a somewhat grim demonstration of the degree to which in fact the government is able to orchestrate the supposedly free and independent British daily press.'[7]

In retrospect, newspapers would claim that they were reflecting anti-war and pro-appeasement public opinion, but expressions of the latter were also suppressed. After the Munich Agreement in 1938, an opinion poll conducted by the *News Chronicle* revealed that 86 per cent of Britons polled did not believe Hitler's protestations that he had no more territorial ambitions. Confronted with this evidence of public scepticism about the effectiveness of appeasement, the editor-in-chief of the paper, Sir Walter Layton, refused to publish the poll and instead passed the data on to Downing Street.[8] Sealed off from reality by their own propaganda efforts, Cockett says that Chamberlain and his senior ministers 'were mesmerized by the game of news control' and 'unable to face any criticism'.[9]

The mechanisms by which the British government sought to control the news agenda in the late 1930s operated at many levels and could be subtle or brutal. Proprietors and editors were courted and journalists brought on side by being given special status as insiders – or they might be denied access to important news development, or, in the last resort their stories not printed and themselves removed from their job. The fate of Norman Ebbutt, Claud's mentor in Berlin, is a sad but telling illustration of the different stages in shutting down a correspondent whose views clash with those of his news outlet.

In 1935 British intelligence sent an officer to interview Ebbutt, who was still the *Times*'s correspondent in Berlin, about Claud. He praised his former protégé, commending him for 'feeding on the crust of an idealist when he could obtain a fat appointment by being untrue to himself'. Unfortunately for Ebbutt, he was himself already coming under strong pressure from the *Times* not to tell what he felt to be the truth about the German regime. To avoid expulsion by the Nazis, he focused on discrimination against the Christian churches rather than the persecution of the Jews. Even so, he regularly complained in letters to the editor that his dispatches were being routinely censored or toned down in London.

His colleague William Shirer, an American correspondent in Berlin, recorded in his diary that 'Ebbutt has complained to me several times in private that *The Times* does not print all he sends, that it does not want to hear too much about the bad side of Nazi Germany and has been captured by pro-Nazis in London. He is extremely discouraged, talks of resigning.' Elsewhere Shirer wrote about Ebbutt's frustration that 'his newspaper, the most esteemed in England, would not publish much of what he reported. The Times in those days was doing its best to appease Hitler and to induce the British government to do likewise. The unpleasant truths that Ebbutt telephones nightly to London from Berlin were often kept out of that great newspaper.'

Ebbutt's frustrations show that Claud had made the correct decision in leaving the *Times*. Dawson, who had tried to keep him on the paper, became a vocal and determined advocate for Britain appeasing Hitler and the Nazis in pursuit of a long-term peace agreement with them. He excised or downplayed news likely to be offensive to Berlin. In a letter dated 23 May 1937, Dawson wrote to Lord Lothian (Philip Kerr) expressing dismay over German anger at the paper's report on the bombing of the Basque town of Guernica, in which 1,650 civilians had died. 'I spend my nights', Dawson wrote, 'in taking out anything that I think will hurt their [German] susceptibilities and in dropping [in] little things which are intended to soothe them.' In a second letter sent the same day, Dawson explained that the article on Guernica had been accurate, but 'there had not been any attempt here to rub it in or to harp on it'.

Censoring of copy critical of Germany was systematic according to journalists working in the *Times* office in London. One of them, Colin Coote, described those who dealt with the Berlin office as 'a carefully selected cabal' who cut out criticism 'in an atmosphere that was quite horrible'. The result of this suppression of news, according to a detailed study of Ebbutt's relations with the paper by historian Frank McDonough, was that from August 1934, Ebbutt found that the paper's 'desire to appease Germany outweighed and finally extinguished any desire to offer criticism or allow Ebbutt to warn the British public of the possible dangers of Nazism. The increased cutting meant that Ebbutt's articles were much less critical of the Nazis in 1935, 1936, 1937.'

But even this was not enough to save Ebbutt from being expelled in August 1937 by the Nazis, who wanted either favourable coverage or none at all. On his return to Britain, Ebbutt complained of the 'half-hearted support' he had received from his superiors at the paper while trying to perform his difficult task of reporting on the Third Reich. Tragically, his troubles had not ended, and he suffered a severe stroke, possibly brought on by Nazi hostility and censorship of his copy, within a month of his return to England, which left him unable to write – meaning he left no memoirs describing his mistreatment – and was able to speak only with difficulty until his death thirty-one years later in 1968.

As crises deepened in Central Europe, Claud spent less of his time in Spain after August 1937. But Jean Ross stayed on as a war correspondent, first for the Spanish government news agency, and then for the *Daily Express*. In the same year that Isherwood presented a slightly modified version of Jean in Berlin as the flighty, apolitical Sally Bowles in his novella of that name, she was in reality reporting from the front line in Spain, where she came close to being killed by German bombers. In the spring of 1937, soon after Claud escaped from Málaga as the Italians captured it, Jean toured the southern towns still in government hands and packed with terrified refugees. Costancia de la Mura, head of the Foreign Press Bureau in Valencia, described Jean as 'a clever and charming English woman working at that time for the government news agency in Paris and London'.

She interviewed women who had fled from Málaga after the men in their families were all executed, and talked to a British businessman who had witnessed German aircraft bombing but was aghast at saying so on the record. Later Jean and an American journalist called Mowrer were watching Republican forces besieging a Nationalist garrison in a monastery when they were attacked by Junker-52 bombers. De la Mura remembers seeing 'in the dusk Mowrer and Jean Ross running down the road. I began to run. The sound of the planes, the low roar of the motors filled my ears and head and heart and throat . . . Suddenly the whole mountain exploded with a sound so hideous, so vast, that the ear was not shaped to comprehend it.'[10]

Jean was uninjured, but she was worn down by the air attacks and the slow strangulation of the Republic.[11] On 15 April 1938, Franco's troops reached the Mediterranean, cutting Republican-held territory in two, and Jean moved temporarily to France to rest. From there she sent a 'very personal and affectionate' letter to Claud on 26 April, saying that she was all right and was recovering from her experiences.[12] Claud came briefly to see her and then moved on to Czechoslovakia.

Jean's younger sister Clare (Billee) and another sister, Peggy, came to see Jean in the late spring: 'Peggy and I travelled together', Billee wrote, 'via Marseilles, to Sclos de Contes, a small village in the hills above Nice, to join Jean.'

> She was recuperating there, in a small Hotel-Rest home. She looked pale and exhausted. The wonderful peace, lying in the shade of the olive groves, and the excellent cuisine, helped to restore her complexion, though it did nothing to lift her spirits. She was very depressed by the outcome of the war, and full of the particular tragedy of the civil war. She described how the two political factions, positioned on the hills on either side of a valley, would be firing at each other all day long, but when night fell they laid down their arms and began to sing sad songs of love and friendship, calling to each other across the valley, brother to brother, friend to friend.

Right-wing supporters of Franco saw Claud's and Jean's activities in Spain and elsewhere in a sinister light. A Mr Pryor, who said he worked for an enquiry agency, sent MI5 a memo in 1939 that was a curious mishmash of accurate and inaccurate information about Claud. He is described 'as one of the most important men working for the Comintern in Western Europe. He is responsible for all political information and the "Cockburn Machine" as it controls military, naval and industrial espionage and would be responsible for sabotage in the event of war.' Pryor, who claimed that Claud and Jean had gone to Spain just prior to Franco's coup in order to plan a Communist revolution, said he later became Moscow's representative on the Foreign Affairs Committee of the Spanish Government. The credibility of the report is sapped by its authors' claim that when in New York, he had 'been in touch with "Time" [magazine] which is secretly associated with the CI [Communist International]'.[13]

MI5 was dubious about unsolicited information like this, and one of its officers wrote a minute on the memo asking if 'this information from alleged enquiry agents of any use to you or any other Govt. Dept? If not, I had better tell him so tactfully.'[14]

On occasion, Claud would reinforce the fears of those who suspected him of planning Red revolution by giving lurid details of the intended uprising. On one occasion, a woman wrote in alarm to MI5 recounting how she had sat next to him at dinner and, presumably aware of his reputation as a dangerous radical, had asked him when he expected revolution to break out. He had appeared to take her question seriously and had informed her confidentially that an uprising was, indeed, imminent and would begin in a surprising place – the Brigade of Guards – whose barracks was located conveniently, for the purposes of seizing power, between the Houses of Parliament and Buckingham Palace.[15]

The idea of a 'Cockburn Machine' is comically out of keeping with Claud's mode of operation, and he admitted to a 'claustrophobic distaste for organization and discipline'.[16] But he did see the Communist Party as a vehicle for effective political action by himself and others. The Communists of whom he speaks with high respect as having a real impact on events include Otto Katz, Egon Irwin Kisch and Mikhail Koltsov.

His third wife, Patricia Arbuthnot, wrote that his attitude towards the Communist Party was very much that of a Central European.[17] But one of those to whom he gives the greatest praise was a French Communist, whom he calls 'Monsieur Bob', describing him as having 'courage, clarity of mind and firm philosophy, which was to be found among the best Comintern agents, without the occupational vices of many of them, such as rigidity, pomposity, affectation, parrot-talk and the arrogance born of basic insecurity'. He adds that the Frenchman was 'one of those men who really do love their fellow-men like brothers and are, literally, prepared to be martyred for their sakes'.[18]

Yet, in 1937–8, amid the great purges of anybody suspected of dissent, failure to march in step was not something likely to be acceptable to Moscow. Claud's highly individualistic Communist associates were particularly vulnerable, however effective they might be as anti-fascist leaders and agitators. Claud himself did not escape suspicion, going by the contents of Comintern files stored in the Russian State Archive of Social and Political History in Bolshaya Dmitrovka Street in Moscow. Documents on Claud are not plentiful compared to the MI5 archive, but they do reveal that Comintern officials had tried to get Claud sacked from the *Daily Worker* for his repeated disregard for the party line. Just as the MI5 chief Colonel Sir Vernon Kell was telling the Americans that Claud 'was a formidable factor on the side of Communism', Comintern officials in Moscow wanted rid of him. Among his sins was cutting a key part of an interview Stalin had given. 'We know him from the negative point of view,' reads a memo written by a Comintern official in Moscow called Bilov on 25 May 1937. 'In the middle of 1936, we suggested to the English Communist Party to sack Cockburn from the senior editorial management as one of the people responsible for the systematic appearance of different types of "mistakes" of a purely provocative character on the pages of the *Daily Worker*.'[19]

The party officials never made up their mind what they thought of Claud, though they all recognised his abilities. In 1936–7, an official in London expressed admiration for him, saying that 'he is held to be one of Fleet Street's cleverest journalists'.[20] Another noted his ability to reveal changes in the cabinet before they were announced: 'He is in touch with bankers and other elements who are in close touch with what goes on in the bourgeois camp and Government circles.'[21] These reports sometimes have the suspicious tone of inquisitors searching for heretics in the conviction that they must be hiding somewhere.

One report in 1936 refers to Jean Ross, saying Harry Pollitt 'distrusts this woman but has no facts to connect her with the enemy'.[22] Another report says,

The mistakes recently made in the *Daily Worker* on the question of the Chinese students' agitation and the omission of a vital part of Comrade Stalin's interview with Ron Howard are to be attributed in the first place to Cockburn. More recently in one of his early dispatches from Spain, where he is working as the *Daily Worker* correspondent, the bad mistake was made of depicting the Communists and the socialist workers' organisations as seizing on the present events to install a regime of socialism.[23]

Party policy at the time was to support the Popular Front government and postpone social revolution until after victory over Franco. Sub-editing the words of Stalin was evidently the greatest offence, since Moscow was still bringing the matter up ten years later.

As the crisis in Europe deepened through 1938, Claud found himself 'looking forward more and more eagerly to conversation with Koltsov, journeys in his company, estimates from him of the course of affairs'.[24] In March Hitler annexed Austria – the Anschluss – without resistance, and the Gestapo began to hunt down Communists, Jews and anybody else on their lists. Eugenie Schwarzwald, the Jewish central figure in the set to which Claud, Berta and many of his friends had belonged in Berlin and Vienna, was, fortunately for her, in Denmark when German troops entered Austria on 12 March. She was advised not to return and took refuge in Zurich, where she was soon joined by her husband Hermann. Her schools and charities were closed down or confiscated in order to 'Aryanise' them, while many of the Jewish students were to be murdered in the death camps.

Six months after the Anschluss, Claud was in Prague with Koltsov for the next phase of Hitler's seizure of Central Europe as he dismembered Czechoslovakia following the Munich conference – the infamous meeting on 30 September attended by Germany, Italy, Britain and France but not by Czechoslovakia or the Soviet Union. Stalin had signed a mutual defence pact with Czechoslovakia to come to its aid if it was attacked by Germany, but only on the condition that France also intervened.[25]

There is a feeling of inevitability about what happened next. The Soviet foreign minister, Maxim Litvinov, had written a few days after the Anschluss to the Soviet envoy in Prague that 'the Hitlerization of Austria has predetermined the fate of

Czechoslovakia'.[26] France and Britain were never prepared to fight for Czechoslovak independence, and it was very unlikely that Stalin would intervene alone. In addition, the Red Army could not reach Czechoslovakia without crossing Poland or Romania, access to which they were unlikely to obtain. There was a possibility that Czechoslovak president Edvard Beneš might order his powerful army to resist the German attack, with the aim of drawing France and the Soviet Union in to the conflict, but hopes of this happening were slender.

Claud found the atmosphere in Prague at the height of the crisis ominously similar to that of Madrid two years earlier: 'You felt that soon there would have to be shells cracking against the hotel to complete the picture.'[27] Claud went with Koltsov to the Soviet Legation, where they could best find out how the crisis was developing. Claud recorded a brief chink of light when, hours after the agreement was signed in Munich, Beneš asked if the Soviet ambassador 'would secure immediately from Moscow an exact, up-to-the-minute verification and reassurance of previous estimates of the pace and volume at which Soviet airpower could get into action from Czechoslovak airbases?'[28]

Claud describes the wild excitement in the Legation at the prospect of Beneš and Czechoslovakia resisting: 'Koltsov [was] dancing and kissing people and throwing his big beret into the air.' But the euphoria soon turned sour when the envoy returned from the presidential palace, having failed to see Beneš and being told that the Czechoslovak government was no longer interested in Moscow's reply. 'With that', wrote Claud apocalyptically, 'it was once again clear that Czechoslovakia would not act with Russia alone as her ally. The shape of the next act was certain. Hitler's next triumph was assured. It was the hour, too, when the Russo-German pact became inevitable.'[29]

The Munich Agreement eliminated any small hope in Madrid that Britain and France might save the Republican government at the last moment. Any hope of an anti-Hitler alliance between Moscow and the two big surviving democracies disappeared with the likelihood that all parties would seek an accommodation with Hitler. Koltsov appears to have sensed the dire consequences for himself of what had just occurred. Claud long remembered his last macabre conversation with him in a café in Prague as they mulled over the disastrous news from Munich. Claud told Koltsov that he was leaving Prague for Geneva on a late plane the same night, so he would need to go to the bank to change his English money into Czech currency to pay for his flight and his hotel bill, run up over the previous ten days. Koltsov, who hated to have a congenial conversation interrupted, said there was no need for Claud to go because he, Koltsov, had plenty of Czech currency in his pocket and could change Claud's pounds sterling himself. He did so and they continued their talk.

'This, of course, could be the death of me,' Koltsov declared. 'How so?'

Koltsov put his hands on the table and began acting out the trial of 'Citizen Koltsov' in Moscow, where the mass extermination of the great purge had been underway for two years, with hundreds of thousands of party members executed as spies and saboteurs. He played the role of public prosecutor addressing Koltsov in the dock:

> Do you deny, Citizen Koltsov, that in Prague on the date in question you received British currency from the well-known British Intelligence Agent Cockburn? Do you deny that you insinuated the same agent into the Legation of the Soviet Union? Do you deny that you discussed the military dispositions of the Soviet Union, including the operation of planes from Prague military airfield?

'You see', said Koltsov to Claud, 'how this might all come to pass?'

Koltsov's last action before Claud left Prague was to appoint him *Pravda*'s correspondent in London.[30] It was not a job likely to last long, though the *Pravda* administration kept insisting that he rent a grand office in keeping with the paper's fame and vast circulation. Claud told them evasively that he did not need an office but could work 'from my own flat, or on a typewriter here and a typewriter there'.

A few weeks later, he was glad that he had dragged his feet on the office question. Koltsov had been arrested in Moscow on

14 December 1938, though he would not be executed until 2 February 1940. Koltsov's former intimacy with Stalin did him no good. Informers were everywhere. A Soviet official in Madrid denounced him in a letter shown to Stalin which gives the flavour of the times, saying that in Madrid, 'Koltsov lives with his two wives with completely equal status', provoking embarrassing questions from Spanish friends as to 'whether polygamy is legal for Soviet writers'. Moreover, the apartment of Koltzov's common law wife, Maria Osten, had been 'turned into a salon where various high-profile comrades of various nationalities gather and where they discuss delicate questions in the presence of not fully verified comrades'.[31]

Claud knew that a plea from him saying, 'do not shoot my boss and friend of my bosom, he is innocent', would not carry much pro-Koltsov weight in the Kremlin. He was, in any case, not entirely sure what had happened to his friend, who had told him in Prague that he was expecting to go shortly on a secret mission to China. But *Pravda* was behaving ominously. First, the newspaper dropped Claud's by-line 'Frank Pitcairn', which upset him since Koltsov had devoted much effort to distinguishing in the Russian translation between the 'a' of Frank and the 'ai' of Pitcairn. Claud's articles went on appearing without a by-line, but then they stopped, as did, sometime later, his salary cheques.

Claud did his best to locate Koltsov, sending letters to Moscow that got no reply. He spoke to the Russian ambassador in London, Ivan Maisky, who gave him a covering letter, but again there was no response. 'Quite a lot of people were probably arrested and jailed or shot just for getting letters from me,' Claud reflected in his memoirs. 'It would have been Stalin's idea of being on the safe side.'[32]

Being a David

Claud with his wife Patricia outside their house in Ireland [author]

After the signing of the Munich Agreement on 30 September 1938, Claud travelled with a *Daily Express* foreign correspondent, Sefton Delmer, from Prague to Uzhhorod, a small city in the eastern tip of Czechoslovakia, where Hungarians, Jews, Poles, Slovaks, Germans, Russians and Ukrainians lived uneasily together. The area, named Carpathian Ruthenia, was a fascinating mix of peoples, languages, religions and political allegiances, the kind of place and society which Claud always liked. But its diversity and location guaranteed instability and, in the savage conflicts of the late 1930s, a growing risk of persecution and even extermination.

'We hardly knew it then', Claud wrote, 'but it was the last smell of the old time east European brew any of us were going to get for a long time.'[1] Different Ruthenian communities were both supported by and at the mercy of predatory foreign powers, who had down the centuries repeatedly turned this impoverished region into a battlefield.

'In the small nick of time that was still left to that type of Europe', Claud described how he and Delmer had interviewed a revered rabbi, famed as a miracle worker, whose predecessor was credited with using his spiritual power to stop the advance of the Russian army towards Uzhhorod in 1915. The current wonder-working rabbi was a man of sophistication and great politeness, who impressed Claud by securing what may have been the first copy of the *Daily Express* to enter Ruthenia, which he casually spread out on his desk, as if it were his daily read. Claud asked him if he could, indeed, genuinely perform miracles, to which the rabbi replied that the Jews in and around Uzhhorod were poor and uneducated, so when they saw a holy man vastly learned in the Talmud like himself, they naturally assumed that he possessed greater, even magical, powers. And were the Ruthenian Jews correct in so thinking? asked Claud and Delmer sceptically. Stroking his long black beard, the rabbi responded by reminding them 'that every false conception contains, nevertheless, a kernel of truth'.

At a nearby Jewish seminary, which Claud says was like a high-class monastery, he encountered 'a blazing-eyed young man', a zealous religious scholar, whom he asked 'what he felt about the Hitler menace. What, if any, preparations were being made for resistance or escape? Or did he think nothing would happen?' The scholar dismissed the fast-approaching danger with some contempt:

He tilted his head back and looked at me over the curling tip of his beard with that searing mix of compassion and disdain with which men of God cannot help regarding the earth-bound.

He was familiar, said he, with the existence and activities of the man Hitler, but as for himself he was interested in certain Talmudic studies and had little time to spare for the kind of question I was asking. Most Jews in that section of the Continent were murdered not long after. Yet who shall say that this man, getting on with his thinking and studies, and sarcastically damning the eyes of the approaching murderers had got things wrongfully summed up?

Claud greatly admired people unintimidated by danger, who continued to say or do what they thought right, whatever the odds against them. His admiration might be for a veteran Communist like Mikhail Koltsov, soon to be purged by Stalin, or a Jewish religious scholar in the backwoods of Ruthenia, piously absorbed in his studies as events crept 'day by day towards the gas chambers'.[2]

Claud instinctively backed any David refusing to admit defeat and striking back with his sling-stone against Goliath, though during the 1930s it was the Goliaths of the world who seemed to be winning the fight. Claud's own resilience in the face of many defeats stemmed in part from a family tradition of dissent stretching back to his great-grandfather Lord Henry Cockburn and the Scottish Enlightenment. But he was influenced also by his exposure from an early age to the desperate insecurities of Central Europe between the wars, where not letting one's day-to-day life be poisoned by approaching danger required a constant fatalistic optimism.

Claud liked to tell the Yiddish story of the young man who goes to his rabbi during the First World War to say that he fears being killed if conscripted into the army. 'Look,' replies the rabbi, 'there are always two possibilities: either you are called up to the army or you are not. If you are not, then you are all right. If you are called up, then you will either [be] sent to the front or you will not. If not, then there is no problem, but if you are you will either be killed or not killed. If you are not killed, then you have nothing to fear, but if you are killed you will either be buried in a Jewish or a non-Jewish cemetery and already' – here Claud's voice would rise to a high pitch as he reached the payoff line of the story – 'you are worrying about whether or not you will be buried in a non-Jewish cemetery!'

On 15 March 1939, six months after Claud had been in Uzhhorod, Hitler invaded the rump of Czechoslovakia, handing this portion of Ruthenia, which had a large Hungarian population, over to Hungary. The Jewish population survived for a few years, but after German troops occupied Hungary in 1944, they entered Uzhhorod, forcing the Jewish population into ghettoes in a brickyard and a lumberyard. From there they were deported in May to Auschwitz, where they were among the 90,000 Ruthenian Jews to be murdered over the course of the year.

Disasters succeeded each other with drum beat regularity in 1939 as the inevitable consequence of non-fascist disunity. It had long been clear that Hitler and Mussolini were emboldened rather than appeased by the string of concessions which had culminated at Munich. The partial breakup of Czechoslovakia was followed in March by the German invasion, which was unresisted by a demoralised Czechoslovak leadership. Sefton Delmer, no longer accompanied by Claud, returning to Prague to report on the German occupation, described how he witnessed 'thousands of Gestapo-hunted political and racial refugees from Germany' trapped and unable to escape, of whom 'hundreds committed suicide'. In Slovakia, even before Delmer's train reached Ruthenia, he saw fascist mobs 'running wild, pillaging Jewish shops, murdering Jewish families, raping Jewish girls'.[3]

At the same moment in southern Europe, the Spanish Civil War was drawing to its murderous close, with similar scenes of slaughter and rapine, as Franco's soldiers captured Barcelona on 26 January and Madrid on 28 March. Those who had fought for the Republic, and did not escape in time, were persecuted, jailed, tortured, disappeared and executed in what historians today call 'the Spanish Holocaust'.[4]

Claud confessed that there was anguish and gloom for people like himself who had denounced the appeasement of the fascist dictators, but he admitted also that it was difficult to suppress a horrible sense of self-satisfaction at being proved so right: 'You spent two years', he wrote, 'saying at the top of your voice that unless the governments of the Western Democracies assisted the Spanish republic against the forces of Fascism, the Western democracies would soon, themselves, get it, as it were, in the neck.' By 1939, whole flocks of political and military chickens were coming home to roost, tempting opponents of appeasement to feel 'a melancholy, perhaps really vicious, satisfaction that the Pharisees were not going to get away with it'.[5]

One of many negative results of Munich was that it helped persuade Stalin that a common front against Hitler was highly unlikely. On 4 May, he sacked the Soviet minister for foreign affairs, Maxim Litvinov, who was most identified with 'collective security' with Britain and France against Germany. His successor, Vyacheslav Molotov, was a long-time close associate of Stalin and more open to a deal with Hitler, though desultory talks continued with Britain and France. In reaction to the Nazi occupation of Czechoslovakia, the two Western democracies guaranteed Poland's sovereignty, but then did nothing effective to protect the Poles from German invasion. Covert British talks with Berlin served only to convince the Russians that they must hurry up and reach an agreement with Hitler before the British and French did so first.

The Central Europe which Claud had known and loved since he first saw it in Budapest as a schoolboy was being torn apart or had already disappeared under fascist rule. When he resigned his job at the *Times* in America and rushed back to Europe in 1932, he could still travel safely to Berlin, Vienna, Prague and Madrid, but by the end of the decade he could no longer visit any of these cities except at great personal peril. Many of those whom he knew well were already dead or had been forced to flee, like Jewish salon hostess Eugenie Schwarzwald, who escaped to Zurich, or the anti-fascist Communist propagandists Otto Katz and Egon Erwin Kisch, who sought safety in Mexico.

Claud was resilient as a matter of temperament, viewing defeatism, however justified by dire events, as self-fulfilling. But by 1939, very real defeats were coming thick and fast, as the

'Popular Fronts' he had advocated as the way to resist fascism and authoritarianism – two forces he was prone to conflate – failed everywhere. Toxic political leaders appeared to be triumphing. He quoted a French artist, whom he encountered at some meeting of statesmen in Paris or Geneva, as saying to him, 'I am by profession a caricaturist, but here photography suffices.' It was, he concluded gloomily, one of those moments in history 'when reality goes bounding past the satirist like a cheetah laughing as it lopes ahead of the greyhound'.

An even more acid comment on current events was expressed by his friend Robert Doll, the ageing but lively diplomatic correspondent of the *Manchester Guardian*, as they sat on the terrace of the Café du Dome in Paris. Doll asked if Claud would care to know how to get a daily scoop for 'your horrid little paper (the *Daily Worker*)'?

> All you have to do . . . is make up your mind what is the vilest action that, in the circumstances, the French, British, Italian or German Governments could undertake, and then, in the leisure of the afternoon, sit down at your typewriter and write a dispatch announcing that that is just what they are going to do. You can't miss. Your news will be denied in two hours and confirmed after twenty-four hours.[6]

Claud's relationship with Jean Ross was coming to an end. They had been together since the second half of 1933, their friends often believing them to be married, not knowing that Hope's dubious 'Mexican divorce' posed an apparently insurmountable obstacle to Claud marrying again. Jean and Claud gave priority to revolutionary politics and little to conventional propriety. Since early adulthood, each had been used to living a cosmopolitan, bohemian life, and were extremely self-reliant.

By the spring of 1938, however, Jean was worn out by months of reporting the horrible end of the Spanish war. After recuperating in the south of France, she returned to London in the summer, when her father Charles died in August at the age of fifty-seven. Having taken against him long before – unfairly according to her younger sister Billee – because of his supposedly reactionary views, she did not go to his funeral. 'Claud reappeared in London in September', Billee noted, 'from Czechoslovakia I think, and Jean and Claud went off to Brighton for a brief week-end at the Queen's Hotel. It was there that Sarah was conceived during what Jean always maintained was the most important weekend of her life.'[7]

Billee believed that Jean and Claud had gone back to Czech-oslovakia, in which case they may have been together in Prague at the time of the Munich conference at the end of the month. Returning to Egypt with her mother in December, Billee received a letter from Jean saying she was pregnant and expecting a baby in May. Several months before the birth, she changed her name by deed poll to Jean Iris Ross Cockburn.[8] On 27 May 1939, Billee received a cable from her brother Pat reading, 'A niece, remarkably like Edward G Robinson. All well.'

Jean stayed in London with baby Sarah, until, believing war to be inevitable, she moved in August to a safer place in the country. 'She had had enough of bombs and bullets,' as Billee explained, and she rented Croft Cottage in Hertfordshire, where Billee and Peggy often came to stay with her. 'Claud came and went as he pleased,' she said, recalling how one night he burst into the bedroom where the three sisters were asleep, holding a bottle of gin and three glasses. He was celebrating 'a giant scoop' that would change history, though Billee could not remember what the scoop was about.

Claud sat on the end of their bed, drinking with them until five in the morning when he left, saying that he hoped he had not bored us, but he must go because he had a train to catch. After war was declared on 3 September, the three Ross sisters lived permanently in Croft Cottage, which 'Claud visited occa-sionally, then less occasionally, then not at all'.[9]

Claud's parting from Jean was indirectly connected to devel-opments in Ruthenia. Claud and Delmer were not the only journalists visiting this out-of-the-way place, foreseeing after Munich that its inhabitants were likely to be among the first casualties of the break-up of Czechoslovakia.

Among those who went to report there was a young woman, Patricia Byron, only twenty-four years old but an experienced traveller who had recently led a Royal Geographic Society expedition making a language map in the Congo. Anglo-Irish by background and from a wealthy family, she was brought up in Ireland during the war of independence and the civil war. Marrying young – her maiden name was Patricia Arbuthnot – she had left her two-year-old baby son Darrel with her mother in Ireland while travelling in Africa. He had died of septicaemia soon after her return, leaving her depressed and feeling guilty about neglecting him.

Her marriage to Arthur Byron, a Lloyds broker, was also breaking down. In early 1939, she had gone to Ruthenia to escape depression and write a series of articles for the *Evening Standard*. Soon after these were published, Claud, who had read them and was keenly interested in Ruthenia following his own visit, asked to be introduced to her at a party in London. They began an affair which soon led to them living together – a relationship that continued until his death in 1981. They were universally assumed to be married after Patricia's divorce from Byron, but Claud's uncertain marital status meant that she, like Jean, changed her name to Cockburn by deed poll. They went through 'a form of marriage' in Sophia, Bulgaria, in 1946 but remarried in London in 1978.[10]

Claud did not quarrel with Jean – he seldom quarrelled on personal matters with anybody but did move on from one intense relationship to another, as Hope had long ago observed. Billee, an eyewitness to the end of their relationship, did not blame him for leaving Jean but did criticise him for losing contact with his daughter Sarah. Jean, asked by Billee many years later why she had never again married or had another full-time partner after Claud, replied that 'nobody else could be as much fun as Claud'.[11]

Claud only mentioned casually to Alexander, his eldest son by Patricia, when he was going up to Oxford as a student, that he might encounter his half-sister Sarah there. 'I did not know I had a half-sister,' said Alexander in amazement. 'You never asked,' Claud replied.

When the German–Soviet Non-aggression Pact was signed in Moscow on 23 August, Claud once again found his personal and political life interweaving: Patricia had just run away with him. 'I felt that now, as a result of the latest turn of events, I might be getting her to jump into a much bigger hole than she could have foreseen a few months before,' he recalled.[12] Der Pakt, under which Hitler and Stalin partitioned Poland and split Eastern Europe into German and Soviet spheres of influence, caused a political, diplomatic and intellectual earthquake. Many were caught by surprise by the accord between the world's greatest ideological enemies, as Realpolitik won out over the genuine hatred between the signatories. The German armed forces – the Wehrmacht – and the Red Army were free to invade Poland, as Stalin gained control of Lithuania, Latvia and Estonia. Hitler avoided the threat of Germany having to fight a war on two fronts, as in 1914–18, and would make war on France, Britain and their allies rather than the USSR. What was to upset Stalin's very reasonable calculations was the speedy and complete victory of Germany over France in 1940, followed by Hitler's overconfident decision to attack the Soviet Union in 1941 before winning the war against Britain.

The pact had a shattering impact on left politics across Europe and America. Communists could no longer present themselves as an iron-willed praetorian guard leading a broad-fronted battle against fascism and in defence of democracy. As Molotov and Ribbentrop shook hands in Moscow, Communists became complicit in a peculiarly ruthless and bloody carve-up of Central and Eastern Europe. Claud says he should not have been entirely surprised that Moscow gave priority to its state interests, since, in May or June, his French Communist friend 'Monsieur Bob' had hinted to him that, if Stalin believed that Britain and France intended to reach a Munich-type deal with Hitler over Poland, he might 'turn the tables on them' by negotiating an agreement with Germany before they did.[13]

Whatever the origins of 'der Pakt', Claud could see that the 'Popular Front' policy, to which he had been dedicated since returning from the US in 1932, was finished. 'However necessary the Pact may have been to the Russians, by signing they had effectively dynamited everywhere all the Popular Fronts, the vague but comforting alliance between Reds and the anti-Nazi Conservatives.' He recognised, nonetheless, that this anti-fascist coalition 'had somehow failed to make the grade' in stopping Hitler, Mussolini and Franco. 'I was, it goes without saying, powerfully and instinctively moved to take that opportunity to break with the Communists there and then and brigade myself with the "Churchillian Tories",' he wrote.

On the other hand, he was unconvinced that Stalin, to escape political and military isolation, had much choice but to make a deal with the Nazis. 'I was dominated by the feeling that I had, of my own free will, joined, so to speak a regiment and I had better soldier along with it, particularly at a moment when it was obviously going to come under pretty heavy fire.'[14] As a socialist, he was very aware of how the European socialist parties in 1914, after proclaiming international solidarity for years, had abruptly reversed course and supported the war aims of their own nationalities. Nor was he persuaded that appeasement was a thing of the past, despite the British and French declaration of war on Germany on 3 September 1939, since this was followed by the so-called Phoney War, a period in which British and French forces were largely passive in Europe, until Hitler attacked westwards in May 1940.

Unsurprisingly, *The Week* was banned for following the anti-war party line in January 1941 and only restarted publishing in September 1942. Retrospectively, Claud understood that by then the situation was 'so entirely different from that which *The Week* had been founded to exploit, and of which it had so successfully taken advantage in the 1930's, [but which] no longer existed – and had not, in fact, existed since, at the latest, the end of the phoney war'.[15]

By the time the ban on *The Week* was lifted, the British Communist leaders wanted to keep it closed, feeling that it was too independent, though widely assumed to be under their control. 'I had a feeling', wrote Claud, irked by this attitude, 'that it might be better to keep my tiny boat in seaworthy condition.'[16]

The most important reason why Claud stuck with the Communists for long after Der Pakt and the end of the Phoney War was probably his abiding hostility to the British government, regardless of whether the prime minister was Chamberlain or Churchill. Patricia, his third wife, wrote at this time that

> its [*The Week*'s] suspicions of those 'on high' were by this time too deeply engrained . . . He [Claud] was unaware that *The Week* was in some respects displaying the same faults that it had so often denounced in others. It was living in the past. It was inclined to confuse slogans with realities. Its former alertness to real shifts in power and direction became notably diminished.[17]

Ironically, the greatest change of which Claud was insufficiently aware was that almost everything that he had campaigned for since fleeing Berlin in 1933 was by the summer of 1941 official British government policy. He had wanted Britain to fight an all-out war against the Nazis and Italian fascists – and this Britain was doing to the limits of its strength. He had advocated a British military alliance with Moscow against Germany, and this too was in place after Hitler invaded the Soviet Union in June 1941.

The Cliveden Set and that pro-appeasement portion of the British ruling class, whom *The Week* had reviled, had either changed their opinions or been reduced to pariah status. The *Times*, so closely associated with appeasement, never wholly regained its pre-appeasement influence and prestige. Churchill's national coalition, combining Tories, Labour and Liberals, was very like the anti-fascist Popular Front government Claud had advocated, though it was the creation of the Churchillian right and excluded the far left. The men of goodwill of all political complexions, whom Claud had nicknamed the 'Dreyfusards', had in fact won without him fully taking the fact on board.

Claud's suspicion of those in authority ran too deep for him to readjust to a British government carrying out policies of which he approved. 'I don't have, I think, the qualities that go to making a "good communist"', Claud later reflected somewhat unnecessarily, 'or a good party man of any denomination.' Yet he was never 'a contrarian', somebody opposing all authority willy nilly. He did accept the necessity of discipline and organisation to resist the powers that be, effectively arguing that without them, opposition became frivolous and ineffectual. This seriousness of purpose had drawn him towards the Communists, beginning in Germany, who 'day after day [were] facing the probability of torture and murder by Goering's young men'.[18] He might not like the party's absolutist tendencies, though he said his own complaint about the Comintern 'was not that it operated with the ruthless and sinister efficiency attributed to it by propagandists and thriller-writers', but that 'for so much of the time it wobbled along in a muddle which was frequently comical, but, at the same time, depressing'.[19]

The political leader whom Claud found most sympathetic in wartime London was General Charles de Gaulle, who, with no assets aside from personal determination, faith in France and high political skills, elevated the Free French into punching far above their weight. At lunch with him in Algiers in 1943, de Gaulle asked Claud why he was a Communist and, having listened attentively to his explanation, commented, 'You don't think your view is somewhat romantic?'

Claud felt that this was the devil rebuking sin, given the general's unwavering devotion to a vision of France with only a distant connection to reality. Claud says he was much influenced by the fact that so far as the Resistance in France was concerned, the Communists were still 'the toughest, supplest muscles in the movement'.[20] He could see, however, that once in power these virtues counted for little. When he and Patricia visited war-battered Eastern Europe in November 1945, they saw 'the chaos of Rumania, the comparative stagnation of Bulgaria, and above all, the arid desert of East Germany'.

Afterword:
Guerrilla Journalist

Claud at *Private Eye* office in the 1960s with Peter Cook behind him, Richard Ingrams on left and John Wells on right [author]

The escalating crises of the 1930s provided an ideal political terrain for Claud's kind of dissident or guerrilla journalism. The rise of the Nazis and the Great Depression were earth-shaking events. Reporting by the traditional media was often ignorant and partisan, creating a pool of politically engaged people eager for well-informed news from an alternative source. Bitter divisions at all levels of state and society ensured that, given sufficient journalistic skill and persistence, the government's near-monopoly control of information could be undermined.

The 1940s were the exact opposite of this, with the British and American governments fighting an all-out war against the Nazis in alliance with the Soviet Union. The Great Depression was finally in retreat, and serious social reforms were underway. Total scepticism about the motives and actions of governments was no longer justified on an almost-daily basis by their misdeeds. As the Second World War proceeded and was followed by the Cold War, people chose sides, and any opposition to the political status quo was interpreted as support for the enemy.

It took Claud a surprisingly long time fully to take on board this transformation of the political landscape, and only in retrospect did he see that he should have closed down *The Week* in 1940, when Neville Chamberlain was replaced by Winston Churchill as prime minister. As total war engulfed Europe – and especially after Hitler invaded the Soviet Union in 1941 – Claud felt he was no longer effective as a journalist, since relations were suddenly so 'cosy' between the British government and left-wing radicals like himself at a time when 'everything was rushing in the right direction'.[1] He did not become disillusioned with the Communists, because he never had many illusions about any political organisation, but he did think they were less and less effective as a vehicle for harrying the government. He found himself in sympathy with de Gaulle and the Free French in London. By the time he travelled to San Francisco for the founding of the United Nations in 1945, he was considering a radical change in his political and personal direction, a feeling he compared to his father's abrupt departure from the Far East and the Foreign Office forty years earlier 'to start leading an entirely different sort of life'.[2]

This determination was brought about not primarily by any change in his views but by a recognition that the type of journalism which he had pioneered was no longer feasible. He had no choice but to shift from news-driven investigative reporting, which had been at the heart of *The Week*'s success, to humorous and satirical writing which was far less polemical and politically engaged. He had previously written books, but only at speed in order to fund his travels, as when he left America in 1932, or for immediate political impact during the Spanish Civil War in 1936. But now he was to start to write fiction, history and his own memoirs. He remained absorbed by politics, but his priority in the future was to provide for his wife and children, in sharp contrast to his life in the 1920s and '30s, when he had passed smoothly from one intense relationship to another. But he was to stay with his third wife, Patricia, for over forty years, until his death in 1981.

This account of Claud's life focuses on how he, an individual journalist without money, battled powerful forces whom he saw as irremediably evil. This fight took place largely in the 1930s, which has been called 'The Devil's Decade', even if the era was not unique in history as a period of multiple crises. Though Claud's way of life and work was to change radically from the late 1940s, he retained two core beliefs. The first was scepticism, to the point of unalloyed cynicism, about the doings of all in authority, high and low. But, secondly, he also believed that decision makers were weaker, more incompetent, more divided, more self-destructively corrupt than they liked people to understand and hence more vulnerable to journalistic attack and exposure. He recognised, realistically, that this level of state vulnerability went up and down. However, it was probably at its highest in the 1930s, the radical decades of the 1960s and '70s, and now again during the deepening turmoil of the 2020s.

Some saw Claud's one-man crusade as romantic knight-errantry on behalf of the poor and needy, but he had very practical ideas about how information wars might be fought and won by the weaker party. At the same time, he did not think this could be done without the underdogs choosing their weapons with professional care and intelligence. Once, he had seen the Communists as providing him with such a weapon with which to resist Nazism abroad and authoritarianism at home. Malcolm Muggeridge, editor of *Punch* magazine, who was to become a close and perceptive friend in the 1950s, understood a certain practicality in Claud's nature. 'No God failed him because Communism never assumed a God-like shape in his eyes,' he wrote. 'He supported it as a cause wholeheartedly and with characteristic verve; and when it ceased to appeal to him as a cause, he ceased to support it. That was all.' Another friend, Maurice Richardson, pointed to another trait in Claud's character, referring to him as 'the Chevalier' because he delighted to fight against the mighty whatever the odds, though this missed out the fact that he had thought profoundly about how these odds might be evened up.[3] Both Muggeridge and Richardson failed to see, however, a strain of ruthless determination in Claud's personality, the product of the formative years he spent among the defeated nations of post–First World War Central Europe.

When Claud did finally decide that the time had come to transform his way of life, he changed virtually every aspect of it. He had considered moving to Mexico as a place of retreat, as had several of his Central European friends, such as Egon Erwin Kisch and Otto Katz. But he and Patricia decided that it made more sense to move to Ireland, where she had grown up and was still the home of part of her family. In 1947, they moved from London to the town of Youghal, in East County Cork. By now, they had two children: Alexander, born in 1941, and Andrew, born at the beginning of the year of their move. The geographical distance travelled by the family might not be great, but the political and social distance between mid-twentieth-century London and rural Ireland, where life was closer to the mid-nineteenth century, was vast. It was also relatively cheap compared to England. In October 1948, they took a fourteen-year lease, at a cost of £265 a year, on Brook Lodge, which was to be their home for the next thirty years.[4]

It took time for MI5, Fleet Street, the Communist Party, and Claud's more distant relatives to realise that his residence in Ireland was going to be permanent. He did not intend his departure from the party to be interpreted as a Pauline conversion to the virtues of Western capitalism and imperialism. It was only in 1949 that the *Daily Express* rang up Harry Pollitt, general secretary of the British Communist Party, to ask if Claud was still a party member. A worried Pollitt subsequently had a comic conversation with another party leader called Johnnie Campbell, which was recorded by MI5:

> Harry says his fear is the Catholic business.
>
> Johnnie says he has not much fear on that. 'She' [Patricia] is a member of the Protestant Ascendancy, The old Protestant . . . Ireland families. For them to go Catholic is almost as bad as a South American Senator marrying a negress. Harry says oh! He says they will keep their fingers crossed.[5]

A journalist from the William Hickey gossip column on the *Daily Express* ran Claud to earth at Brook Lodge, the tumbledown house he and Patricia had rented, and asked him if he had left the party. 'I have absolutely no statement to make,' Claud replied. 'I consider the question impertinent.' The *Express* journalist described Claud bicycling into Youghal, a mile away, where 'he drops into the Royal Bar for an Irish whiskey. Then he pedals home, head down against wind. Against rain. And against the party line?'[6] A few months later, Special Branch reported informants told them that 'Cockburn had profound disagreements with the Communist Party. Curiously they are alleged to be principally over the question of Lysenko [the fraudulent biologist supported by Stalin].'[7] A first cousin of Claud's called George Cruikshank wrote to the security services from Singapore with an intriguing explanation of Claud's apparent change in ideological direction: 'Family rumour has it that he has joined or is about to join the Catholic Church. If this is true, I think it most unlikely that the conversion it [sic] is a faked conversion. He was very seriously ill about three years ago, when he was also shaken by his mother's death.'[8] George was correct about his illness, but Claud had never been close to his mother, who died in 1947.

Finally, MI5 sent a real defector, Douglas Hyde, to Ireland. He spoke to the parish priest in Youghal, 'who informed him that Cockburn showed no signs of conversion to Roman Catholicism. Hyde's own view is that Cockburn may have severed his connections with the Party without necessarily ceasing to be a

Communist.'⁹ This was not so far off the mark, since Claud's politics remained as radical as ever.

Claud's immediate preoccupations, however, were practical rather than ideological. He had to relearn non-polemical journalism designed to amuse or otherwise attract the attention of editors and readers. Equally important, he had to find a publication that would print and pay for what he wrote. His name and professional abilities might be known, but they reeked of subversion and revolution. Eventually, he found a niche in a magazine called *Lilliput*, edited by Richard Bennett, who was unworried by Claud's political associations. MI5 clipped his first articles in *Lilliput*, noting that they were a humorous account of his long-distance contact with Lord Louis Mountbatten during the abdication crisis in 1936. They wondered if it was a sign that Claud was distancing himself from radical politics.

During the Cold War, British and American editors and proprietors were edgy about publishing any criticism of the political and social status quo. Before the Second World War, Claud had both produced *The Week* and worked for *Fortune*, the American business magazine, which was owned by the right-wing media mogul Henry Luce. But now, in the era of McCarthyism, this was no longer possible, and Claud had to conceal his identity behind a bewildering array of pseudonyms. Freelance journalists do not make much money at the best of times, but Claud's near pariah status made the task of earning a living particularly complicated.

He was aware that one simple way to rehabilitate himself swiftly in the eyes of mainstream publishers was to denounce his former comrades. This would necessarily have involved writing 'the familiar 50,000 words entitled "My fifteen years in a Snakepit" which would certainly shake the [financial] coconut trees, but otherwise be undesirable'.¹⁰ The alternative was to produce a stream of articles, books and scripts that would eventually find a publisher because they were funny and original.

Claud later wrote sardonically about how a visitor to Brook Lodge had described discovering an entire literary colony at work there:

He claimed to have met Frank Pitcairn, ex-correspondent of the *Daily Worker* – a grouchy, disillusioned type secretly itching to dash out and describe a barricade. There was Claud Cockburn, founder and editor of *The Week*, talkative, boastful of past achievements, and apt, at the drop of a hat, to tell, at length, the inside story of some forgotten diplomatic crisis of the 1930's. Patrick Cork would look in – a brash little number and something of a professional Irishman, seeking no doubt to live up to his name. James Helvick lived in and on the establishment, claiming that he needed good food and drink to enable him to finish a play and a novel which soon would bring [in] enough money to repay all costs. In the background, despised by the others as a mere commercial hack, Kenneth Drew hammered away at the articles which supplied the necessities of the colony's life.[11]

Disappointments were frequent, such as a play that long hung fire, but there were successes, such as his novel *Beat the Devil*, rights to which he sold for £5,000 to John Huston and Humphrey Bogart, whose film appeared in 1953 and subsequently achieved cult status. But with McCarthyism ascendant in the US, this had to be published under the name of James Helvick, so its success did not lead to a flood of other commissions. When the first volume of his autobiography, *In Time of Trouble*, became a bestseller in the UK three years later, he noticed that his publisher, Rupert Hart-Davis, was disconcerted rather than pleased by the success of a memoir by a former Communist unapologetic about his past. Twice during the early 1950s, Claud played a leading role in the planning for new newspapers that were supposedly going to shake up the dead-in-the-water world of British journalism, only for the proprietors to lose their nerve and abandon the projects at the last minute.

More satisfactory employment came from an unexpected quarter when the novelist Anthony Powell, a friend from Oxford and now literary editor of *Punch*, commissioned Claud to write for the magazine. Expecting requests to tone down his contributions to this venerable publication, whose gentle humour had long been geared to offending nobody, he was surprised when

Powell asked him to be 'somewhat astringent'.[12] The change of tack was explained when he met *Punch*'s new editor, Malcolm Muggeridge, appointed in 1952 to shake up the publication and arrest falling circulation.

A fierce anti-Communist since he had briefly worked as a correspondent for the *Guardian* in Moscow in the early 1930s, Muggeridge was vociferously anti-establishment and shared Claud's amused scepticism about all received wisdom and suspicion of almost all political and cultural icons. 'Malcolm was a cynic who got great fun out of it,' wrote the historian A. J. P. Taylor, a description that might equally be applied to Claud.[13] Others criticised Muggeridge for zigzagging between passionately held beliefs during the course of his life, but to Claud this was, on the contrary, a sign of intellectual vigour and receptivity to new ideas and situations. Claud expressed instant enthusiasm about the atmosphere in the *Punch* office in Bouverie Street, off Fleet Street: 'You felt some life crackling behind the desk, as though somebody, for a joke, had thrown a firecracker into a mausoleum.'[14]

As with *The Week* twenty years earlier, the shameless self-censorship of the British media on significant issues created great opportunities for any editor who dared risk pariah status by doing so. In the early fifties, the press had maintained a respectful silence about the growing senility of Winston Churchill, the seventy-nine-year-old prime minister, who had suffered an undisclosed stroke. Uproar followed when in 1954, *Punch* published a cartoon showing Churchill at his desk, slack jawed and eyes vacant, accompanied by a satiric piece by Muggeridge on the great Byzantine general Belisarius in his dotage. When Claud wrote 'a modest proposal' to exterminate the English, parodying arguments used by those supporting the use of myxomatosis – an exceptionally cruel virus being employed to exterminate rabbits – readers took this literally, as demonic advocacy for mass murder. Two collections of Claud's *Punch* articles, one of them with an introduction by Muggeridge, called 'Nine Bald Men' – invoking a mysterious Chinese proverb: 'Of nine bald men, eight are deceitful and the ninth is dumb.'[15]

No sooner had Claud's professional career reached calmer and reasonably profitable waters than he and his family were hit by two devastating health disasters, one after the other. Claud and Patricia viewed rural County Cork as a safe haven politically, but this was not true of personal health. Inured as they were to downplaying dangers that would have intimidated others, they returned to Brook Lodge from London during a polio epidemic that was raging in Cork city in the summer of 1956. It is at this point that I begin to have vivid memories of what happened next. My parents felt that deep in the Irish countryside, our family would be safe. I, then six years old, caught the virus, nearly died in hospital and was left with a severe limp. Overconfident as Claud and Patricia may have been about the chances of avoiding the virus, they certainly saved my life by taking me out of hospital, against the doctors' advice, as I was fading away. Claud wrote movingly and perceptively about the grim experience, writing that Patrick, 'who had been so gay, so alert, inquisitive, talkative, was sinking into a sort of voiceless apathy ... There came a week when throughout our visit he never raised his voice above a whisper, and much of the time lay in total silence on his bed.'[16]

I had not been the only member of the family to contract the illness. My brother Andrew, who was three years older than me, had gone back to school in Dublin, from which he was hurriedly sent home by the headmaster. Claud met him at Cork railway station. 'I really thought', he wrote, 'all might be well up to the very the last moment when the diesel train pulled into the station and Andrew got out. I then saw that his body was bowed slightly forward in an awkward way and that he was moving his legs sluggishly.'[17] In a few months, Andrew recovered entirely, while I graduated from a wheelchair to crutches, which I discarded after three or four years.[18]

It was while I was walking with a crutch under each arm in the winter of 1957 that Claud – who had seldom been ill in his life for more than two or three days, despite smoking two or three packets of Woodbine cigarettes a day and heavy consumption of Irish whiskey – began to feel exhausted after only a short walk. We had gone to a Christmas house party in the Wicklow mountains when he felt his energy draining away after even a short walks with me to a mountain lake less than a mile away.

Diagnosed with advanced tuberculosis, he was sent to a sanatorium on the outskirts of Cork city, where he stayed for ten months. Claud survived, though at one moment the TB bacterium showed signs of being reinforced by lung cancer, but he never fully recovered his health. Nevertheless, he lived another productive twenty years longer, outlasting several doctors who had predicted his imminent demise. He continued to pour out columns and articles for newspapers and magazines, though not for *Punch*, after Muggeridge's repeated refusal to stay within boundaries acceptable to the proprietors' led to his sacking. Muggeridge soon got into deeper trouble when he wrote an article in the *Saturday Evening Post* magazine in the US about 'the Royal Soap Opera', which was primarily a contemptuous critique of the hysterical fervour of the British media's quasi-religious adulation of the monarchy. Savagely denounced by the *Daily Express* and the *People*, Muggeridge received quantities of hate mail, including some rejoicing in the death of his son in a skiing accident. Claud was generally dismissive of criticism of himself and his writings, or even being spat at in public. 'I can write. They can spit,' he wrote. 'Let us see which is more effective.'[19] Nevertheless, the hysterical abuse of Muggeridge, very much Claud's best friend, soured him further with aspects of English life.

After Muggeridge departed from *Punch*, Claud saw that his type of writing was soon going to be out of keeping with the magazine as it reverted to its traditional harmlessness. The venom with which Muggeridge had been pursued made Claud feel even less at home in England. He wrote a column for the *Sunday Telegraph*, whose editor, Donald McLachlan, was seeking to broaden its appeal beyond the Tory faithful. A little later, he started writing a weekly column for the *Irish Times*, which suited him well because the paper in this period almost invariably took a more original and less sceptical view than did the British press on goings-on across the Irish Sea and in the world in general.

Fortunately for Claud, it soon became clear that *Punch* had got rid of Muggeridge and turned away from sharp-edged anti-establishment writing at the very moment that such sharp critiques were emerging as the wave of the future. Defanged by proprietorial decree, the magazine went into lengthy but terminal decline. From about 1960 on, the cultural mood was being set on stage by *Beyond the Fringe*, on television by *That Was the Week That Was*, and in the print press by *Private Eye*. Claud and Muggeridge had discussed starting an independent magazine freed from the prejudices of owners and advertising departments. 'Then the Eye came along in answer to their prayers,' explained Richard Ingrams, who was to edit it for many years. 'Claud and Malcolm subsequently acted as Godfathers to the fledgling organ.'[20] Ingrams knew about Claud through Sefton Delmer, the *Daily Express* journalist who had travelled with Claud through eastern Czechoslovakia at the time of the Munich Agreement in 1938. As a very young man, Ingrams had said to Delmer that journalists seldom wrote good memoirs; Delme, by way of contradiction, had handed him a copy of *In Time of Trouble*.

Claud guest-edited a special issue of *Private Eye* in August 1963 at the height of the Profumo scandal, which appeared to reveal sex and espionage at the top of the British establishment in a way that showed the whole system to be rotten to the core. Conscious of being a generation older than the circle revolving around *Private Eye*, notably Ingrams and Peter Cook, he thought of turning down the job. But, having accepted it, he found that the formula that had worked for *The Week* thirty years earlier still worked. 'I had for long battered away at the point that a satirical paper cannot justify its existence by only satirizing what is already known,' he wrote. 'It must disclose news, too.'[21] The issue contained many scoops, one of which was simply to publish the name of the head of MI6, Sir Dick White, already known to at least some in Fleet Street but not to the public at large. The revelation appeared in a small paragraph under his own name, marked 'Note to Foreign Agents', saying that Sir Dick was chief of 'what you romantically term the British Secret Service'. Claud was soon afterwards told by a source that the disclosure was causing uproar in Whitehall, and he was urged to return promptly to Ireland to avoid official retribution. When the cabinet papers of the time were published in 2000, it

was clear that Claud's source had been correct about govern-
mental outrage. Sir Burke Trend, the cabinet secretary, had
summoned a top-level meeting to decide what to do. It had
regretfully decided that it would be unwise to arrest Claud
because he certainly would not reveal the identity of his informant. In addition, Sir Dick's job might be a state secret but was
known to an inner circle of journalists. In a splendid piece of
elusive mandarin-speak, which Claud would have enjoyed, Sir
Burke wrote that 'it is not so much a matter of concealing as
withholding the truth and what is withheld is not so much the
truth as the facts.'[22]

Claud's life after he moved to Ireland had many successes and
achievements, but this book – part biography, part description
of opposition journalism in action – concentrates on the first
half of Claud's career up to 1940, a period of savage conflict. It
was then that he put into practice his ideas about how the weak
might best combat the strong in the information wars. He took
it for granted that these wars were never ending, both within
and between nations. Anybody who pretended differently was
misleading the public. The journalistic tactics he developed in
the 1930s worked equally well in the 1960s and '70s. They are
even more relevant in the 2020s, a period which is shaping up
to be a new 'devil's decade' as fresh crises explode every few
months and, at the time of writing, wars rage in Ukraine and
Gaza. The political landscape is not dissimilar from that ninety
years ago, as once again societies begin to shake or disintegrate
because of cumulative stresses. A partisan mass media is selec-
tive and propagandistic in what news it reports, while political
establishments are dysfunctional and riven by divisions. In many
countries, populist, undemocratic parties are in power (or getting close to it) from Washington to Buenos Aires, and Rome
to Delhi.

Claud relied on the humble mimeograph to spread his dissident news and views to a few thousand politically active
people. The internet provides an infinitely larger platform for
opposition through online publications, blogs, podcasts, Substacks, and the like. Government control of the news agenda,
though it remains stronger than the public imagine, is reduced

from what it once was. A dissident podcast can now command an audience of hundreds of thousands, or even millions. Yet big media has also vastly expanded its reach, and small, piratical purveyors of information are still far outgunned by the giant battleships of the news business.

Yet media platforms, big and small, are not the only weapons of those who seek to break the media monopoly of the powerful and wealthy. Personal courage and resolution count for much, as do a willingness to endure poverty and danger. Claud believed that professional journalistic skills of a high order were essential if journalistic guerrilla warfare, of which he was an arch-exponent, was to be fought with any chance of victory. He disbelieved strongly in the axiom about 'telling truth to power', knowing that the rulers of the earth have no wish to hear any such thing. Much more effective, he believed, is to tell truth to *the powerless* so they have a fighting chance in any struggle against the big battalions.

Notes

Preface: 'A Maquis of His Own Devising'

1. Claud Cockburn, *I, Claud: The Autobiography of Claud Cockburn*, Penguin, 1967, p. 141.
2. Malcolm Muggeridge, *Tread Softly Because You Tread on My Jokes*, Collins, 1966, p. 282.
3. Claud Cockburn, *Discord of Trumpets: An Autobiography*, Simon & Schuster, 1958, pp. 190–1.
4. Ibid., p. 204.
5. Cockburn, *I, Claud*, p. 17.

1. 'This Small Monstrosity'

1. Claud Cockburn to Geoffrey Dawson, n.d. (ca. November 1931), TNL Archive TT/ED/GGD/1, Claud Cockburn file.
2. Geoffrey Dawson to Claud Cockburn, 15 November 1931, TNL Archive TT/ED/GGD/1, Claud Cockburn file.
3. Claud Cockburn, *A Discord of Trumpets: An Autobiography*, Simon & Schuster, 1958, pp. 209–13.
4. Ibid., pp. 230–1.
5. Claud Cockburn, letters (excerpts describing Claud's voyage back to Europe and his impressions of Vienna and Berlin), Hope Hale Davis Papers, Schlesinger Library, Harvard Radcliffe Institute, MC 533 2.14.
6. Cockburn, *Discord of Trumpets*, p. 93.

7. Hope Hale Davis Papers MC 533 2.14, letter sent by Claud to Davis from Berlin, n.d., ca. late 1932.

8. Cockburn, *Discord of Trumpets*, p. 233.

9. Ibid.

10. Correlli Barnet, *The Collapse of British Power*, Sutton, 1972, p. 389; Ian Gilmour, review of *The Cliveden Set: Portrait of an Exclusive Fraternity* by Norman Rose, *London Review of Books*, 19 October 2000.

11. *New York Times*, 31 January 1933.

12. [Claud Cockburn] Anon., *High Low Washington*, J. B. Littincott, 1932, pp. 168–212.

13. Cockburn, *Discord of Trumpets*, pp. 236–40.

14. Ibid., p. 244.

15. Claud Cockburn, *In Time of Trouble: An Autobiography*, Rupert Hart-Davis, 1956, p. 210.

16. MI5 to the Foreign Office, 5 November 1933, National Archives, KV2/546.

17. *The Week*, 8 June 1933.

18. Ibid.

19. 'London Economic Conference of 1933,' Encyclopedia.com.

20. [Cockburn], *High Low Washington*, pp. 203–6. Claud describes how the big radio companies were provoked by Schuette into unwisely attacking him and thereby gave him free publicity and the opportunity to counterattack them.

21. Cockburn, *I, Claud*, p. 139.

22. I requested MI5 to release the files on Claud Cockburn a year earlier, but I received no direct reply and am not certain whether or not this led them to be placed in the National Archives.

23. Report from 'casual' agent, 23 October 1933, National Archives, KV2/546.

24. Military Intelligence communication, 10 April 1924, National Archives, KV2/546.

25. AOH to Commander Bardwell NID, 18 January 1934, National Archives, KV2/546.

26. Claud Cockburn File, 18 January 1942, National Archives, KV2/546.

27. P Colonel Sir Vernon Kell to Major N. G. Hind, MC, 19 June 1934, National Archives, KV2/546.

28. Mr Wright of the Foreign Office, 20 July 1933, KV2/546.

29. Hope Hale Davis, 'Miss Sally Bowles, Claud Cockburn and Others', Hope Hale Davis Papers, Schlesinger Library, Harvard Radcliffe Institute, MC 533 2.14. This is an unpublished manuscript submitted to the magazine *Grand Street* in 1989, based on her contemporary journals and letters.
30. Hope Hale Davis, *Great Day Coming: A Memoir of the 1930s*, Steerforth Press, 1994, p. 2.
31. Ibid., p. 20.
32. Ibid., p. 2.
33. Patricia Cockburn, *The Years of The Week*, Penguin, 1971, p. 228.
34. Cockburn, *Discord of Trumpets*, p. 236.
35. Cockburn, *Years of The Week*, p. 85.

2. The Limits of Diplomacy

1. Susanna Hoe, *Women in the Siege of Peking, 1900*, Holo Books, 2000, pp. 160–2. The guest quoted was Deaconess Jessie Ransome.
2. Claud Cockburn, private conversation with the author.
3. Henry Cockburn letter book, 1896–1905, in the author's possession. These are mostly to brother Frank and his mother. His official dispatches are much more interesting.
4. Hoe, *Siege of Peking*, p. 31, quoting a letter from Lady Claude MacDonald.
5. Claud Cockburn, *I, Claud: The Autobiography of Claud Cockburn*, Penguin, 1967, p. 26.
6. This was Claud's longest stay in Scotland, though he always expressed great affection for the country. Out of respect for Scottish education, he sent his three sons – Alexander, Andrew and myself – to Trinity College, Glenalmond, in Perthshire.
7. For details of the complicated set of events that ended Henry's diplomatic career, see Chin Sok-Chong, *The Korean Problem in Anglo-Japanese Relations, 1904–1910*, Nanam Publications, 1987. This is the only study drawing on British, Japanese and Korean documents. See also Patrick Cockburn, 'A Prehistory of Extraordinary Rendition', *London Review of Books*, 13 September 2012; Patrick Cockburn, 'Henry's War: One Man's War

Against Rendition,' *Independent*, 6 December 2007.

8. For an acute account of the uprising in Korea, see Henry Cockburn to Sir Edward Grey, Annual Report for 1907, National Archives KV 371/238.

9. Chong, *Korean Problem*, p. 187, indirectly quoting from a letter dated 5 June 1907.

10. Henry Cockburn to Edward Grey, 7 May 1908, National Archives KV 371/238.

11. Henry Cockburn to Edward Grey 27 July 1908, National Archives KV 371/238.

12. Henry Cockburn to Edward Grey, 18 August 1908, National Archives KV 371/238; Chong, *Korean Problem*, p. 281. A consular official and two doctors sent subsequently by Henry to further examine Yang found that he was suffering from carbon-monoxide poisoning as a result of being confined in a small room with nineteen other prisoners.

13. Henry Cockburn to Edward Grey, 3 August 1908, National Archives KV 371/238.

14. Cockburn to Grey, 18 August 1908. The Japanese official may not have been so wrong in that Henry shows increasing animus towards the Japanese officials he dealt with, or on occasion refused to deal with, in Seoul.

15. Chong, *Korean Problem*, p. 289.

16. Henry Cockburn to Sir Claude Macdonald, 20 September 1908, National Archives KV 371/238.

17. Henry Cockburn to Sir Claude Macdonald, 3 August 1908, National Archives KV 371/238.

18. Sir Claude Macdonald to Henry Cockburn, 20 September 1908, National Archives KV 371/238.

19. Henry Cockburn to Edward Grey, 12 July 1909, Archives KV 371/238.

20. Patricia Cockburn as related to Janet Montefiore.

21. Cockburn, *I, Claud*, p. 29.

22. William J. Oudendyk, *Ways and By-ways in Diplomacy*, Peter Davies, 1936, pp. 34–5.

23. Ibid.

24. Claud Cockburn, *In Time of Trouble: An Autobiography*, Rupert Hart-Davis, 1956, pp. 1–2.

25. Claud Cockburn, *A Discord of Trumpets: An Autobiography*,

Simon & Schuster, 1958, p. 21.

26. Cockburn, *In Time of Trouble*, pp. 35–6. Henry may have yearned to live in China, but not to use his expertise as 'a China expert' in any new job. Claud says that he turned down an offer for him to act as a paid consultant on Chinese affairs because 'it was too much like a continuation of his former work'.

3. 'First Experiences in Revolution'

1. Lesley Koulouris (Berkhamsted School archivist), letter citing school records, 24 May 2021.
2. Claud Cockburn, *A Discord of Trumpets: An Autobiography*, Simon & Schuster, 1958, p. 33.
3. Claud Cockburn, *I, Claud: The Autobiography of Claud Cockburn*, Penguin, 1967, p. 31.
4. William J. Oudendyk, *Ways and By-ways in Diplomacy*, Peter Davies, 1936. The Dutch diplomat Sir William Oudendyk ran into Henry in the street by the Aldwych in London during the First World War, and Henry told him that he was working in censorship.
5. Cockburn, *Discord of Trumpets*, p. 34.
6. Ibid., p. 39.
7. Norman Sherry, *The Life of Graham Greene: Volume 1: 1904–1939*, Jonathan Cape, 1989, p. 43. Charles Greene is described by Ben Greene, a cousin of Graham, as being 'bewildered by sex. He just didn't understand it.'
8. Koulouris, school records.
9. Cockburn, *Discord of Trumpets*, p. 40.
10. Ibid., p. 41.
11. Ibid. I used to play him in the 1950s when I was convalescing during my recovery from polio and found him a strong player.
12. Ibid., p. 42.
13. Sherry, *Graham Greene*, p. 60. Claud gave a lengthy and detailed interview to Sherry about Berkhamsted School and the Greene family on 18 June 1977.
14. Ibid., pp. 57–8.
15. Ibid., pp. 59–60.

16. Ibid.
17. Ibid., pp. 60–2. In his autobiography *In Time of Trouble* (Rupert Hart-Davis, 1956), pp. 44–5, Claud somewhat misremembered the riot, saying that it took place some months after the Armistice, when the soldiers stationed in and around Berkhamsted were becoming 'drunker and drunker, and once rioted, breaking into the school itself and threatening to throw the headmaster into the canal'. The probable explanation for Claud's reticence is that he was not comfortable with his role in harassing Charles Greene, whom he deeply admired in the company of soldiers who believed, though mistakenly, that Greene was opposed to the war.
18. Ibid., p. 61.
19. Certificate in possession of the author.
20. Berkhamsted School Report, 21 December 1920.
21. *Illiterary Magazine* 'mid-October 1919' is one of the few possessions dating from Claud's schooldays that he retained, or possibly somebody sent him in later life.
22. *World Press News*, 26 September 1935.
23. Graham Greene, *A Sort of Life*, Vintage, 1971, pp. 82–3.
24. Cockburn, *In Time of Trouble*, p. 46.
25. Ibid., p. 57.
26. Communication from Peter Monteith, archivist and record manager, Keble College, Oxford, 14 July 2021.
27. Cockburn, *In Time of Trouble*, p. 58. The Keble College register gives the date of Claud joining the college as 13 October 1922.

4. 'Budapest Rather Than Berkhamstead'

1. Evelyn Waugh, *A Little Learning*, Penguin, 1990.
2. Ibid., pp. 284–6. Waugh's letters and diaries showed that he and Claud were constantly in each other's company over the five years spanning 1922–27.
3. Claud Cockburn Remembers, Fintan O'Toole, *In Dublin*, June–July 1981.
4. By the time Claud came to write his autobiography *In Time of Trouble* in 1956, he had become impatient with this attitude. He describes himself depicting to an aunt 'the realities of Hungary'

compared to the 'artificiality of Oxford'. 'I did it badly, because I did not in the fullest sense of the term know what I was talking about.' Claud Cockburn, *In Time of Trouble: An Autobiography*, Rupert Hart-Davis, 1956, p. 63.

5. Obituary of Henry Cockburn, *Times*, 2 April 1927, p. 17.

6. Cockburn, *In Time of Trouble*, pp. 46–7.

7. *Guardian*, 4 June 2020. Such was the traumatic impact of the Treaty of Trianon that its hundredth anniversary was commemorated as a day of national mourning.

8. Claud Cockburn, *A Discord of Trumpets: An Autobiography*, Simon & Schuster, 1958, p. 46.

9. Cockburn, *In Time of Trouble*, p. 48.

10. Cockburn, *Discord of Trumpets*, p. 46.

11. Ibid., p. 66.

12. Cockburn, *In Time of Trouble*, p. 52.

13. Ibid., p. 52.

14. Ibid., pp. 59–60.

15. Ibid., p. 52.

16. Cockburn, *Discord of Trumpets* pp. 52–3.

17. Claud Cockburn, *Evelyn Waugh's Ear Trumpet*, reprinted in *Counterpunch*, 23 April 2003.

18. Waugh, *A Little Learning*, pp. 284–5.

19. Cockburn, *Discord of Trumpets*, p. 63.

20. Claud told this to Janet Montefiore in 1977.

21. Cockburn, *Discord of Trumpets*, pp. 64–5.

22. Waugh, *A Little Learning*, p. 239.

23. Graham Greene, *A Sort of Life*, Vintage, 1971, p. 94.

24. This network of Oxford friends was largely to stay with him for the rest of his life. One lent him forty pounds to start *The Week*, while doing so he stayed with another, in the 1950s Anthony Powell as the newly appointed literary editor of *Punch* immediately commissioned him to write articles and introduced him to Malcolm Muggeridge, the editor, who became his closest friend.

25. Claud Cockburn, *I, Claud: The Autobiography of Claud Cockburn*, Penguin, 1967, p. 61.

26. Waugh, *A Little Learning*, p. 271.

27. Greene, *A Sort of Life*, p. 108.

28. Norman Sherry, *The Life of Graham Greene: Volume 1: 1909–*

1939, Jonathan Cape, 1989, p. 130.

29. Claud Cockburn Remembers, Fintan O'Toole, *In Dublin*, June–July 1981.

30. Waugh, *A Little Learning*, p. 260.

31. Ibid., p. 106.

32. Shelly, *Graham Greene*, p. 734, citing an interview with Raymond Greene, Graham's elder brother.

33. Graham Greene, foreword to Claud Cockburn, *Cockburn Sums Up: An Autobiography*, Quartet Books, 1980.

34. Graham Greene, review of *The Years of The Week* by Patricia Cockburn, *New Statesman*, 31 May 1968.

5. 'A Damned Odd Sort of Englishman'

1. Military Intelligence, National Archives, KV2/546, 10 April 1924.

2. Graham Greene, *A Sort of Life*, Vintage, 1971, pp. 110–16.

3. For a detailed account of Graham and Claud's trip to the Ruhr, see the chapter entitled 'The Art of Spying' in Norman Sherry, *The Life of Graham Greene: Volume 1: 1909–1939*, Jonathan Cape, 1989, pp. 132–40. This includes an interview with Claud about the trip dated 18 June 1977 and another interview with Edward 'Tooter' Greene dated 19 December 1976.

4. Ibid., p. 137.

5. Military Intelligence, National Archives, KV2/546, 10 April 1924.

6. Greene, *A Sort of Life*, p. 112. Graham quotes the letter to his mother, though the letter itself omits the detail about the patriotic German woman dancer being naked.

7. Sherry, *Graham Greene*, p. 138, citing interview with Claud on 18 June 1977.

8. *Oxford Chronicle*, 9 May 1924.

9. Claud Cockburn, *A Discord of Trumpets: An Autobiography*, Simon & Schuster, 1958, p. 66.

10. Ibid., p. 67.

11. Ibid., p. 68.

12. Ibid., p. 66.

13. Ibid., p. 68.

14. Ibid., p. 67.
15. Keble College Register of scholars, exhibitioners and undergraduates, p. 349.
16. Cockburn, *Discord of Trumpets*, p. 69.
17. Michael Davie, ed., *Diaries of Evelyn Waugh 1911–65*, Penguin, 1979, p. 271.
18. Cockburn, *Discord of Trumpets*, p. 78.
19. W. H. Auden, *Forewords and After Words*, Faber & Faber, 1972, pp. 492–524.
20. Keble Archives, deposited personal papers: material relating to Claud Cockburn.
21. Claud Cockburn, *I, Claud: The Autobiography of Claud Cockburn*, Penguin, 1967, p. 48.
22. Claud Cockburn, *Cockburn Sums Up: An Autobiography*, Quartet Books, 1980, p. 32.
23. Davie, *Diaries of Evelyn Waugh*, pp. 283–4.

6. 'Of Course, You Will Write for the Paper'

1. Claud Cockburn, *A Discord of Trumpets: An Autobiography*, Simon & Schuster, 1958, p. 101.
2. F. McDonough, 'The Times, Norman Ebbut and the Nazis 1927–37, *Journal of Contemporary History* 27, no. 3 (July 1992), pp. 4–7n424.
3. Claud Cockburn, *In Time of Trouble: An Autobiography*, Rupert Hart-Davis, 1956, p. 9.
4. Ibid., p. 100.
5. Captain Liddell of MI5 to V,V, National Archives KV/1548, 28 October 1935.
6. A sign that Ebbutt was correct in his understanding that the *Times* would be quick to forget that it had initially vetoed Claud writing for them once he had made his mark is confirmed by a short potted biography of him in the official history of the *Times*, which says that he was their correspondent in Berlin in 1927 and in Paris in 1928, though he only officially joined the paper in 1929.
7. Cockburn, *Discord of Trumpets*, p. 105.

8. *Times*, 27 May 1927.
9. Cockburn, *Discord of Trumpets*, p. 111; Norman Ebbutt to Ralph Deakin, 9 June 1933 (praising Claud's contribution in covering the transatlantic flyers story), TNL Archive, Deakin Papers. 'It does not seem to me to be quite clearly recognised how much we owe to Cockburn's keenness and how little reason there is to fear that we shall fall under any financial obligation to him.'
10. Cockburn, *Discord of Trumpets*, p. 128.
11. *World Press News*, 26 September 1935. There are no other references to a stolen car.
12. *Times*, 11 July 1927.
13. Cockburn, *Discord of Trumpets*, p. 128.
14. Scoops that cause rejoicing in newsrooms are often unnoticed by the public, who do not necessarily notice datelines or the superior coverage of one news source compared to others.
15. Ralph Deakin to Claud Cockburn, 11 July 1927, TNL Archive, Deakin Papers. This telegram from Deakin to Claud warmly congratulates him on the Saxon floor story and suggests various job options in London or Berlin.
16. Claud Cockburn, *I, Claud: The Autobiography of Claud Cockburn*, Penguin, 1967, p. 65; *Times*, 2 April 1927.
17. Cockburn, *In Time of Trouble*, p. 88.
18. Ibid., p. 89.
19. Cockburn, *Discord of Trumpets*, pp. 98–9.
20. Ibid., p. 106.
21. Peter Gay, *Weimar Culture*, W. W. Norton, 2002, pp. 25–8, gives a slightly more positive take on the contradictions of Stresemann's political stance. Nominally a right-wing royalist who had fully supported German war aims, he oversaw crucial diplomatic achievements that briefly stabilised the Weimar Republic.
22. Cockburn, *Discord of Trumpets*, p. 105.
23. Many people whom Claud denounced after the Nazis came to power in 1933 persisted in the belief, right up to 1939, that if the wrongs of the Treaty of Versailles were to be righted, then peace in Europe could yet be preserved.
24. *The Dial*, January 1928, pp. 8–24.
25. Pound was an early admirer of Claud's short story. A few months after it was published, Claud received a letter from Pound in

Vienna. He says it was 'the first and only written communication I received from him – a note written apparently on lavatory paper in blue chalk, saying, 'Hail. Dial story great. Can we meet? What chance you coming this city merry month May?' Claud hurried down to Vienna to see the great poet.

26. He also may have been influenced by Joseph Conrad, whose few short stories are terse and effective. Conrad was one of the few writers in English who gave his fiction a European setting (most unusual for a British writer). I owe these insights to Professor Janet Montefiore.

27. I owe this insight to Professor Janet Montefiore. Claud and Isher-wood did not know each other in Berlin in the twenties, as Claud left in 1929, just as Isherwood was arriving. They may have met in Berlin in the winter of 1932–3 and met frequently when they were both back in London.

7. Love and Revolutionary Politics

1. Claud Cockburn, *A Discord of Trumpets: An Autobiography*, Simon & Schuster, 1958, pp. 112–13.
2. Claud Cockburn, *In Time of Trouble: An Autobiography*, Rupert Hart-Davis, 1956, pp. 101–2.
3. Ibid., pp. 103–4.
4. Cockburn, *Discord of Trumpets*, p. 124.
5. Cockburn, *In Time of Trouble*, p. 105.
6. Peter Gay, *Weimar Culture*, W. W. Norton, 2002, p. xiii.
7. Ibid., p.25.
8. Cockburn, *Discord of Trumpets*, p. 124.
9. Cockburn, *In Time of Trouble*, p. 105.
10. Hope Hale Davis, unpublished manuscript, Hope Hale Davis Papers, MC 533 2.14.
11. Cockburn, *Discord of Trumpets*, pp. 120–3.
12. Hans Hautmann, *Die verlorene Räterepublik. Am Beispiel der Kommunistischen Partei Deutschösterreichs*, 1971, p. 27; Hans Hautmann, *Geschichte der Rätebewegung in Österreich 1918–1924*, 1987, p. 185.
13. Cockburn, *In Time of Trouble*, pp. 110–11.
14. Hope Hale Davis, *Great Day Coming: A Memoir of the 1930s*,

Steerforth Press, 1994, p. 21.

15. Davis, *Great Day Coming*, pp. 49–50. Davis found it confusing that 'Claud's two most important political influences should have almost the same name [Berta and Berti].' Cockburn, *Discord of Trumpets*, p. 119.
16. *Daily Telegraph*, 8 April 2012.
17. Cockburn, *In Time of Trouble*, p. 122.
18. Norman Ebbutt to Ralph Ebbutt, 28 February 1928, TNL Archive, Deakin Papers.
19. *Times* Archive, Claud Cockburn personal file, 30 October 1928.
20. Cockburn, *In Time of Trouble*, p. 127.
21. Cockburn, *Discord of Trumpets*, p. 135.
22. Ibid., p. 136.
23. Ibid., p. 138.
24. *Times*, 17 December 1981.
25. Cockburn, *Discord of Trumpets*, p. 148.
26. Cockburn File, TNL Archive, 30 July 1929.

8. 'The Word "Panic" Is Not to Be Used'

1. Claud Cockburn, *A Discord of Trumpets: An Autobiography*, Simon & Schuster, 1958, p. 156.
2. Ibid., p. 160. J. K. Galbraith, *The Great Crash 1929*, Mariner Books, 1955, pp. 94–5, makes a similar point about the mood of America in the summer months of 1929.
3. Ibid., pp. 163–4.
4. Ibid., p. 166.
5. Claud Cockburn, *In Time of Trouble: An Autobiography*, Rupert Hart-Davis, 1956, p. 147.
6. Cockburn, *Discord of Trumpets*, p. 179.
7. Ibid., p. 188.
8. Galbraith, *Great Crash*, p. 121.
9. Cockburn, *In Time of Trouble*, p. 167.
10. Cockburn, *Discord of Trumpets*, p. 189.
11. Galbraith, *Great Crash*, p. 123.
12. Cockburn, *In Time of Trouble*, p. 168.
13. Cockburn, *Discord of Trumpets*, p. 190.

14. Cockburn, *Discord of Trumpets*, pp. 192–4.

15. Ibid., pp. 194–6.

16. DNB Sir Willmott Lewis (1877–1950). Times correspondent in Washington 1920–48. Knighted 1931, D. W. Brogan revised by Marc Brady 2004.

17. Cockburn, *Discord of Trumpets*, pp. 197–9.

18. Ibid., pp. 204–5. In his memoir Claud misremembered the date of his arrival in Washington as 31 December, but the fire occurred on Christmas Eve, not New Year's Eve.

19. DNB Sir Willmott Lewis (1877–1950).

20. Cockburn, *Discord of Trumpets*, pp. 200–1.

21. Ibid., pp. 204–5.

22. *Chicago Tribune*, 19 December 2007.

23. Cockburn, *In Time of Trouble*, pp. 188–9.

24. Cockburn, *Discord of Trumpets*, p. 215.

25. Ibid., p. 216.

26. Claud Cockburn, interview by Fintan O'Toole, *In Dublin*, 25 June 1981.

27. Cockburn, *Discord of Trumpets*, p. 217.

28. Ibid., p. 218.

29. Cockburn, *In Time of Trouble*, p. 191.

30. Ibid., p. 192.

9. With Hope

1. Hope Hale Davis, 'Miss Sally Bowles, Claud Cockburn and Others', Hope Hale Davis Papers, Schlesinger Library, Harvard Radcliffe Institute, MC 533 2.14.

2. Hope Hale Davis, *Great Day Coming: A Memoir of the 1930s*, Steerforth Press, 1994, p. 1.

3. Davis, 'Sally Bowles, Claud Cockburn and Others'.

4. Davis, *Great Day Coming*, p. 2.

5. Davis, 'Sally Bowles, Claud Cockburn and Others'.

6. Claud Cockburn, *A Discord of Trumpets: An Autobiography*, Simon & Schuster, 1958, p. 208.

7. J. K. Galbraith, *The Great Crash of 1929*, Mariner Books, 1955, p. 186.

8. Cockburn, *Discord of Trumpets*, p. 209.

9. Ibid., p. 214.

10. Davis, 'Sally Bowles, Claud Cockburn and Others'.

11. Davis, *Great Day Coming*, p. 5.

12. Davis, 'Sally Bowles, Claud Cockburn and Others'.

13. Cockburn, *Discord of Trumpets*, p. 221. He always deliberately talked up the prospects for radical change for morale-building purposes because he believed it necessary to counteract the way in which the powers that be talked it down.

14. Claud Cockburn, interview by Fintan O'Toole, *In Dublin*, 25 June 1981. Claud liked to think of his father as most closely resembling a Chinese mandarin since he had spent almost his entire career in China.

15. Davis, *Great Day Coming*, p. 2.

16. Suzanne La Follette to Claud Cockburn, Hope Hale David papers, MC 533 2.14. The letter is dated 'Sunday' but was evidently sent soon after he had started his affair with Hope Hale.

17. Excerpts from HHD's Journal, Summer of 1931, Hope Hale Davis Papers, MC 533 2.14.

18. Ibid., p. 5.

19. Ibid.

20. Ibid., p. 211.

21. Wolfgang Zu Putlitz, 'The Putlitz Dossier', 1957. Despite Putlitz providing high-quality and immediate news about Nazi plans, this was largely ignored by the Chamberlain government.

22. Cockburn, *In Time of Trouble*, p. 192.

23. Claud Cockburn to Geoffrey Dawson, n.d. (ca. November 1931), TNL Archive TT/ED/GGD/1, Claud Cockburn file. The slightly contorted grammar and punctuation of the letter suggests that Claud was agonising up to the last moment over his decision to resign. The previous letters between Claud and Dawson referred to here have not survived.

24. Geoffrey Dawson to Claud Cockburn, 15 November 1931, TNL Archive, TT/ED/GGD/1, Claud Cockburn file.

25. Cockburn, *Discord of Trumpets*, pp. 227–8.

26. Ibid., p. 231.

27. Claud Cockburn to Hope Hale Davis, n.d., Hope Hale Davis Papers, MC 533 2.14.

28. A copy of this letter is missing from the Hope Hale Davis papers.

29. Claud Cockburn to Hope Hale Davis, n.d., Hope Hale Davis Papers, MC 533 2.14.

10. *The Week*

1. Patricia Cockburn, *The Years of The Week*, Penguin, 1971, pp. 22–3.

2. Claud Cockburn, *I, Claud: The Autobiography of Claud Cockburn*, Penguin, 1967, p. 137–8.

3. This belief that litigants sue to make money may sound cynical but was the experience of *Private Eye*, according to its former editor Richard Ingrams. Private conversation with the author.

4. Claud Cockburn, *A Discord of Trumpets: An Autobiography*, Simon & Schuster, 1958, p. 238.

5. Ibid.

6. Claud Cockburn to Nancy Cunard, 9 July 1933, National Archives, KV2/546.

7. Cockburn, *Discord of Trumpets*, p. 240.

8. [Claud Cockburn] Anon., *High Low Washington*, J. B. Littincott, 1932, pp. 132–68.

9. Cockburn, *I, Claud*, p. 139.

10. Claude Cockburn, letter to potential subscribers, 3 April 1933, National Archives, MI5, Claud Cockburn file, KV2/546.

11. Ibid.

12. *The Week*, 29 March 1933.

13. Cockburn, *Years of The Week*, p. 16.

14. The Rumbold dispatch is quoted in Corelli Barnett, *The Collapse of British Power*, Methuen, 1972, p. 386.

15. *The Week*, 5 July 1933.

16. Ibid. Evidently Claud had not seen the original text of Rumbold's telegram but knew of its general content since there are no direct quotes in his piece.

17. Claud Cockburn Letter to Captain Liddell, letter marked 'personal and secret', 4 September 1933, National Archives, Claud Cockburn file, KV2/546.

18. *The Week*, 18 September.

19. Cockburn File, 24 September 1934, National Archives, KV2/546,

MI5, Claud Cockburn file.

20. Cockburn, *Discord of Trumpets*, p. 253.
21. Obituary, Frederick Kuh, *New York Times*, 4 February 1978.
22. 'Paul Scheffer Out as Editor', *New York Times*, 3 January 1937.
23. Cockburn, *Years of The Week*, pp. 41–6.
24. Ibid., p. 255.
25. *The Week*, 16 August 1933.
26. *The Week*, 24 April 1933.
27. *The Week*, 16 August 1933.
28. *The Week*, 24 April 1933.
29. Cockburn, *Discord of Trumpets*, p. 255.
30. *The Week*, 23 August 1933.
31. *The Week*, 17 August 1934.
32. *The Week*, 23 August 1933.
33. *The Week*, 20 June 1934.
34. *The Week*, 3 July 1934. Other accounts of von Bose's murder differ a little from this.
35. *The Week*, 11 July 1934.

11. Frank Pitcairn of the *Daily Worker*

1. Cockburn File, 23 October 1933, National Archives, KV2/546.
2. Cockburn File, 10 November 1933, National Archives, KV2/546.
3. Ibid. Professional journalists are usually suspicious of freelance journalists whose by-lines they and their colleagues have never seen.
4. Patricia Cockburn, *The Years of The Week*, Penguin, 1971, pp. 77–80.
5. *The Week*, 23 September 1935, National Archives, KV2/546.
6. Sir Vernon Kell to Major N. G. Hind MC, Committee of Imperial Defence, 19 June 1934, National Archives, KV2/546.
7. Cockburn File, 19 March 1934, National Archives, KV2/546.
8. Ibid.
9. Claud Cockburn, *I, Claud: The Autobiography of Claud Cockburn*, Penguin, 1967, p. 152.
10. *Daily Worker*, 24 September 1934.
11. Claud Cockburn, *A Discord of Trumpets: An Autobiography*,

Simon & Schuster, 1958, p. 276.

12. Cockburn, *I, Claud*, p. 153.

13. Ibid., p. 276.

14. Cockburn, *Years of The Week*, p. 229.

15. Ibid., pp. 110–11.

16. Unpublished ms, n.d. (ca. 1933 or early 1934), Hope Davis papers, MC 533, box 214.

17. Records of Liberty, Hull History Centre, catalogue.hullhistory centre.org.uk.

18. Cockburn, *Discord of Trumpets*, p. 271.

19. Ibid., p. 272.

20. Obituary, Sylvia Scaffardi, *Guardian*, 30 January 2000.

21. Cockburn, *Discord of Trumpets*, p. 273.

22. Ibid.

23. *The Week*, 21 February 1934.

24. Ibid.

25. *Guardian*, 3 August 1934.

26. Cockburn File, Copy sent to MI5, 2 August 1934, National Archives, KV2/584.

27. *Guardian*, 3 August 1934.

12. Project Revolutionary Baby

1. Hope Hale Davis, *Great Day Coming: A Memoir of the 1930s*, Steerforth Press, 1994, p. 4.

2. Hope Hale Davis, 'Miss Sally Bowles, Claud Cockburn and Others', Hope Hale Davis Papers, Schlesinger Library, Harvard Radcliffe Institute, MC 533 2.14, pp. 5–6.

3. Davis, *Great Day Coming*, p. 3.

4. Ibid.

5. Ibid., p. 11.

6. Davis, 'Sally Bowles, Claud Cockburn and Others', p. 7.

7. Davis, *Great Day Coming*, p. 6.

8. Ibid., p. 9.

9. Ibid., p. 10.

10. Ibid., p. 54.

11. Ibid., p. 55.

12. Davis, *Great Day Coming*, pp. 56–7.
13. Ibid., 60.
14. Davis, 'Sally Bowles, Claud Cockburn and Others', p. 15.
15. Davis, *Great Day Coming*, p. 61.
16. There were other claimants to be the subject of the song, including Machwitz's estranged wife Hermione Gingold, but the balance of scholarly opinion is that the song was addressed to Jean.
17. Davis, 'Sally Bowles, Claud Cockburn and Others', p. 16.
18. Ibid., pp. 1–2. Hope says that *I Am a Camera*, in which Sally Bowles/Jean Ross was playing on Broadway at the time, which would date this episode to 1951–2.
19. This is not quite accurate. Jean appears to have returned at the end of 1932, some months before Hitler became chancellor on 30 January 1933. See Peter Parker, *Isherwood: A Life Revealed*, Picador, 2004.
20. Davis, 'Sally Bowles, Claud Cockburn and Others', p. 2.
21. Christopher Isherwood, *Christopher and His Kind*, Eyre Methuen, 1956, p. 51. The book is written in a mix of third- and first-person narratives.
22. This was occasionally even true of Hope, who otherwise presented Jean as a much deeper and more intelligent person than her fictional counterpart.
23. *I Am a Camera*, trailer, YouTube.com.
24. *Caberet*, trailer, YouTube.com.
25. Parker, *Isherwood*, pp. 207–8.
26. Davis, 'Sally Bowles, Claud Cockburn and Others'.
27. Ibid., p. 26.
28. Sarah Caudwell, 'Reply to Berlin', *New Statesman*, 3 October 1986.
29. Ibid.

13. Sally Bowles and the Party

1. Clare 'Billee' Hughes, *A Cotton Thread*, 2004, p. 70. Many myths accumulated about Jean's early life, some of which she authenticated or denied, but this account by her sister is the most persuasive eyewitness account.
2. Peter Parker, *Isherwood: A Life Revealed*, Picador, 2004, p. 206.

This information is at least in part drawn from direct communications between Parker, Billee and Jean's daughter Sarah Cockburn, whose pen name was Sarah Caudwell.

3. Hughes, *A Cotton Thread*, p. 69.
4. Possibly she could have been referring to her period.
5. Ibid., pp. 69–70.
6. Ibid.
7. Ibid., p. 75.
8. Parker, *Isherwood*, pp. 206–7.
9. Ibid., p. 207.
10. Peter Gay, *Weimar Culture*, W. W. Norton, 2002, p. xiii.
11. Hughes, *A Cotton Thread*, p. 85.
12. Parker, *Isherwood*, p. 205.
13. 'Day at Night: Christopher Isherwood', YouTube.com.
14. Parker, *Isherwood*, pp. 205–6.
15. Ibid., p. 207.
16. Hope Hale Davis, 'Miss Sally Bowles, Claud Cockburn and Others', Hope Hale Davis Papers, Schlesinger Library, Harvard Radcliffe Institute, MC 533 2.14, p. 20.
17. Sarah Caudwell, 'Reply to Berlin', *New Statesman*, 28 October 1986.
18. Ibid.
19. Christopher Isherwood, *Christopher and His Kind*, Eyre Methuen, 1956.
20. Ibid., p. 52.
21. Ibid., p. 53.
22. Ibid.
23. Hughes, *A Cotton Thread*, p. 92. Other sources dispute this, but Billee, Jean's youngest sister, is likely to have heard this directly from Jean.
24. Ibid., pp. xiii–iv.
25. Hope Hale Davis, unpublished ms of 'Miss Sally Bowles, Claud Cockburn and Others', written for *Grand Street*, 1989.
26. Berta Pölz (1927–9), Hope Hale (1930–2), Jean Ross (1933–9), Patricia Byron (1940–81).
27. Parker, *Isherwood*, p. 94.
28. Claud Cockburn, *A Discord of Trumpets: An Autobiography*, Simon & Schuster, 1958, p. 245.

29. Isherwood, *Christopher and His Kind*, p. 94.

30. Jean Ross, phone call to Claud Cockburn, 7 November 1933. 'She seems to be connected in some way with the film business,' comments the note. National Archives, KV2/546.

31. *Guardian*, 8 June 1934.

32. Davis, 'Miss Sally Bowles, Claud Cockburn and Others', p. 18.

33. Hughes, *A Cotton Thread*, p. 93.

34. Dictionary of National Biography (DNB), 'Jean Ross', Peter Parker.

35. Hughes, *A Cotton Thread*, p. 91.

36. The first favour was involuntary, which was to serve as a model for Sally Bowles.

37. Isherwood, *Christopher and His Kind*, pp. 115–16. DNB Jean Ross.

38. Hope Hale Davis, *Great Day Coming: A Memoir of the 1930s*, Steerforth Press, 1994, p. 65.

39. Ibid., p. 67.

40. Cockburn File, National Archives, No VI. The document is damaged but is between two others dated respectively 4.3.38 and 6.5.38.

41. Patrick Cockburn, *Broken Boy*, Jonathan Cape, 2006, pp. 220–1. When I wrote this book, I had discovered the marriage certificate but did not understand why my parents had gone to such pains to give the impression they were married when they were not, suspecting it might have something to do with Patricia's divorce from her first husband, Arthur Byron. On the 1978 marriage under the heading 'Condition', the registrar wrote: 'Previously went through a form of marriage at Sofia, Bulgaria on the 2nd March 1946.'

14. 'If a Mistake Can be Made, They'll Make It'

1. Claud Cockburn, *A Discord of Trumpets: An Autobiography*, Simon & Schuster, 1958, p. 249.

2. Peter Parker, *Isherwood: A Life Revealed*, Picador, 2004, p. 289, citing a letter from Isherwood to John Lehman, 22 July 1934.

3. Cockburn, *Discord of Trumpets*, p. 277.

4. Ibid., p. 278.

5. Ibid.

6. Patricia Cockburn, *The Years of The Week*, Penguin, 1971, p. 110.

7. MI5 noted the change on 25 March 1937. National Archives.

8. Cockburn, *Years of The Week*, p. 120.

9. Claud had been a London stringer for *Time* in 1933 but does not seem to have done much for them.

10. Claud Cockburn, 'On Fortune's Fringe', *Atlantic*, July 1974.

11. Ibid.

12. MI5 list of intercepted phone calls and telegrams, 1 November 1933, National Archives.

13. MI5 intercepted a message from Ingersoll to Claud later in 1935 (it is undated but is filed in between other MI5 documents that indicate the general time frame). This is very unlikely to have been because of in-house censorship. Ingersoll wanted Claud to help a visiting staff correspondent. R. Ingersoll to C. Cockburn PF 42675, National Archives.

14. *Fortune* editors, *Arms and the Men*, Doubleday, 1934.

15. Cockburn, 'On Fortune's Fringe'.

16. 'The Ghost Army', Facebook.com, 13 February 2021.

17. It is difficult to be precise about dates, but MI5 lists Hilton Howell Raines in France as being in touch with Claud on 16 August 1934. National Archives.

18. Ibid.

19. Cockburn, 'On Fortune's Fringe'.

20. Ibid.

21. Jonathan Miles, *The Nine Lives of Otto Katz*, Bantam Press, 2010, p. 76.

22. Cockburn, *Years of The Week*, p. 121.

23. Ibid., pp. 126–7.

24. Miles, *Nine Lives of Otto Katz*, pp. 76–100.

25. Ibid., p. 92.

26. *I, Claud*, pp. 190–1.

27. Ibid., p. 191.

28. Ibid., p. 198.

29. Ibid., p. 197.

30. Claud Cockburn, *Cockburn Sums Up: An Autobiography*, Quartet Books, 1980, p. 137.

31. Claud Cockburn, *I, Claud: The Autobiography of Claud Cockburn*, Penguin, 1967, pp. 188–9.

32. Ibid., p. 190.
33. Cockburn, *Cockburn Sums Up*, p. 139.
34. Special Branch to Home Office, 31 May 1934, National Archives.

15. *Reporter in Spain*

1. Paul Preston, *The Spanish Civil War*, William Collins, 2016.
2. Claud Cockburn, *A Discord of Trumpets: An Autobiography*, Simon & Schuster, 1958, p. 288.
3. Claud Cockburn, *Reporter in Spain*, Lawrence & Wishart, 1936.
4. Ibid., p. 16.
5. *The Week*, 4 June 1936.
6. Cockburn, *Reporter in Spain*, p. 34.
7. Ibid., p. 44–5.
8. Anthony Beevor, *The Battle for Spain: The Spanish Civil War 1936–1939*, Weidenfeld & Nicolson, 2012.
9. Ibid., p. 289.
10. Ibid., p. 290.
11. Cockburn, *Discord of Trumpets*, p. 293. The account of Claud's encounter with Durruti is in this book but not in any of the British editions of his memoirs.
12. Paul Callan, letter to *Spectator*, 23 January 1982.
13. Beevor, *Battle for Spain*, p. 87.
14. Preston, *Spanish Civil War*, pp. 176–7.
15. Cockburn File, 31 August 1936, National Archives.
16. Cockburn, *Reporter in Spain*, pp. 84–91.
17. Cockburn File, National Archives Kew. Undated, but other dated documents indicate that this suggestion was made between 31 August and 18 September 1936.
18. Cockburn, *Reporter in Spain*, pp. 103–4.
19. Ibid., p. 106.
20. Ibid., p. 117.
21. Ibid., p. 126.
22. Ibid., p. 127.
23. Ibid., p. 128.
24. Cockburn, *Discord of Trumpets*, p. 298.
25. Claud Cockburn, interview by Fintan O'Toole, *In Dublin*, 25

June 1981.

26. Cockburn, *Reporter in Spain*, p. 132.

27. Ibid., pp. 132–3. According to an MI5 file dated 23 September 1936, 'Cockburn was reported missing for two days and later it was reported that he was killed.' National Archives.

28. Fintan O'Toole, *In Dublin*, p. 19.

16. The Sinking of the *Llandovery Castle*

1. An AP newsreel report shows the ship down by the bows and passengers being taken to land by boats. It says that divers found the hole in the ship's side.

2. *Daily Worker*, 27 February 1937.

3. Claud was to write later, in *Discord of Trumpets*, that it was an Italian torpedo rather than a mine. At the time he and the shipping authorities all refer to a mine, but it has always been difficult to distinguish between the two as the source of an explosion, as was shown repeatedly in both world wars.

4. Telegram dated 26 February 1937, National Archives, MI5 file.

5. Claud Cockburn, *A Discord of Trumpets: An Autobiography*, Simon & Schuster, 1958, p. 299.

6. Ibid., p. 300.

7. A blurred typed reference to Claud's membership gives 1937 as the year, but the month appears to have been omitted by accident.

8. Cockburn, *Discord of Trumpets*, pp. 300–2.

9. *Daily Worker*, 17 December 1936.

10. *Daily Worker*, 4 January 1937.

11. Anthony Beevor, *The Battle for Spain: The Spanish Civil War 1936–1939*, Weidenfeld & Nicolson, 2012, pp. 211–23.

12. Claud Cockburn, conversation with the author in the 1970s.

13. *Daily Worker*, 6 February 1937.

14. *Daily Worker*, 8 February 1937.

15. *Daily Worker*, 10 February 1937.

16. Paul Preston, *The Spanish Civil War*, William Collins, 2016, p. 194.

17. Beevor, *Battle for Spain*, p. 223.

18. Letter dated 25 February 1937 to Captain E. A. Airy, Defence

Security Officer, Gibraltar, National Archives, MI5 file.

19. Cockburn, *Discord of Trumpets*, p. 306.

20. Ibid., p 308.

21. Ibid.

22. Claud Cockburn, *Crossing the Line*, McGibbon and Kee, 1958, p. 27.

23. Philip Knightley, *The First Casualty*, Andre Deutsch, rev. ed., 2000, pp. 212–13.

24. Patricia Cockburn, *The Years of The Week*, Penguin, 1971, p. 212.

25. Fintan O'Toole, *In Dublin*, pp. 14–20.

26. *Daily Worker*, 24 March 1937; Cockburn File, 25 May 1937, National Archives, MI5 file, KV2/546.

27. *Daily Worker*, 29 March 1937.

28. Cockburn File, 26 March 1937, National Archives, MI5 file, KV2/546.

29. Cockburn, *Years of The Week*, p. 206.

30. George Orwell, *Homage to Catalonia*, Penguin, 1962, p. 197.

31. Alberto Lawaza, *George Orwell and Claud Cockburn: Parallel Lives and Divergent Thinking*, Universitadde Alcala, 2012, pp. 1–11.

32. Cockburn, *Discord of Trumpets*, p. 291.

33. *Daily Worker*, 11 May 1937.

34. *Daily Worker*, 17 May 1937.

35. Orwell, *Homage to Catalonia*, p. 237.

36. In fact, the Soviet advisers in Spain were to be singled out by Stalin for imprisonment and execution.

37. 'A Conversation with Claud Cockburn', *Review*, 1964, nos. 11–12, pp. 51–4.

38. George Orwell, *Looking Back on the Spanish Civil War*, 1943, p. 240.

17. Scoops and Abdications

1. *The Week*, 14 October 1936.

2. Archbishop Cosmo Lang was a strong opponent of the king's marriage to Mrs Simpson.

3. *The Week*, 28 October 1936.

4. Cockburn File, dated November 1936 and signed 'Chief CON-

STABLE Consyavle', National Archives, MI5 file, KV3/546.

5. Cockburn, *Discord of Trumpets*, p. 282.

6. Ibid., pp. 281–5.

7. *The Week*, 16 December 1936.

8. *Daily Worker*, 5 December 1936.

9. 'A Conversation with Claud Cockburn', *Review*, 1964, nos. 11–12, pp. 51–3.

10. Interview with Friedman, who says that this picture was taken as untrained Republican militiamen repeatedly charged a Francoist machine gun position despite heavy casualties. YouTube.com. Many of these photographs are in the hands of the International Center for Photography in New York.

11. Richard Whelan, *Capa*, Bison, 1985, pp. 121–2.

12. Patrick Cockburn, 'How My Father's Face Turned Up in Robert Capa's Suitcase', *Independent*, 3 August 2013.

13. Ibid.

14. Stanley Weintraub, *The Last Great Cause*, W. H. Allen, 1968, pp. 179–80.

15. Cockburn, *Discord of Trumpets* pp. 302–3. Going by Hemingway's account, the incident took place in September 1937.

16. 'A Conversation with Claud Cockburn', p. 50.

17. Richard Davenport-Hines, *Auden*, Vintage, 1995, p. 164.

18. Ibid., pp. 165–6.

19. 'A Conversation with Claud Cockburn', p. 50.

20. In fact, Kolzov was born in Kyiv.

21. Cockburn, *Discord of Trumpets*, p. 304.

22. Ibid., p. 305.

18. The Cliveden Set

1. Claud Cockburn, *A Discord of Trumpets: An Autobiography*, Simon & Schuster, 1958, p. 298.

2. Cockburn File, 1934 (day and month not given), National Archives, MI5 file, KV2/546.

3. Cockburn File, 14 July 1938, National Archives, MI5 file, KV2/546.

4. Cockburn File, 1 April 1940, National Archives, MI5 file,

KV2/555.

5. Cockburn File, 1 February 1935, National Archives, MI5 file, KV2/546.

6. Clare 'Billee' Hughes, *A Cotton Thread*, 2004, p. 92.

7. Cockburn File, 14 July 1937, citing *Daily Worker*, National Archives, MI5 file, KV2/546.

8. Special Branch Report, 1935 (exact date destroyed), National Archives, KV2/546.

9. Cockburn File 1937 National Archive, MI5 file, KV2/546.

10. *The Week*, 17 June 1936.

11. Ibid.

12. Ibid.

13. *The Week*, 17 November 1937.

14. Ibid. 'Der Tag' was supposedly a German naval toast pre-1914 referring to 'the day' Germany would go to war with Britain.

15. Claud Cockburn, *I, Claud: The Autobiography of Claud Cockburn*, Penguin, 1967, p. 179.

16. *The Week*, 22 December 1937.

17. Cockburn, *I, Claud*, p. 179.

18. James Fox, *Langhorne Sisters*, Granta Books, 1998, p. 499.

19. Ibid., p. 506.

20. Cockburn, *I, Claud*, p. 180.

21. Fox, *Langhore Sisters*, p. 496.

22. Ibid., p. 500.

23. Bruce T. Riggs, 'Geoffrey Dawson, Editor of the Times and His Contribution to the Appeasement Movement', PhD thesis, University of North Texas, 1993.

24. Cockburn, *I, Claud*.

25. Ibid., 181.

26. Jan Montefiore who was told of the rhyme by her mother Elisabeth Paton who went up to Oxford in 1938.

19. Press Censorship, British Style

1. Claud Cockburn, *I, Claud: The Autobiography of Claud Cockburn*, Penguin, 1967, pp. 150–1.

2. Richard Cockett, *Twilight of Truth*, Weidenfeld & Nicolson,

1989, p. 40.

3. Ibid., p. 40.
4. Cockett, *Twilight of Truth*, pp. 1–2.
5. Ibid., pp. 40–1.
6. *The Week*, 31 August 1937.
7. Ibid.
8. Cockett, *Twilight of Truth*, p. 190.
9. Ibid., pp. 190–1.
10. Costancia de la Mura, *In Place of Splendour*, Clapton Press, 2021, pp. 245–51.
11. Clare 'Billee' Hughes, *A Cotton Thread*, 2004, pp. 113–14.
12. 26 April 1938, National Archives, MI5 files.
13. Cockburn File, 2 May 1939, National Archives, MI5 file, KV2/55a.
14. Cockburn File, 6 May 1939, National Archives, MI5 file, KV2/55a.
15. Ibid.
16. Claud Cockburn, *A Discord of Trumpets: An Autobiography*, Simon & Schuster, 1958, p. 298. He goes on to say that, even given these personal preferences, the 'makeshift ramshackle nature of Spanish War was terrifying' because it meant that the odds against the Republican side winning were very high.
17. Patricia Cockburn, *The Years of The Week*, Penguin, 1971.
18. Cockburn, *I, Claud*, p. 205.
19. Memo from Bilov, 28 May 1937, RASPI (Russian State Archive for Social and Political History), Fund 495, OPIC 198, item 1370.
20. Robert J. Stewart, 7 April 1937, RASPI, Fund 495, OPIC 198, item 1370.
21. James Shields, 28 August 1936, RASPI, Fund 495, OPIC 198, item 1370.
22. Robert J. Stewart, 7 April 1937, RASPI, Fund 495, OPIC 198, item 1370.
23. James Shields, 28 August 1936, RASPI, Fund 495, OPIC 198, item 1370.
24. Cockburn, *I, Claud*, p. 169.
25. Stephen Kotkin, *Stalin*, vol. 2, p. 560.
26. Ibid.
27. Cockburn, *I, Claud*, p. 204.
28. Ibid., p. 172.
29. Ibid., pp. 162–73.

30. Cockburn, *Years of The Week*, pp. 259–60.
31. Kotkin, *Stalin*, pp. 459–60.
32. Cockburn, *I, Claud*, p. 176.

20. Being a David

1. Claud Cockburn, *Crossing the Line*, McGibbon and Kee, 1958, pp. 9–11.
2. Ibid., p. 11.
3. Sefton Delmer, *Trail Sinister*, Secker, 1971, pp. 370–7.
4. Paul Preston, *The Spanish Holocaust*, HarperPress, 2013.
5. Cockburn, *Crossing the Line*, p. 12.
6. Ibid., p. 13.
7. Clare 'Billee' Hughes, *A Cotton Thread*, 2004, p. 114.
8. *London Gazette*, 3 March 1939.
9. Ibid., p. 115.
10. Patrick Cockburn, *Broken Boy*, Jonathan Cape, 2006, p. 221.
11. Clare 'Billee' Hughes in conversation with Janet Montefiore, March 2000.
12. Cockburn, *Crossing the Line*, p. 44.
13. Claud Cockburn, *I, Claud: The Autobiography of Claud Cockburn*, Penguin, 1967, p. 204.
14. Cockburn, *Crossing the Line*, p. 44.
15. Ibid., p. 76.
16. Ibid.
17. Patricia Cockburn, *The Years of The Week*, Penguin, 1971, p. 271.
18. Ibid., pp. 75–6; Cockburn, *Crossing the Line*, p. 49. He is speaking specifically of Dmitrov, the Bulgarian Communist who defied Goering at the Leipzig trial of Communists accused of responsibility for the Reichstag Fire.
19. Cockburn, *Crossing the Line*, p. 50.
20. Cockburn, *I, Claud*, p. 239.

Afterword: Guerrilla Journalist

1. Claud Cockburn, *I, Claud: The Autobiography of Claud Cock-*

burn, Penguin, 1967, p. 244.

2. Ibid., p. 29.

3. Malcolm Muggeridge, *Tread Softly Because You Tread on My Jokes*, Collins, 1966, pp. 279–84.

4. Copy of leasehold agreement 1 October 1948, in possession of author. Claud and Patricia stayed there until 1977, when they moved to Rock House, Ardmore, Co Waterford, some five miles away.

5. MI5 report, 8 September 1949, National Archives, KV2/955.

6. *Daily Express*, 9 September 1939.

7. Special Branch report, 3 November 1949, National Archives, KV2/555.

8. George Cruikshank to security services, 11 April 1950, National Archives, KV2/555.

9. MI5 report, 12 February 1951, National Archives, KV2/555.

10. Claud Cockburn, *Crossing the Line*, McGibbon and Kee, 1958, p. 187.

11. Ibid., p. 187.

12. Cockburn, *I, Claud*, p. 358.

13. Richard Ingrams, *Muggeridge*, HarperCollins, 1995, p. 247.

14. Ibid., p. 1965. Claud was not alone.

15. Claud Cockburn, *Nine Bald Men*, Rupert Hart-Davis, 1956.

16. Cockburn, *I, Claud*.

17. Ibid., pp. 383–4.

18. Patrick Cockburn, *Broken Boy*, Jonathan Cape, 2006, gives a full account of my experiences when I contracted polio and the history of the epidemic, among the last in Western Europe before use of the polio vaccine became widespread.

19. Cockburn, *I, Claud*, p. 393.

20. Ingrams, *Muggeridge*, p. xi.

21. Cockburn, *I, Claud*, p. 409.

22. *Guardian*, 16 February 2000.

Index

Page numbers in **bold** refer to illustrations

Hyde, Douglas 243–4
Hypocrites Club 43, 45

The Illiterary Digest (school magazine)
34–5
In Time of Trouble (Cockburn) 245,
249
Incitement to Disaffection
Bill 122–3
Independent Labour Party 185
information wars xvi, xx, 241
Ingersoll, Ralph 150–1
Ingrams, Richard xx, **239**, 249
Institute of Irish Studies, Queen's
University Belfast xv
International Steel Cartel 56
internet, the xx–xxi, 250
Iraq xvii
Ireland xi, xiv, 143, 242–3, 247
Irish Times (newspaper) 248
Isherwood, Christopher 71–2, 130–3,
138–41, 141, 142, 144–5, 148,
160, 219
Isis (magazine) 45
Italy 177–9, 179–80, 181
Spanish Civil War involvement
Ito, Prince 21, 23

J. P. Morgan & Company 87
Japan 89
Jews
Czechoslovakia 227–30
persecution 10–11, 110
Johnson, Boris xvii, xix
journalistic freebooting 216
journalistic guerrilla warfare ix,
xiv, 6, 250–1

Kaiserhof Hotel, Berlin 75–6
Katz, Otto xii, 157, 159–62, 182–4,
221, 231
Keble College Oxford 28, 36,
43–7
Kell, Sir Vernon 13–14, 116,
222
Keynes, John Maynard 41, 42
Khashoggi, Jamal xix
Kidd, Ronald 120–1
Kipling, Rudyard 24, 71
Kisch, Egon Erwin 78, 158–9, 161–2,
221, 231, 242

Knightley, Phillip 183–4
Koestler, Arthur 180
Koltsov, Mikhail 199–201, 221,
223, 224–6, 229
Korea, Japanese occupation
of 18–23
Korea Daily News (newspaper)
20
Kuh, Frederick 109
Kun, Béla 39

La Follette, Suzanne 97–8
Labour Party 119
Lamont, Thomas W. xviii–xix,
87
Latvia 235
Layton, Walter 217
Lazarsfeld, Paul 78
Le Canard Enchaîné 8
Leatherhead Court 135–6
Leeper, Rex 108–9
Lehman, John 132, 141
Lenin, Vladimir 79, 80
Lennox, Hamish 43
Lewis, Sir Wilmott xix, 88–91
Liberal Party 30, 45
Libya xvii
Lilliput (magazine) 244
Lingle, Jake, murder of 91
Lithuania 235
Littauer, Paul 109
Litvinov, Maxim 223–4, 231
Llandovery Castle, SS, sinking
of 177–9
Lloyd George, David 45
London, Café Royal 142–3
Lothian, Philip Kerr, Lord 204,
211, 218
Low, David 210
Luce, Henry 150, 244
Luftwaffe 164, 186–7
Luxembourg 55, 56, 69–72

McCarthy, Joe xii, xiv
McCarthyism 244, 245
MacDonald, Sir Claude 21–2
MacDonald, Ramsay 10, 11–12
McDonough, Frank 218
McLachlan, Donald 248
McLennan, Graham 122
Madam T 77–9, 95

offal-eaters, the 43
Orwell, George 185–8
Osten, Maria 226
O'Toole, Fintan 91–3
Oudendyk, William 25
Oxford University
  Keble College 28, 36, 43–7
  Queen's College 52–8

Papen, Franz von 111–12, 113
Paris 4, 80–1
Peking, siege of 16–17, **16**
Phoney War, the 236
Pitcairn, Frank 119
Poland 231, 235
Poliakoff, Vladimir 208
Polish News Agency 109
Pollitt, Harry 117, 119, 175, 185,
  242–3
Pölz, Berta (Madam T) 77–9, 95,
  99, 102, 158
populism xvii
Pound, Ezra 68
poverty 120
Powell, Anthony 245–6
Prague 223, 224–5, 230
Pravda (newspaper) 225, 226
Preiss, Hans 110
press control 214–19
Private Eye (magazine) xx, **239**,
  249–50
propaganda xxi, 156–7, 183, 215
proprietorial bias xxiii
public interest xxiii
public opinion 215
Punch (magazine) 245–6, 248,
  248–9
Putin, Vladimir xix
Putlitz, Wolfgang zu 2, 99

Queen's College, Oxford 52–8
Queen's University Belfast, Institute
  of Irish Studies xv
Quennell, Peter 36

radical insurgent journalism xx
Radio Trust 2–3, 7
Railey, Hilton 152–4
Realpolitik xvi, 9, 107, 235
Red Army 223–4
Reichstag fire 156

Reichsverband Deutscher Schifts-
  teller 113
Reinhardt, Max 137–8
Reporter in Spain (Cockburn) 165–6,
  175
revolutionary romanticism 125
revolutionary upsurge, expectations
  of 120
Rhineland, the 13, 48–52, **48**
Ribbentrop, Joachim von 214–15, 235
Richardson, Maurice 241–2
Rökk, Marika 137
Rose, Norman 211
Ross, Billee 132, 134, 136, 143,
  144, 220, 232–3, 233–4
Ross, Charles 134, 135, 232–3
Ross, Clara, 134
Ross, Jean. *see* Cockburn, Jean
  (nee Ross)
Ross, Peggy 135, 136, 220, 233
Royal Academy of Dramatic Art
  (RADA) 136–7
Royal Institute of International
  Affairs 147
Royal Navy 19
Ruhr, the 48–52
Rumania 238
Rumbold, Sir Horace 107–8
Russia, invasion of Ukraine 250
Russian Revolution 79
Russian State Archive of Social and
  Political History 22
Russo-Japanese War 18

Saddam Hussein xvii
Salou 165
Salzburg 74
Saragossa 166–9, 185
Saturday Evening Post (magazine)
  248
Saxony, flood 59, 63–5
Scheffer, Paul 109
Schleicher, General Kurt von 7–8
Schuette, Oswald 2–3, 7
Schwarzwald, Eugenie 76–7, 223,
  231
Schwarzwald, Hermann 76
Scotland 23, 26
Scott Moncrieff, C. K. 81
Second World War 161, 240
  outbreak 234–8

Index